STAR WARS®

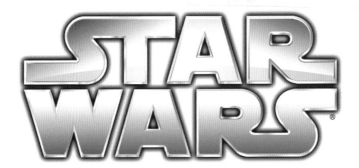

publisher
Mike Richardson

designer
Scott Cook

art director
Lia Ribacchi

assisting editor
Dave Marshall

editor
Randy Stradley

The editor gratefully acknowledges the assistance
of Elaine Mederer, Jann Moorhead, David Anderman, Leland Chee,
Sue Rostoni, and Amy Gary at Lucas Licensing.

Star Wars®: Episode II — Attack of the Clones
PhotoComic

Published by Dark Horse Books, a division of Dark Horse Comics, Inc.
10956 SE Main Street
Milwaukie, OR 97222

Originally published by TOKYOPOP, Inc.

www.darkhorse.com
www.starwars.com

To find a comics shop in your area,
call the Comic Shop Locator Service toll-free at 1-888-266-4226

First edition: November 2007

ISBN-10: 1-59307-855-2
ISBN-13/EAN: 978-1-59307-855-3

10 9 8 7 6 5 4 3 2 1

Printed in China

STAR WARS

EPISODE II
ATTACK OF THE CLONES

STORY AND SCREENPLAY BY
GEORGE LUCAS

DARK HORSE BOOKS®

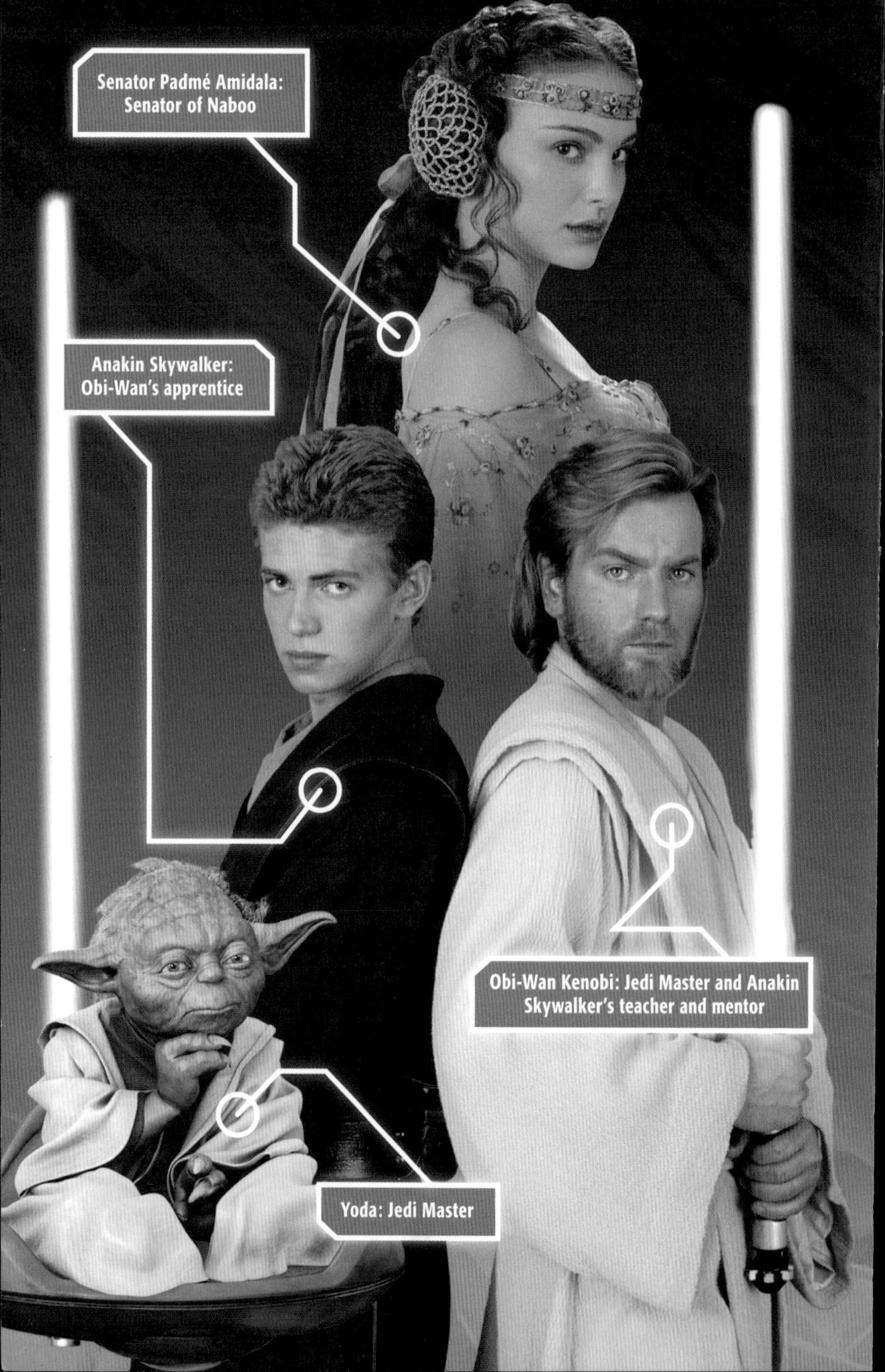
Senator Padmé Amidala: Senator of Naboo
Anakin Skywalker: Obi-Wan's apprentice
Obi-Wan Kenobi: Jedi Master and Anakin Skywalker's teacher and mentor
Yoda: Jedi Master

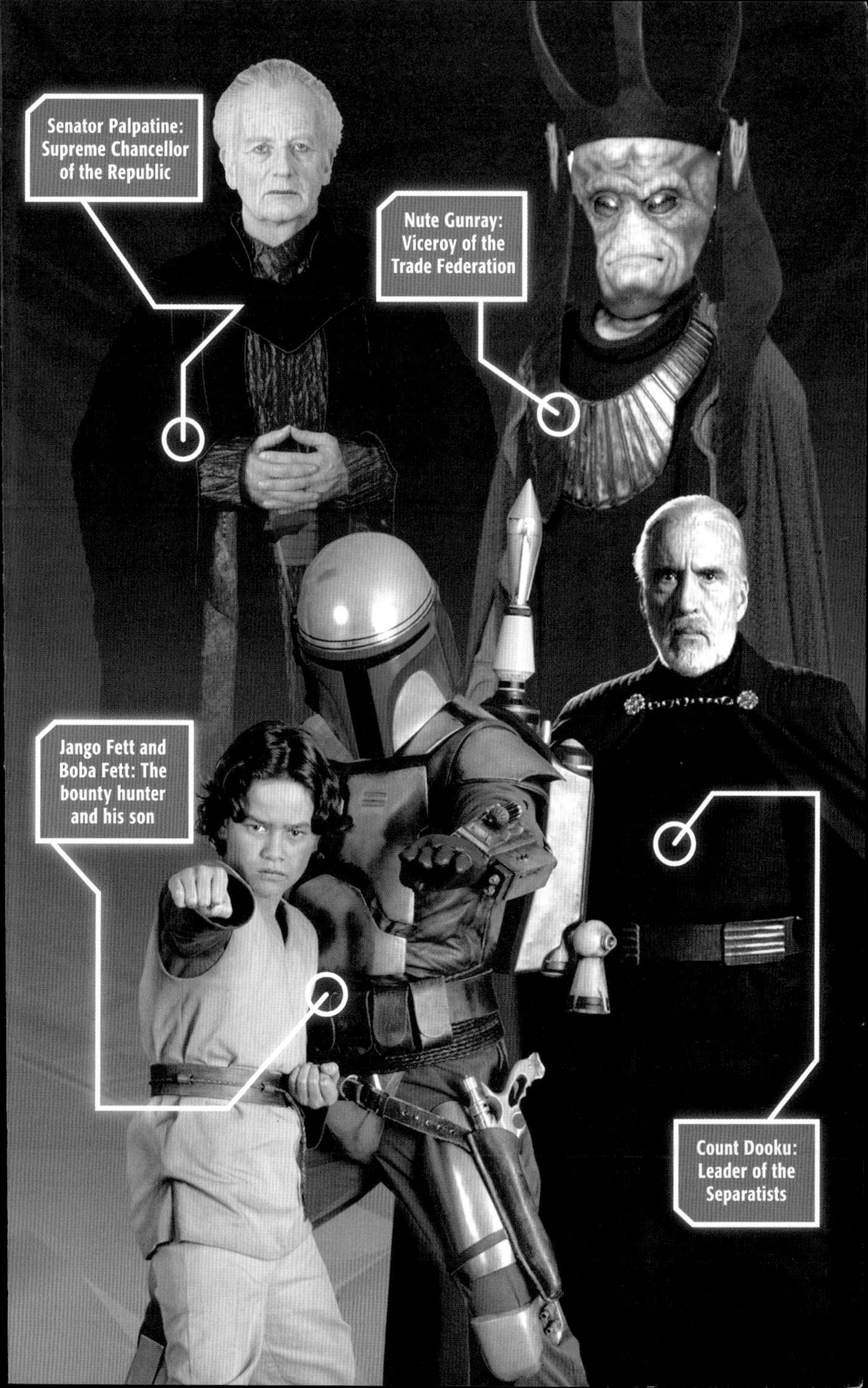
Senator Palpatine: Supreme Chancellor of the Republic
Nute Gunray: Viceroy of the Trade Federation
Jango Fett and Boba Fett: The bounty hunter and his son
Count Dooku: Leader of the Separatists

A long time ago in a galaxy far, far away....

There is unrest in the Galactic Senate.
Several thousand solar systems have declared
their intentions to leave the Republic.

This separatist movement,
under the leadership of Count Dooku,
has made it difficult for the limited
number of Jedi Knights to maintain peace
and order in the galaxy.

Senator Amidala, the former Queen of
Naboo, is returning to the Galactic Senate
to vote on the critical issue of creating
an ARMY OF THE REPUBLIC to
assist the overwhelmed Jedi....

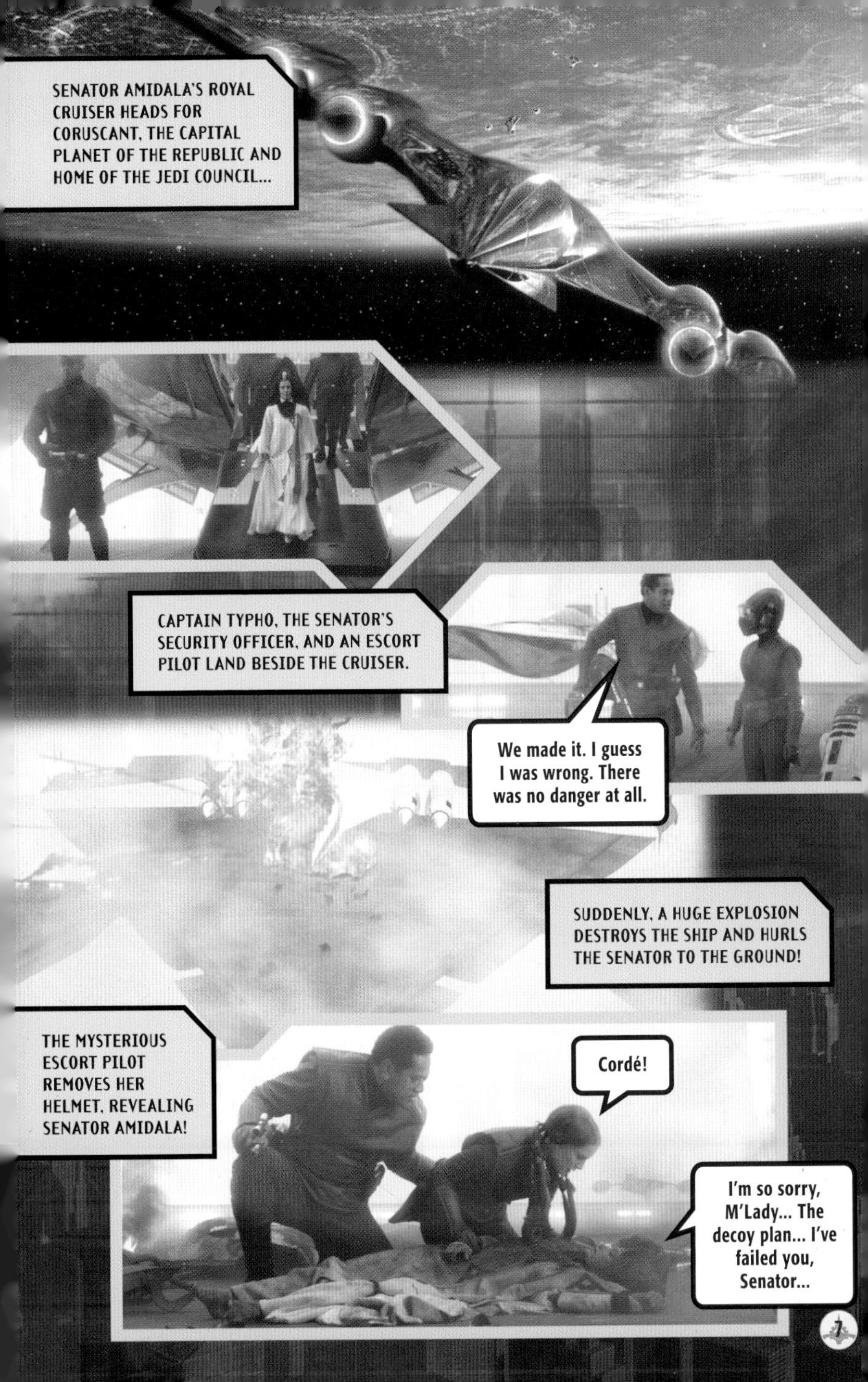
SENATOR AMIDALA'S ROYAL CRUISER HEADS FOR CORUSCANT, THE CAPITAL PLANET OF THE REPUBLIC AND HOME OF THE JEDI COUNCIL...
CAPTAIN TYPHO, THE SENATOR'S SECURITY OFFICER, AND AN ESCORT PILOT LAND BESIDE THE CRUISER.
We made it. I guess I was wrong. There was no danger at all.
SUDDENLY, A HUGE EXPLOSION DESTROYS THE SHIP AND HURLS THE SENATOR TO THE GROUND!
THE MYSTERIOUS ESCORT PILOT REMOVES HER HELMET, REVEALING SENATOR AMIDALA!
Cordé!
I'm so sorry, M'Lady... The decoy plan... I've failed you, Senator...

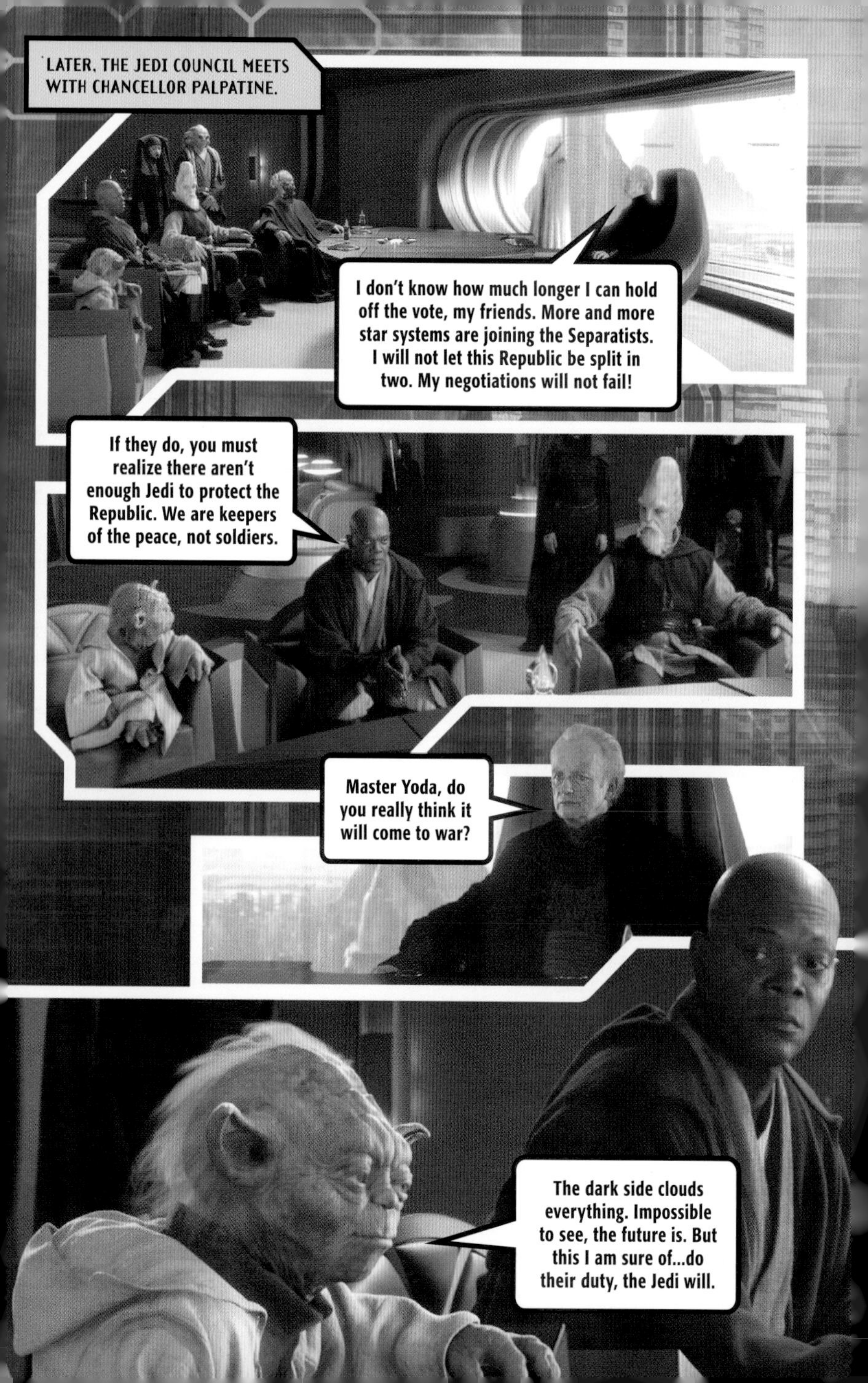
LATER, THE JEDI COUNCIL MEETS WITH CHANCELLOR PALPATINE.
I don't know how much longer I can hold off the vote, my friends. More and more star systems are joining the Separatists. I will not let this Republic be split in two. My negotiations will not fail!
If they do, you must realize there aren't enough Jedi to protect the Republic. We are keepers of the peace, not soldiers.
Master Yoda, do you really think it will come to war?
The dark side clouds everything. Impossible to see, the future is. But this I am sure of...do their duty, the Jedi will.

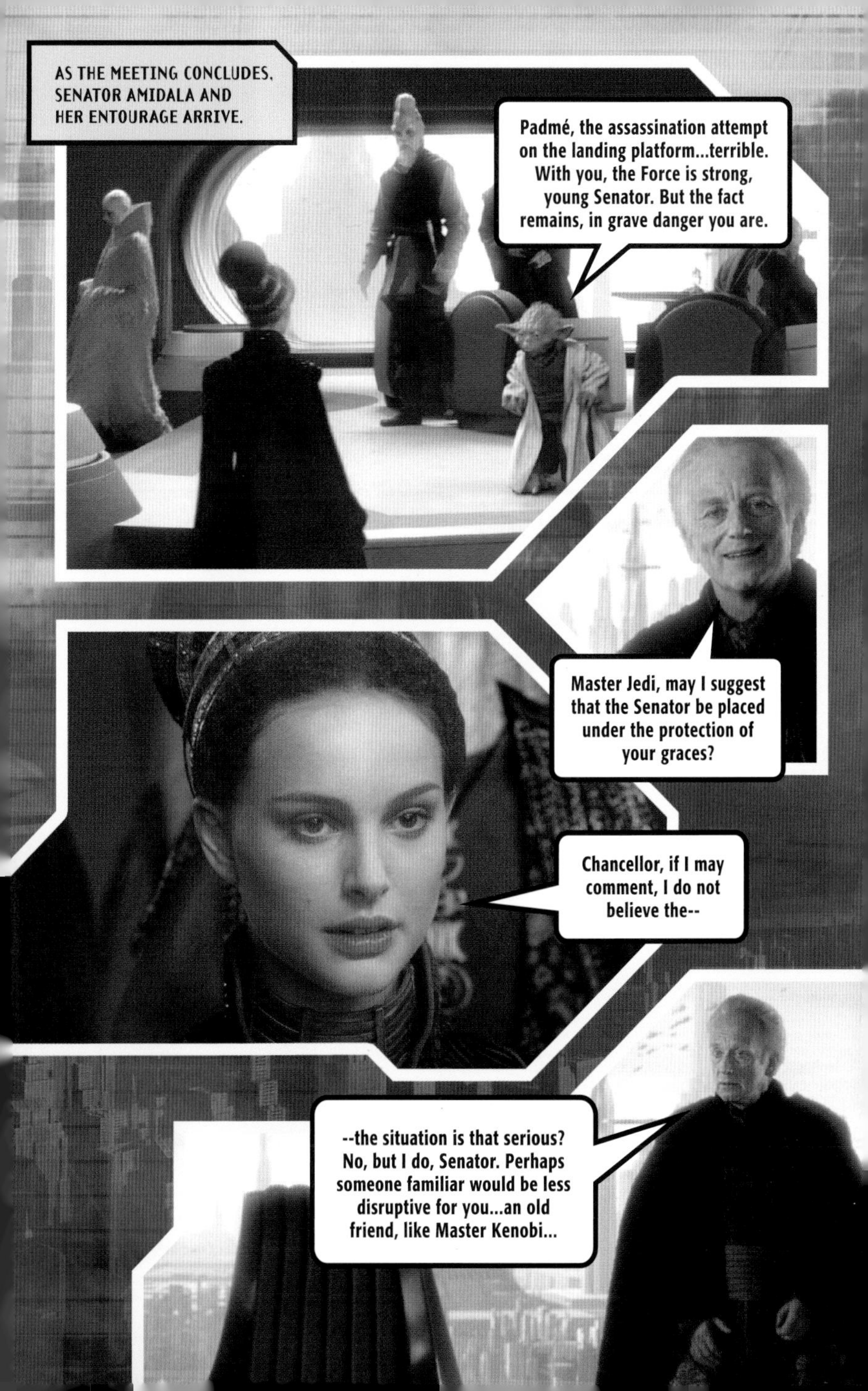
AS THE MEETING CONCLUDES, SENATOR AMIDALA AND HER ENTOURAGE ARRIVE.
Padmé, the assassination attempt on the landing platform...terrible. With you, the Force is strong, young Senator. But the fact remains, in grave danger you are.
Master Jedi, may I suggest that the Senator be placed under the protection of your graces?
Chancellor, if I may comment, I do not believe the--
--the situation is that serious? No, but I do, Senator. Perhaps someone familiar would be less disruptive for you...an old friend, like Master Kenobi...

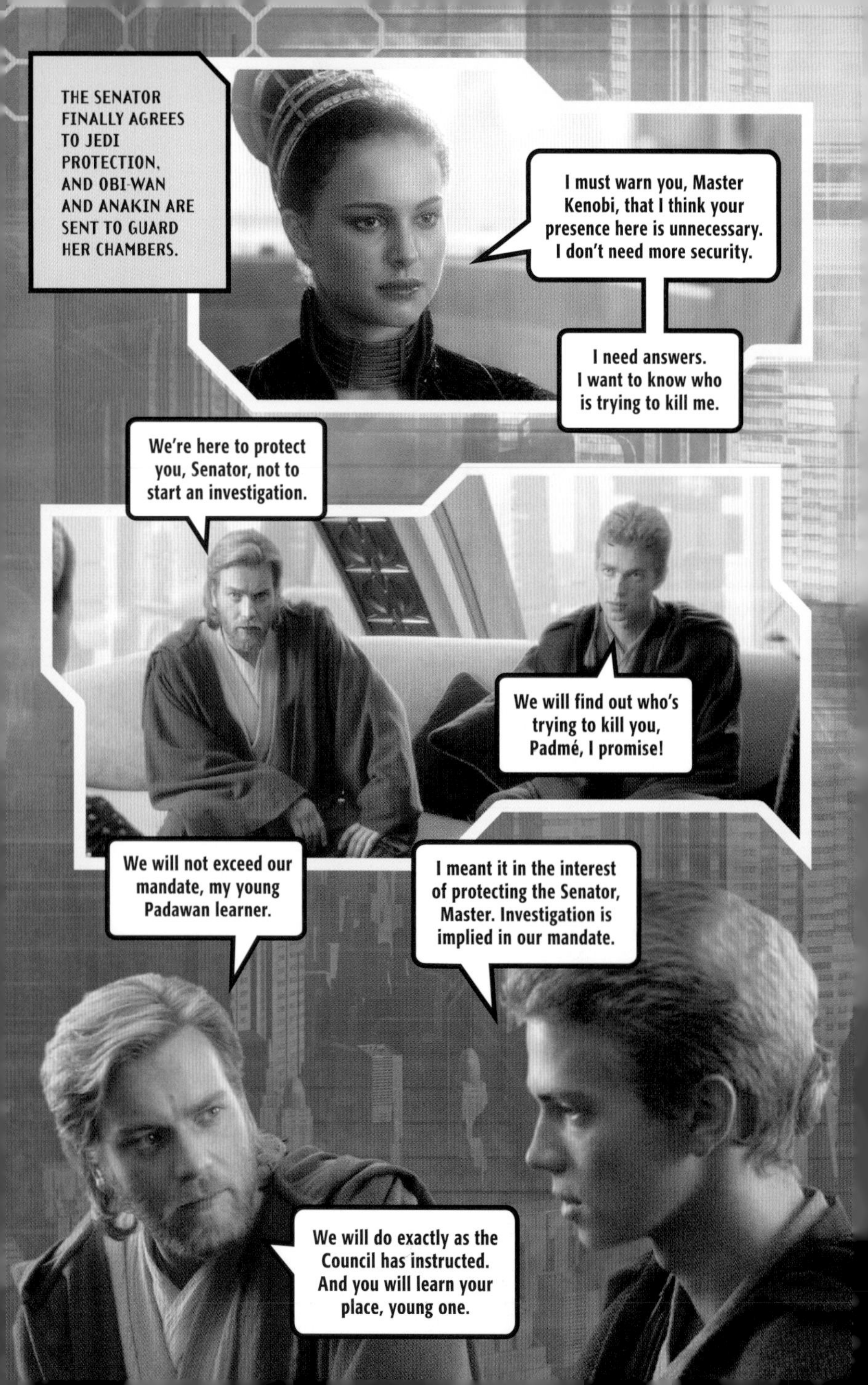
THE SENATOR FINALLY AGREES TO JEDI PROTECTION, AND OBI-WAN AND ANAKIN ARE SENT TO GUARD HER CHAMBERS.
I must warn you, Master Kenobi, that I think your presence here is unnecessary. I don't need more security.
I need answers. I want to know who is trying to kill me.
We're here to protect you, Senator, not to start an investigation.
We will find out who's trying to kill you, Padmé, I promise!
We will not exceed our mandate, my young Padawan learner.
I meant it in the interest of protecting the Senator, Master. Investigation is implied in our mandate.
We will do exactly as the Council has instructed. And you will learn your place, young one.

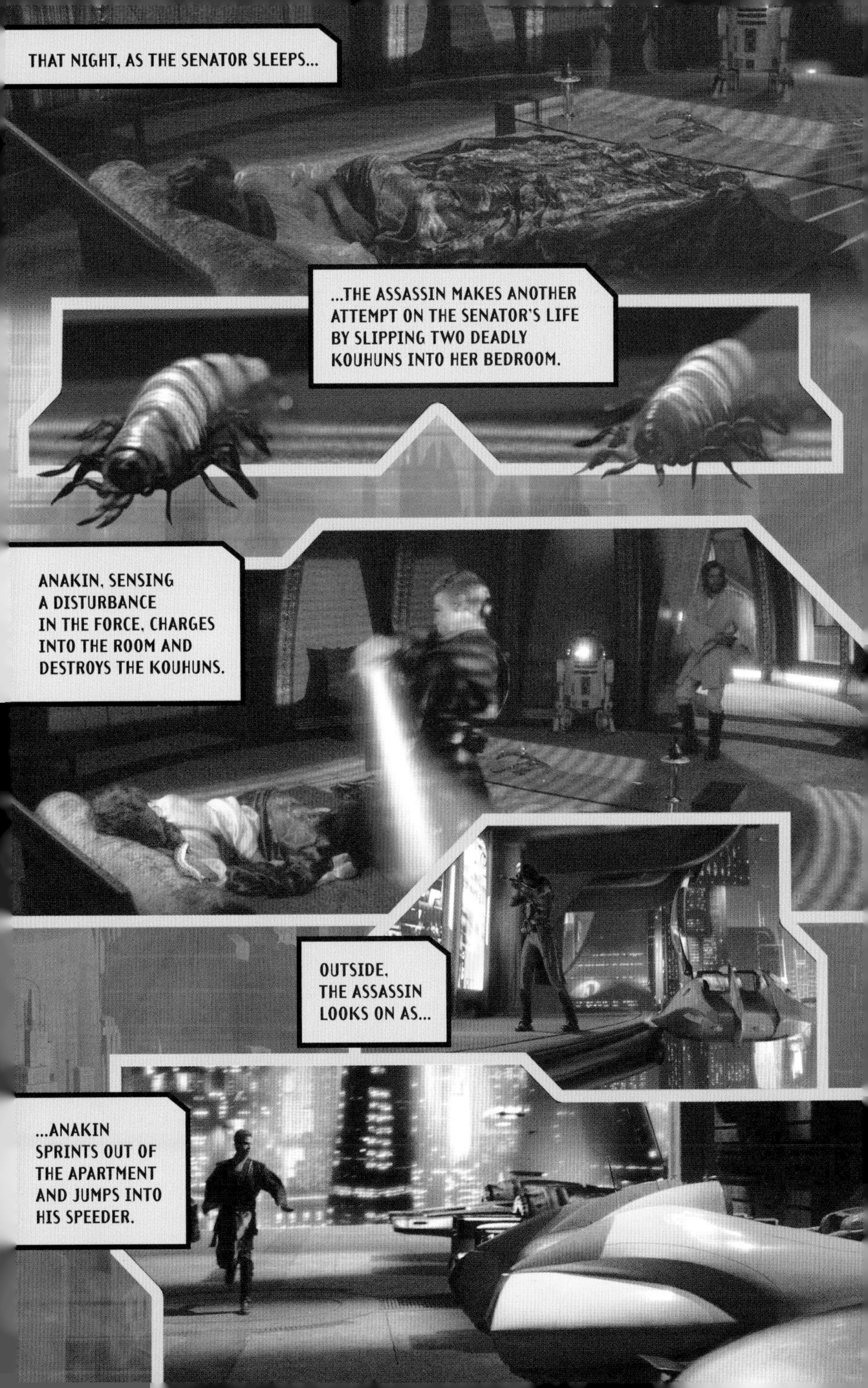
THAT NIGHT, AS THE SENATOR SLEEPS...
...THE ASSASSIN MAKES ANOTHER ATTEMPT ON THE SENATOR'S LIFE BY SLIPPING TWO DEADLY KOUHUNS INTO HER BEDROOM.
ANAKIN, SENSING A DISTURBANCE IN THE FORCE, CHARGES INTO THE ROOM AND DESTROYS THE KOUHUNS.
OUTSIDE, THE ASSASSIN LOOKS ON AS...
...ANAKIN SPRINTS OUT OF THE APARTMENT AND JUMPS INTO HIS SPEEDER.

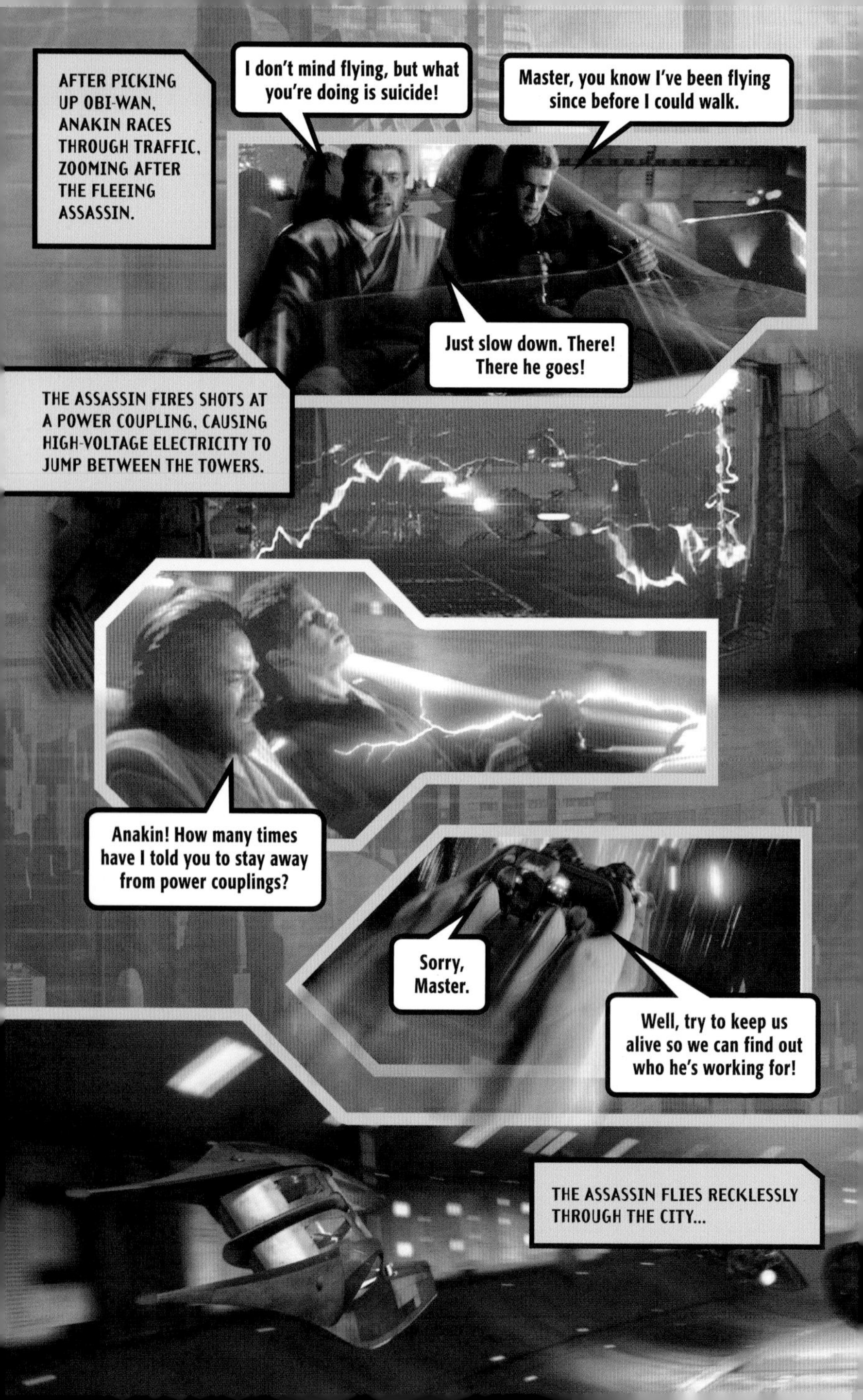
AFTER PICKING UP OBI-WAN, ANAKIN RACES THROUGH TRAFFIC, ZOOMING AFTER THE FLEEING ASSASSIN.
I don't mind flying, but what you're doing is suicide!
Master, you know I've been flying since before I could walk.
Just slow down. There! There he goes!
THE ASSASSIN FIRES SHOTS AT A POWER COUPLING, CAUSING HIGH-VOLTAGE ELECTRICITY TO JUMP BETWEEN THE TOWERS.
Anakin! How many times have I told you to stay away from power couplings?
Sorry, Master.
Well, try to keep us alive so we can find out who he's working for!
THE ASSASSIN FLIES RECKLESSLY THROUGH THE CITY...

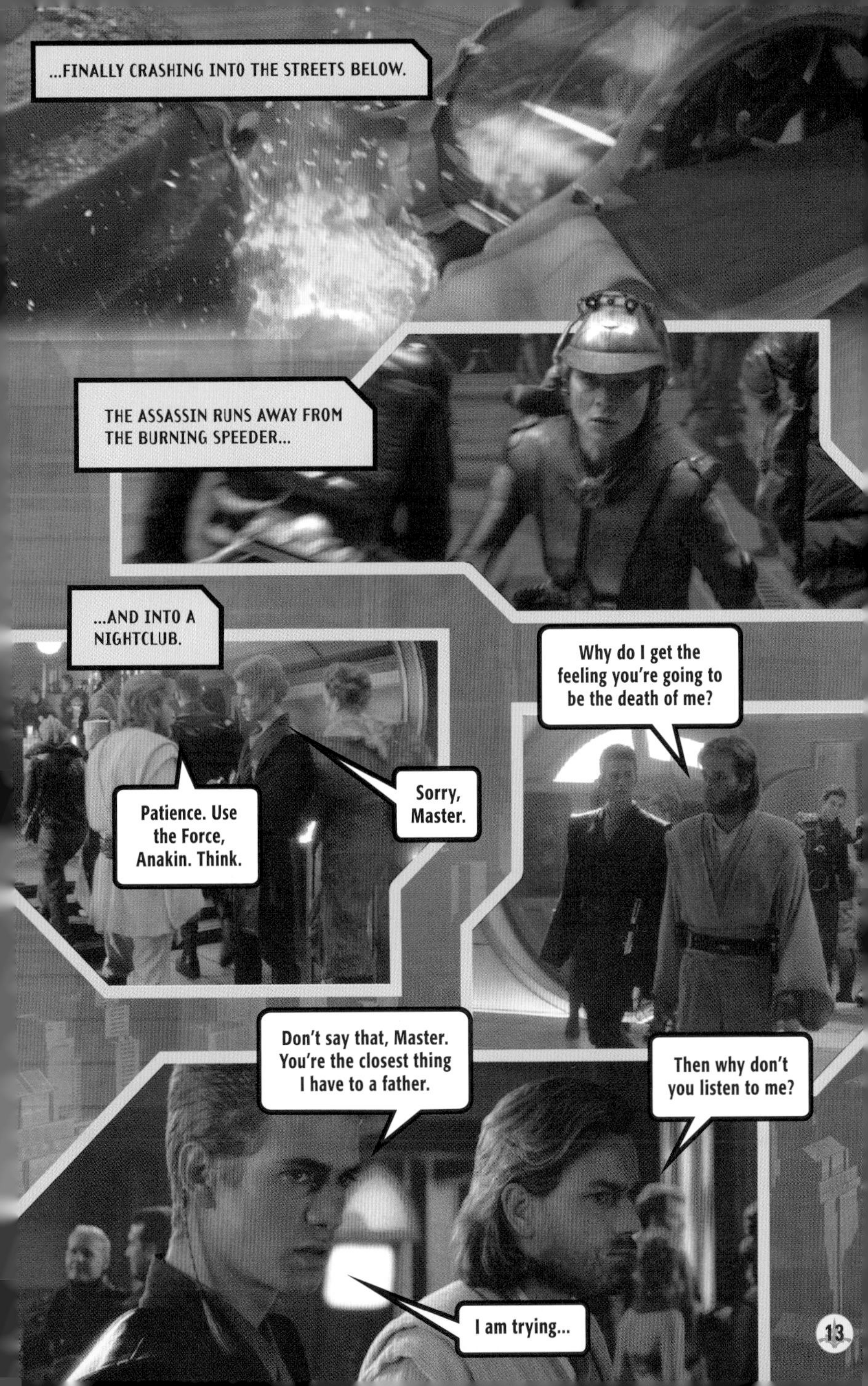
...FINALLY CRASHING INTO THE STREETS BELOW.
THE ASSASSIN RUNS AWAY FROM THE BURNING SPEEDER...
...AND INTO A NIGHTCLUB.
Patience. Use the Force, Anakin. Think.
Sorry, Master.
Why do I get the feeling you're going to be the death of me?
Don't say that, Master. You're the closest thing I have to a father.
Then why don't you listen to me?
I am trying...

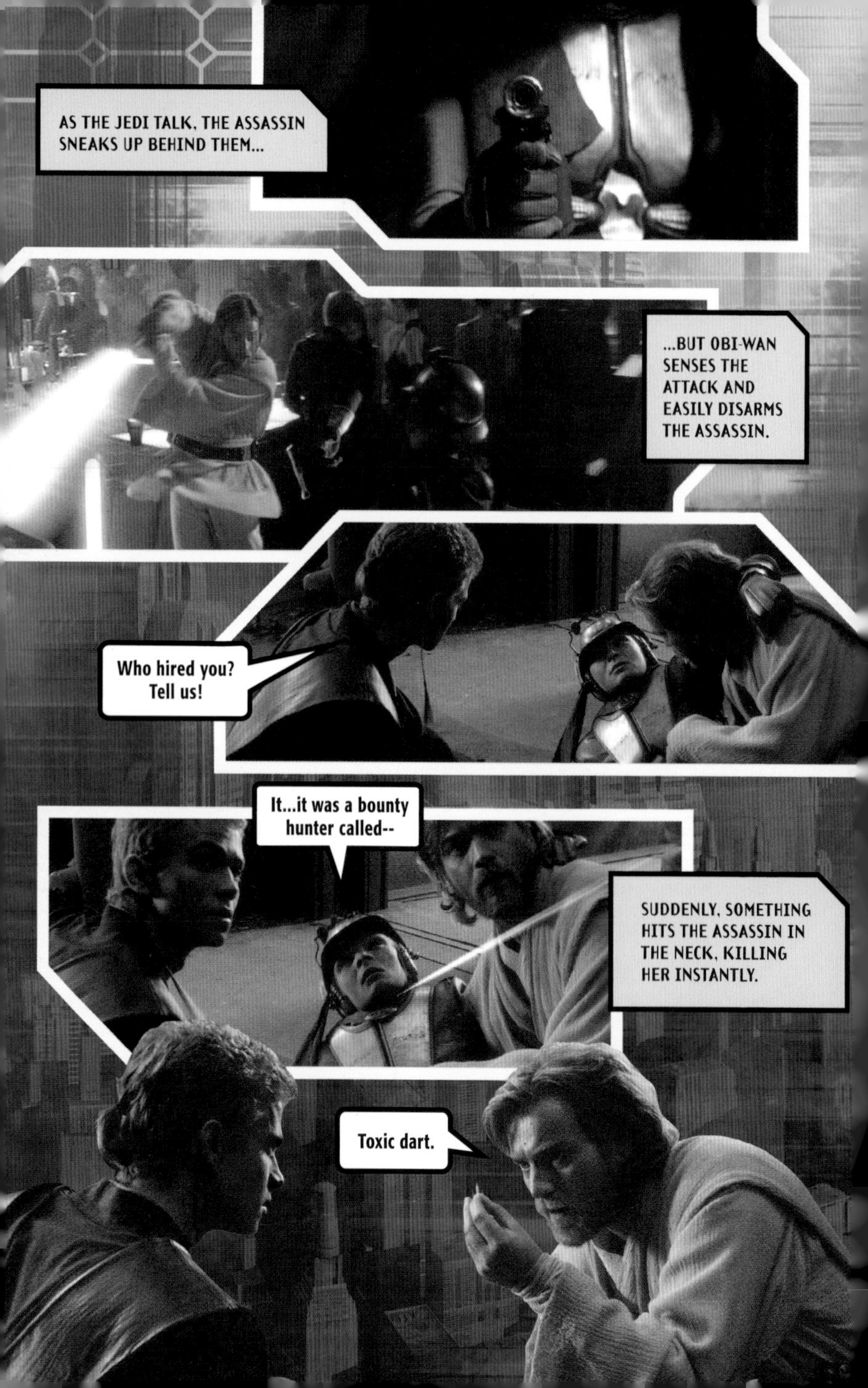
AS THE JEDI TALK, THE ASSASSIN SNEAKS UP BEHIND THEM...
...BUT OBI-WAN SENSES THE ATTACK AND EASILY DISARMS THE ASSASSIN.
Who hired you? Tell us!
It...it was a bounty hunter called--
SUDDENLY, SOMETHING HITS THE ASSASSIN IN THE NECK, KILLING HER INSTANTLY.
Toxic dart.

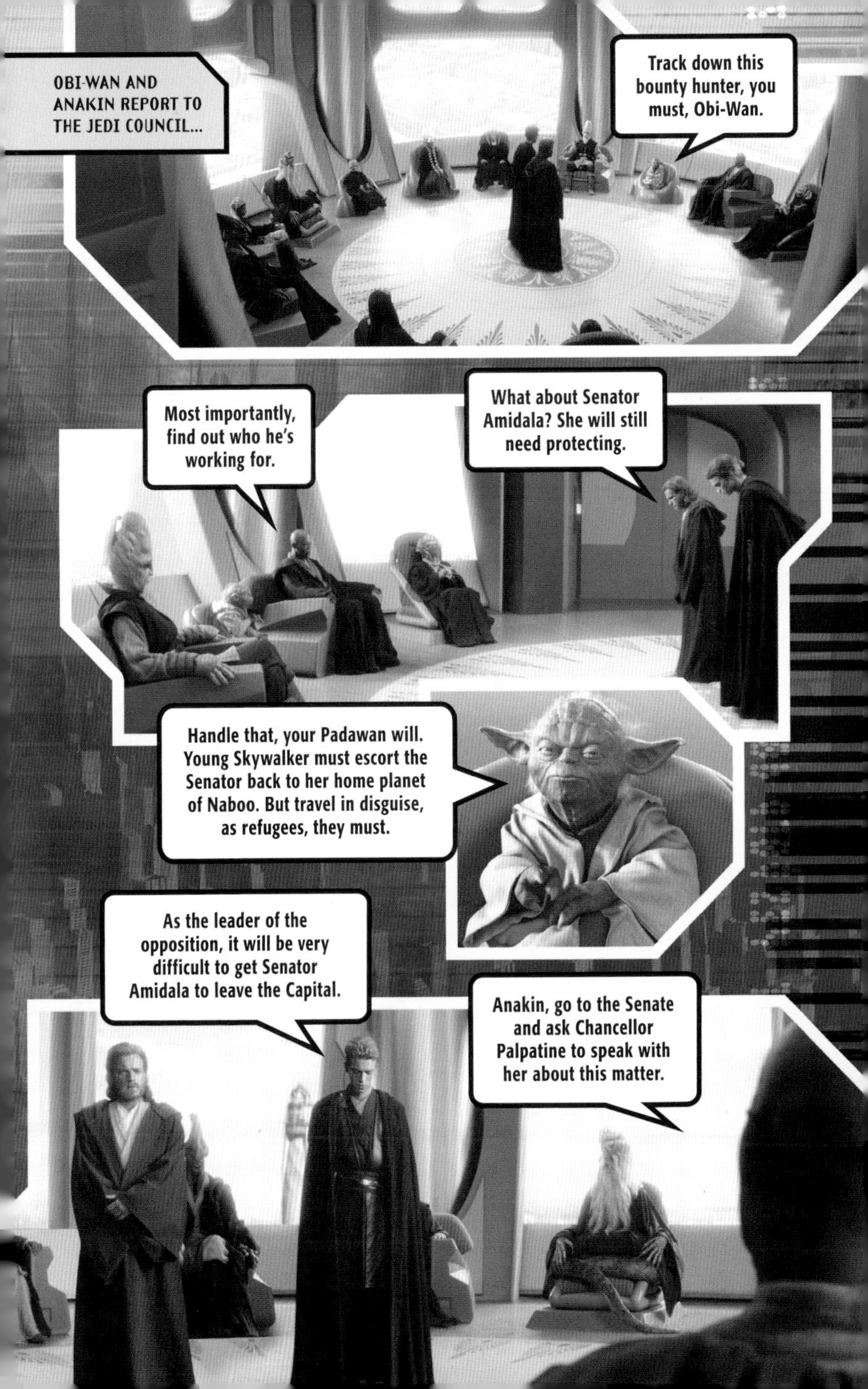
OBI-WAN AND ANAKIN REPORT TO THE JEDI COUNCIL...
Track down this bounty hunter, you must, Obi-Wan.
Most importantly, find out who he's working for.
What about Senator Amidala? She will still need protecting.
Handle that, your Padawan will. Young Skywalker must escort the Senator back to her home planet of Naboo. But travel in disguise, as refugees, they must.
As the leader of the opposition, it will be very difficult to get Senator Amidala to leave the Capital.
Anakin, go to the Senate and ask Chancellor Palpatine to speak with her about this matter.

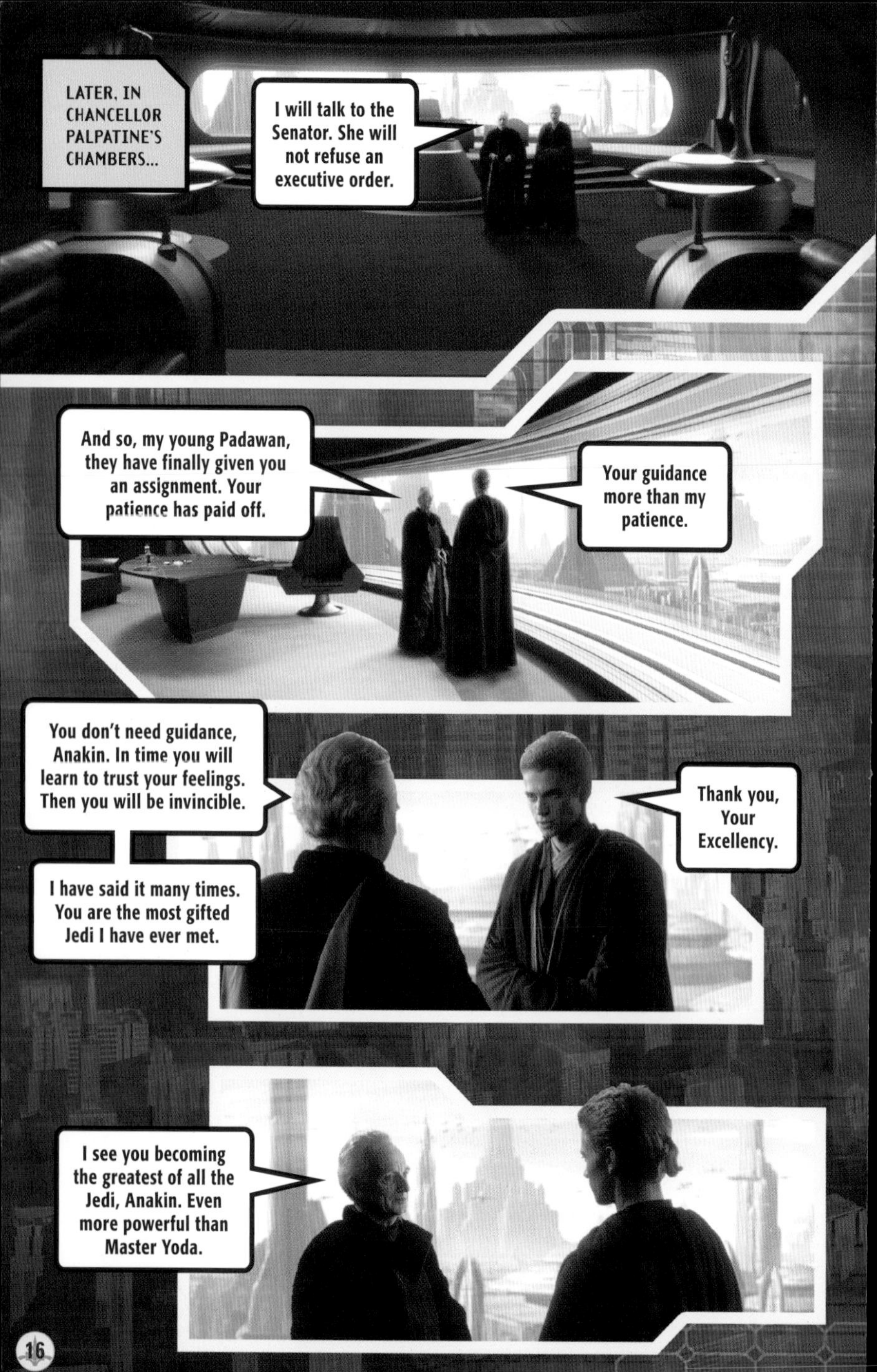
LATER, IN CHANCELLOR PALPATINE'S CHAMBERS...
I will talk to the Senator. She will not refuse an executive order.
And so, my young Padawan, they have finally given you an assignment. Your patience has paid off.
Your guidance more than my patience.
You don't need guidance, Anakin. In time you will learn to trust your feelings. Then you will be invincible.
I have said it many times. You are the most gifted Jedi I have ever met.
Thank you, Your Excellency.
I see you becoming the greatest of all the Jedi, Anakin. Even more powerful than Master Yoda.

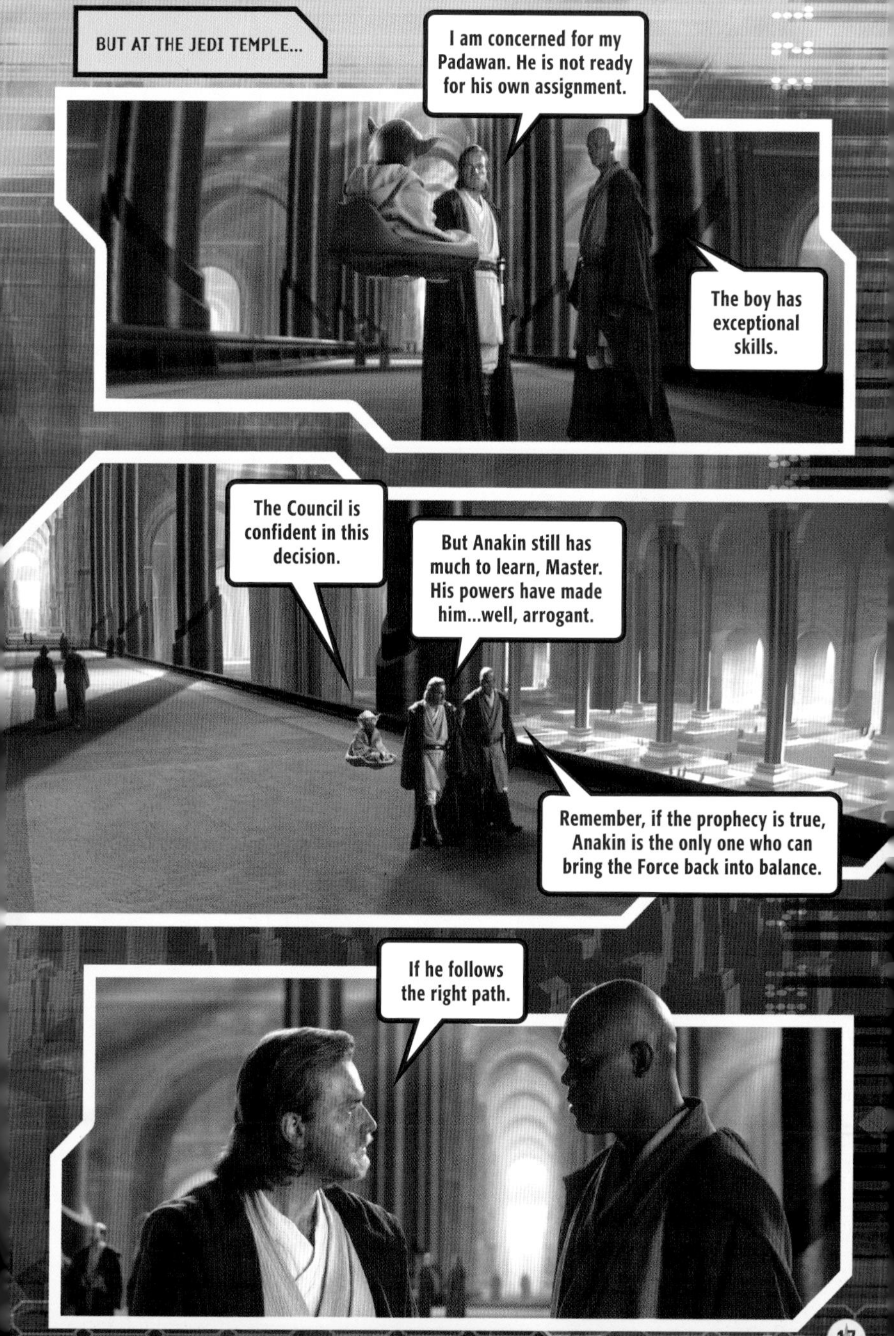
BUT AT THE JEDI TEMPLE...
I am concerned for my Padawan. He is not ready for his own assignment.
The boy has exceptional skills.
The Council is confident in this decision.
But Anakin still has much to learn, Master. His powers have made him...well, arrogant.
Remember, if the prophecy is true, Anakin is the only one who can bring the Force back into balance.
If he follows the right path.

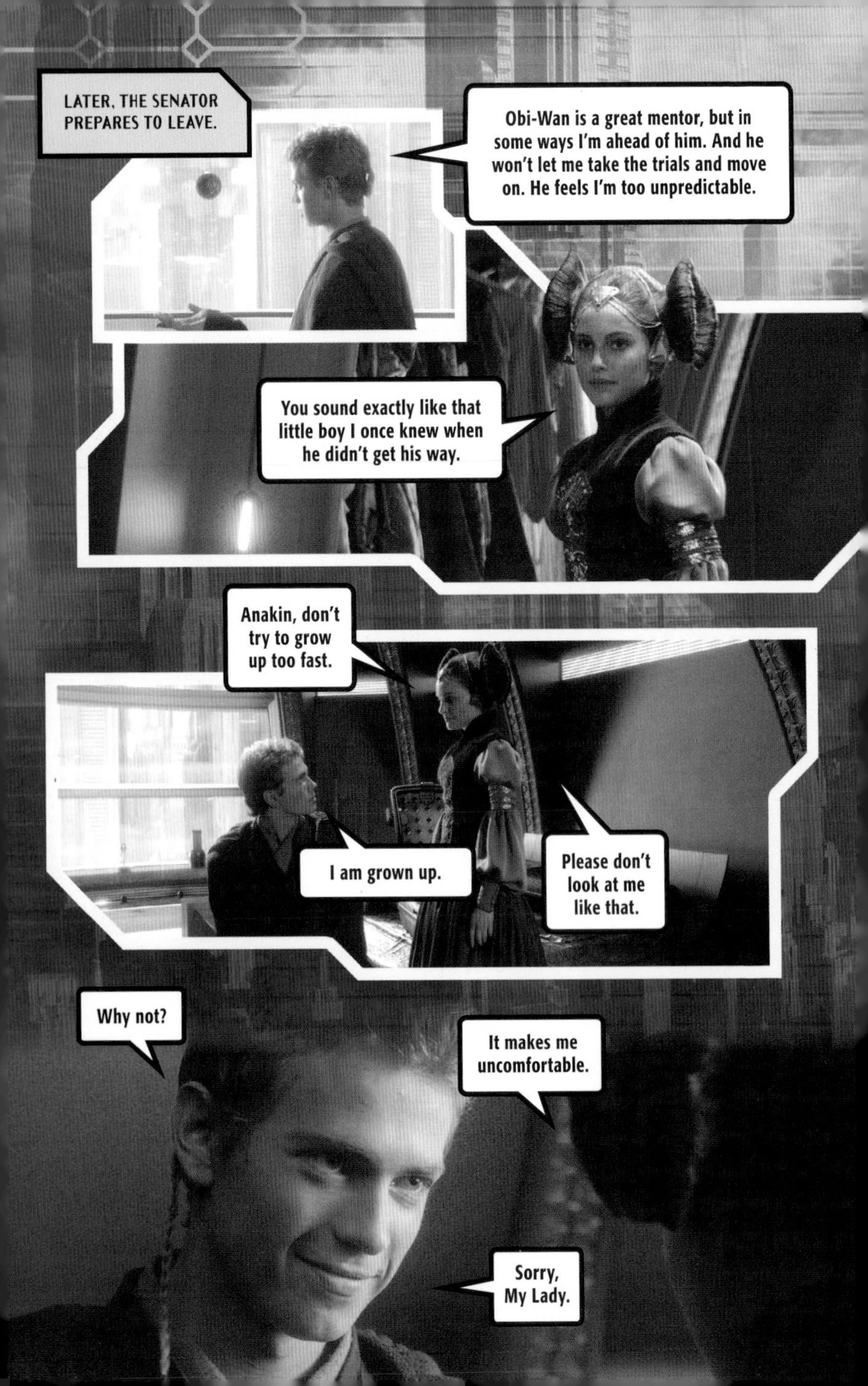
LATER, THE SENATOR PREPARES TO LEAVE.
Obi-Wan is a great mentor, but in some ways I'm ahead of him. And he won't let me take the trials and move on. He feels I'm too unpredictable.
You sound exactly like that little boy I once knew when he didn't get his way.
Anakin, don't try to grow up too fast.
I am grown up.
Please don't look at me like that.
Why not?
It makes me uncomfortable.
Sorry, My Lady.

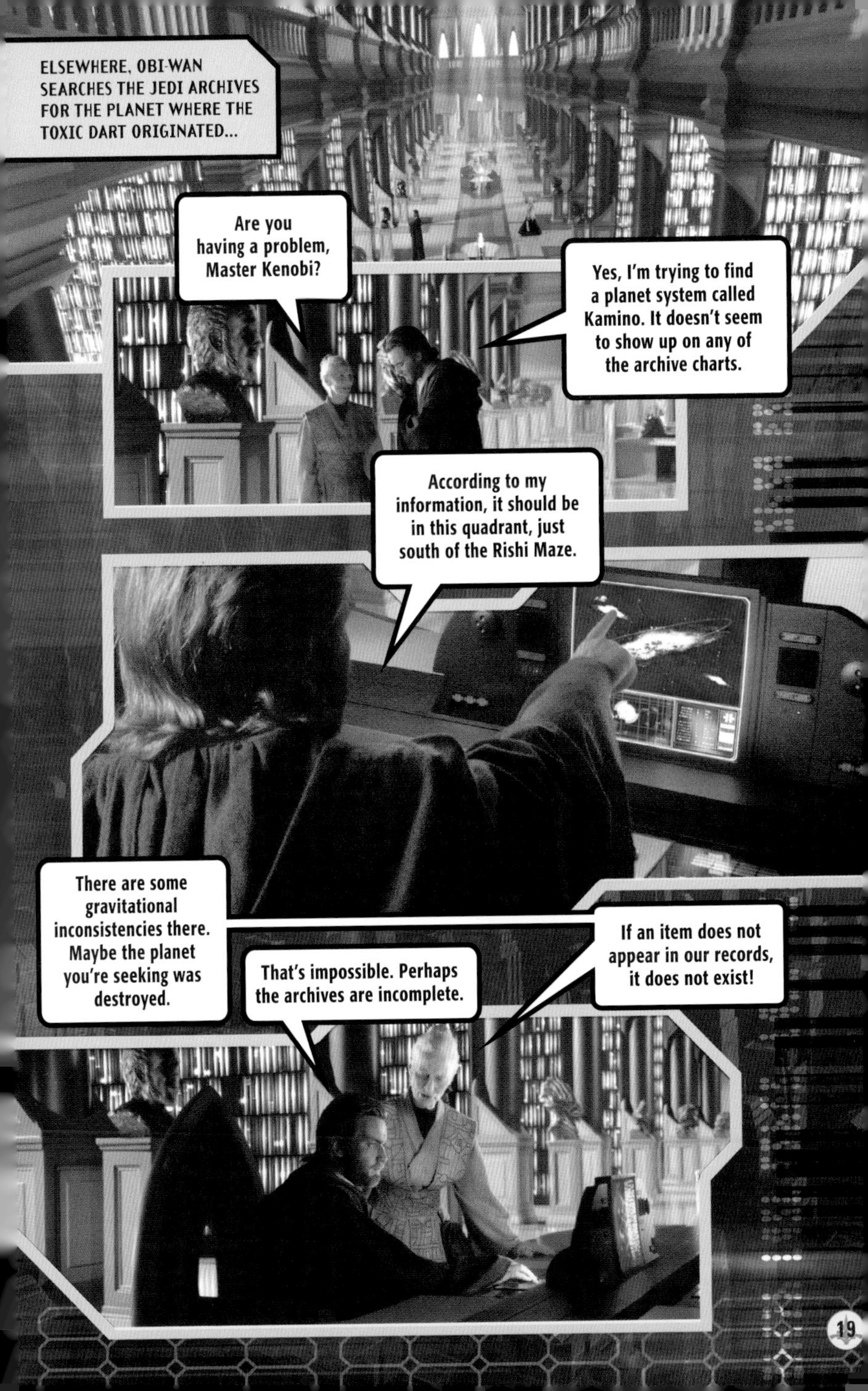
ELSEWHERE, OBI-WAN SEARCHES THE JEDI ARCHIVES FOR THE PLANET WHERE THE TOXIC DART ORIGINATED...
Are you having a problem, Master Kenobi?
Yes, I'm trying to find a planet system called Kamino. It doesn't seem to show up on any of the archive charts.
According to my information, it should be in this quadrant, just south of the Rishi Maze.
There are some gravitational inconsistencies there. Maybe the planet you're seeking was destroyed.
That's impossible. Perhaps the archives are incomplete.
If an item does not appear in our records, it does not exist!

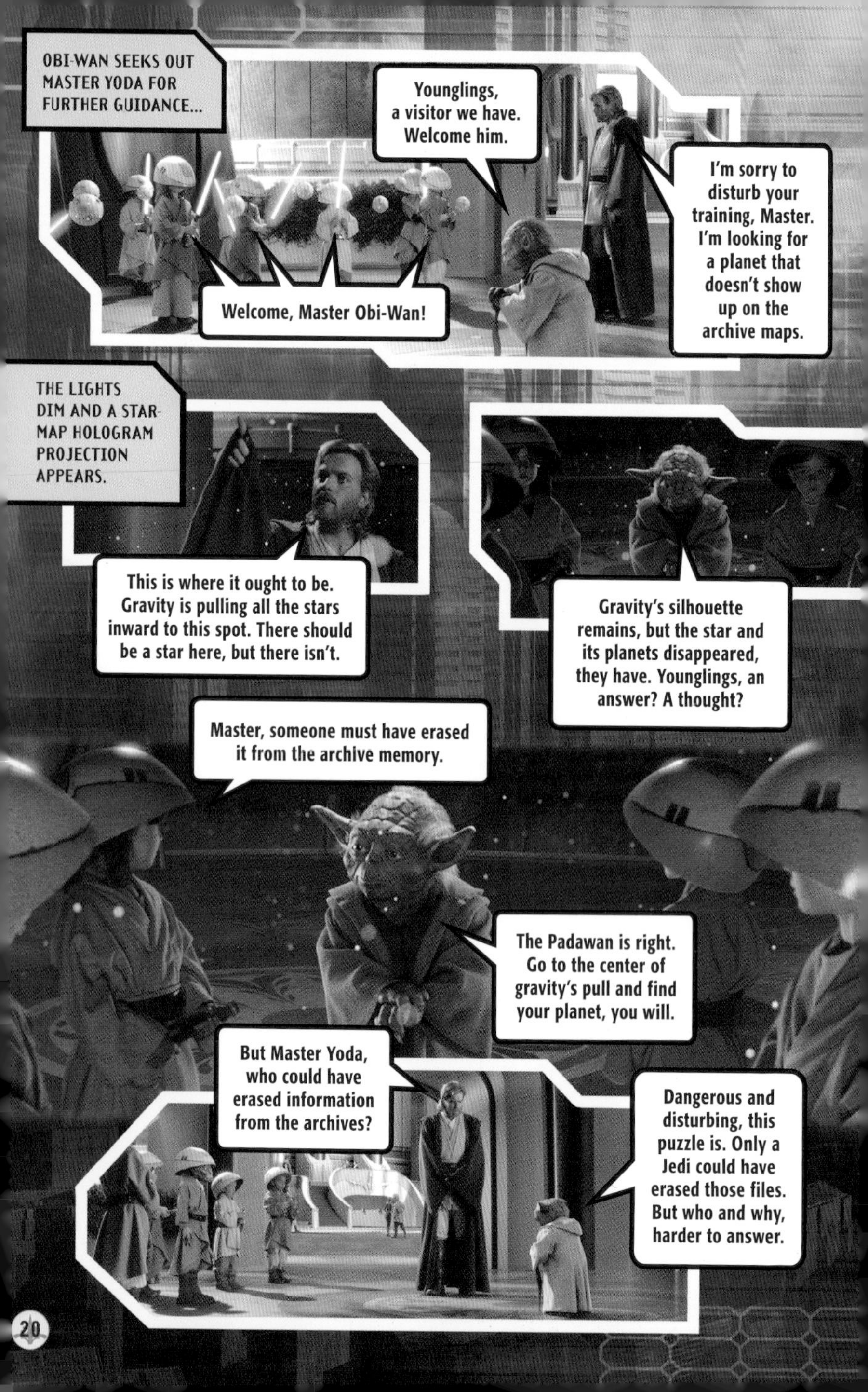

OBI-WAN SEEKS OUT MASTER YODA FOR FURTHER GUIDANCE...
Younglings, a visitor we have. Welcome him.
Welcome, Master Obi-Wan!
I'm sorry to disturb your training, Master. I'm looking for a planet that doesn't show up on the archive maps.
THE LIGHTS DIM AND A STAR-MAP HOLOGRAM PROJECTION APPEARS.
This is where it ought to be. Gravity is pulling all the stars inward to this spot. There should be a star here, but there isn't.
Gravity's silhouette remains, but the star and its planets disappeared, they have. Younglings, an answer? A thought?
Master, someone must have erased it from the archive memory.
The Padawan is right. Go to the center of gravity's pull and find your planet, you will.
But Master Yoda, who could have erased information from the archives?
Dangerous and disturbing, this puzzle is. Only a Jedi could have erased those files. But who and why, harder to answer.

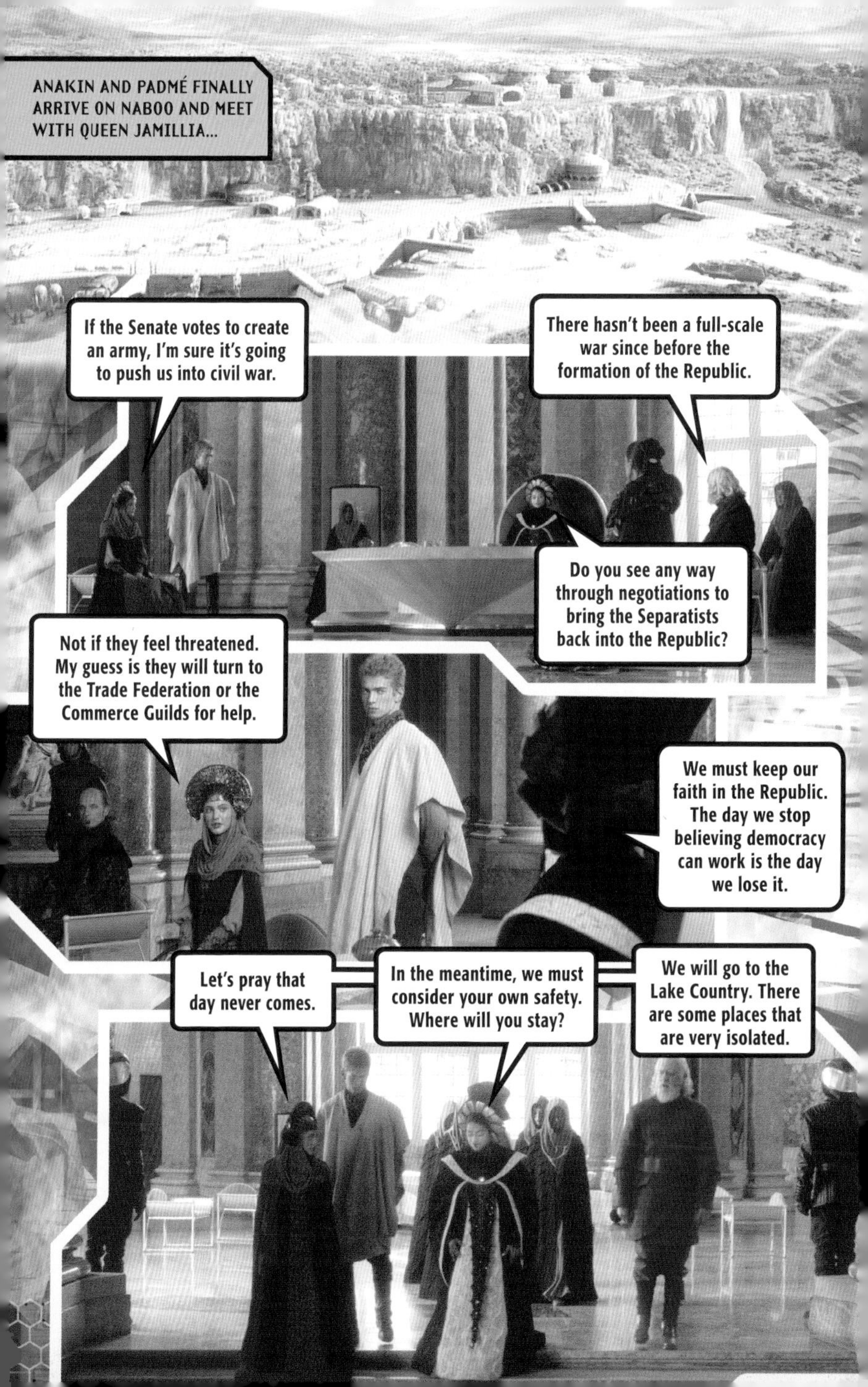
ANAKIN AND PADMÉ FINALLY ARRIVE ON NABOO AND MEET WITH QUEEN JAMILLIA...
If the Senate votes to create an army, I'm sure it's going to push us into civil war.
There hasn't been a full-scale war since before the formation of the Republic.
Do you see any way through negotiations to bring the Separatists back into the Republic?
Not if they feel threatened. My guess is they will turn to the Trade Federation or the Commerce Guilds for help.
We must keep our faith in the Republic. The day we stop believing democracy can work is the day we lose it.
Let's pray that day never comes.
In the meantime, we must consider your own safety. Where will you stay?
We will go to the Lake Country. There are some places that are very isolated.

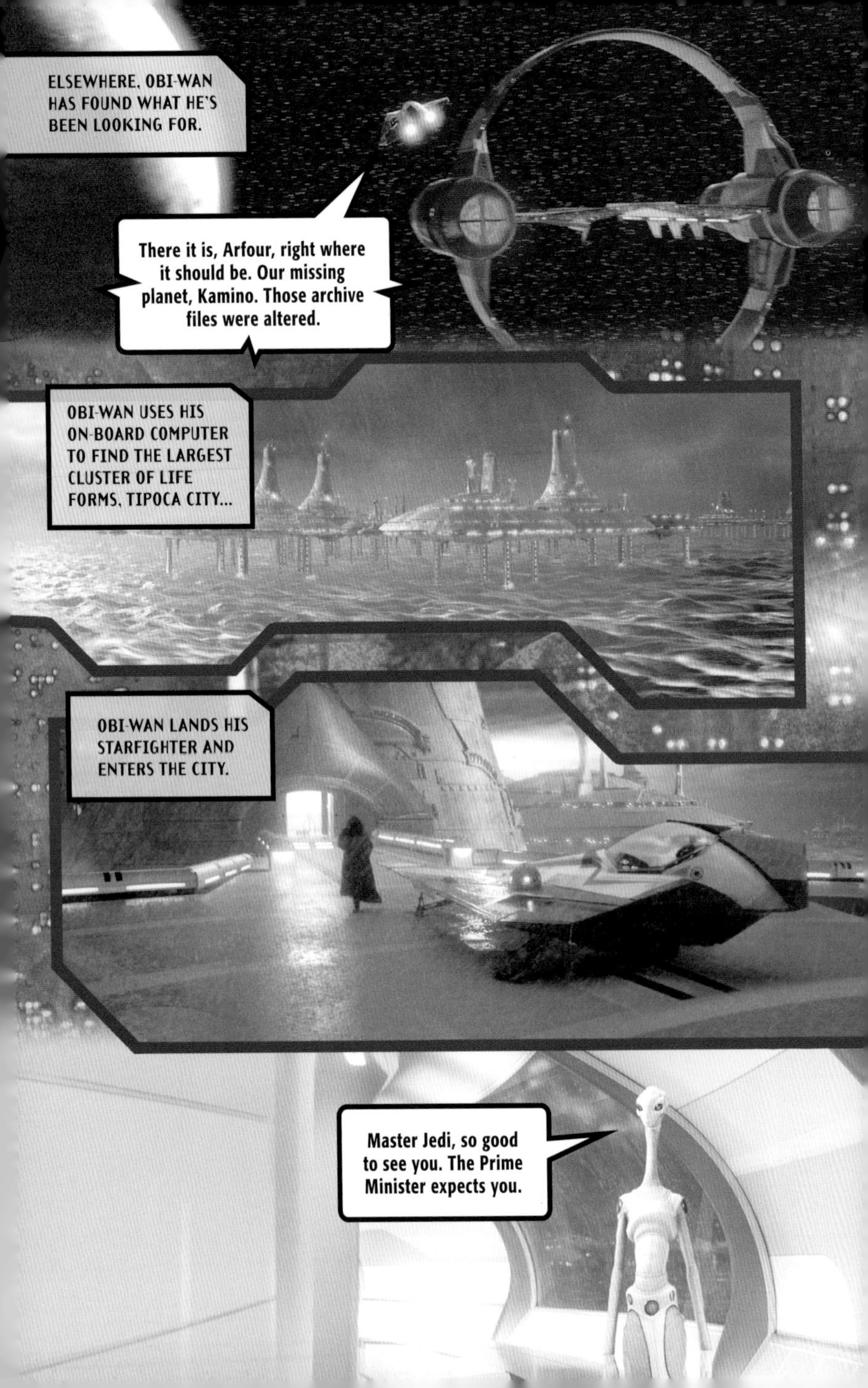
ELSEWHERE, OBI-WAN HAS FOUND WHAT HE'S BEEN LOOKING FOR.
There it is, Arfour, right where it should be. Our missing planet, Kamino. Those archive files were altered.
OBI-WAN USES HIS ON-BOARD COMPUTER TO FIND THE LARGEST CLUSTER OF LIFE FORMS, TIPOCA CITY...
OBI-WAN LANDS HIS STARFIGHTER AND ENTERS THE CITY.
Master Jedi, so good to see you. The Prime Minister expects you.

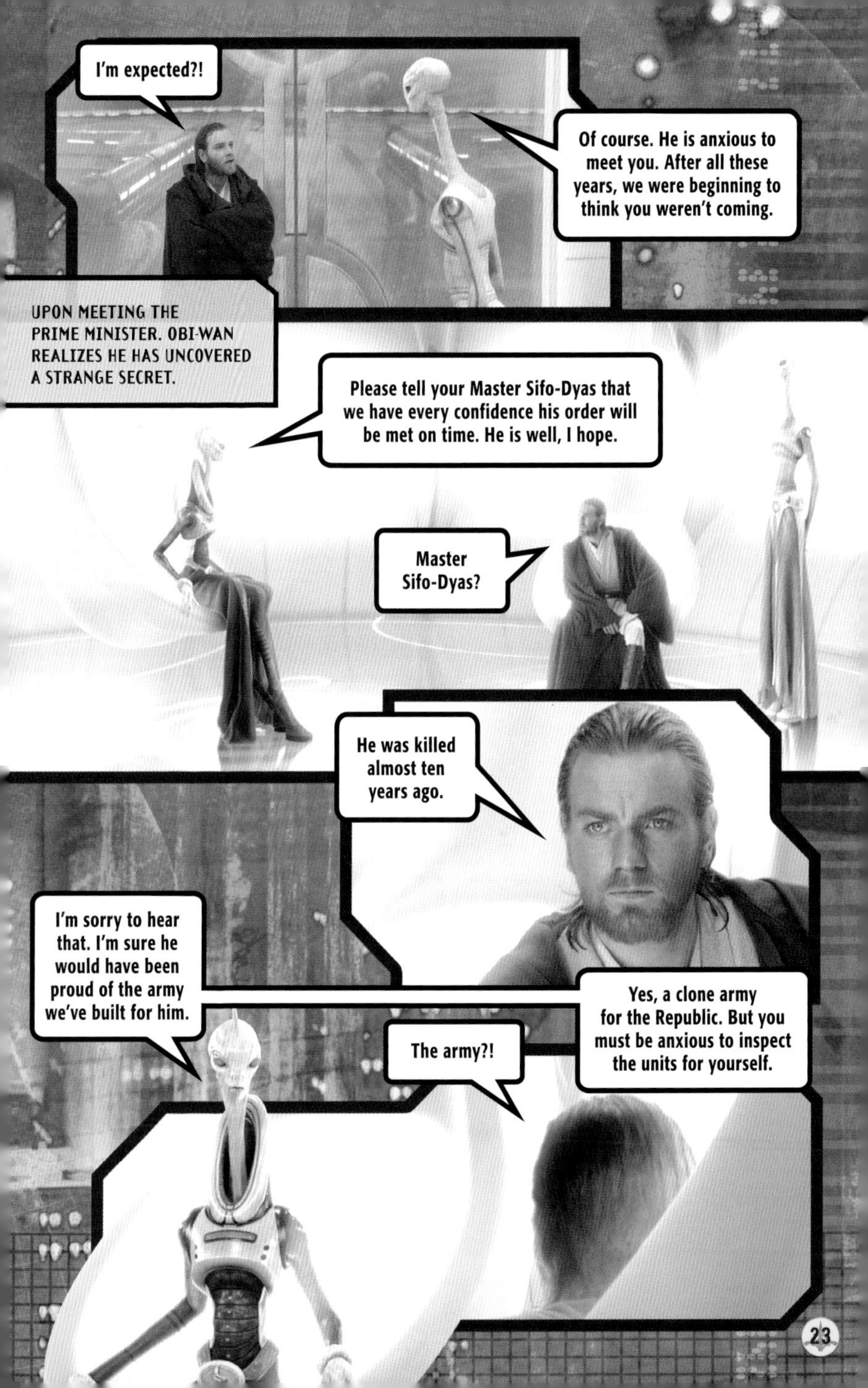

I'm expected?!
Of course. He is anxious to meet you. After all these years, we were beginning to think you weren't coming.
UPON MEETING THE PRIME MINISTER. OBI-WAN REALIZES HE HAS UNCOVERED A STRANGE SECRET.
Please tell your Master Sifo-Dyas that we have every confidence his order will be met on time. He is well, I hope.
Master Sifo-Dyas?
He was killed almost ten years ago.
I'm sorry to hear that. I'm sure he would have been proud of the army we've built for him.
The army?!
Yes, a clone army for the Republic. But you must be anxious to inspect the units for yourself.

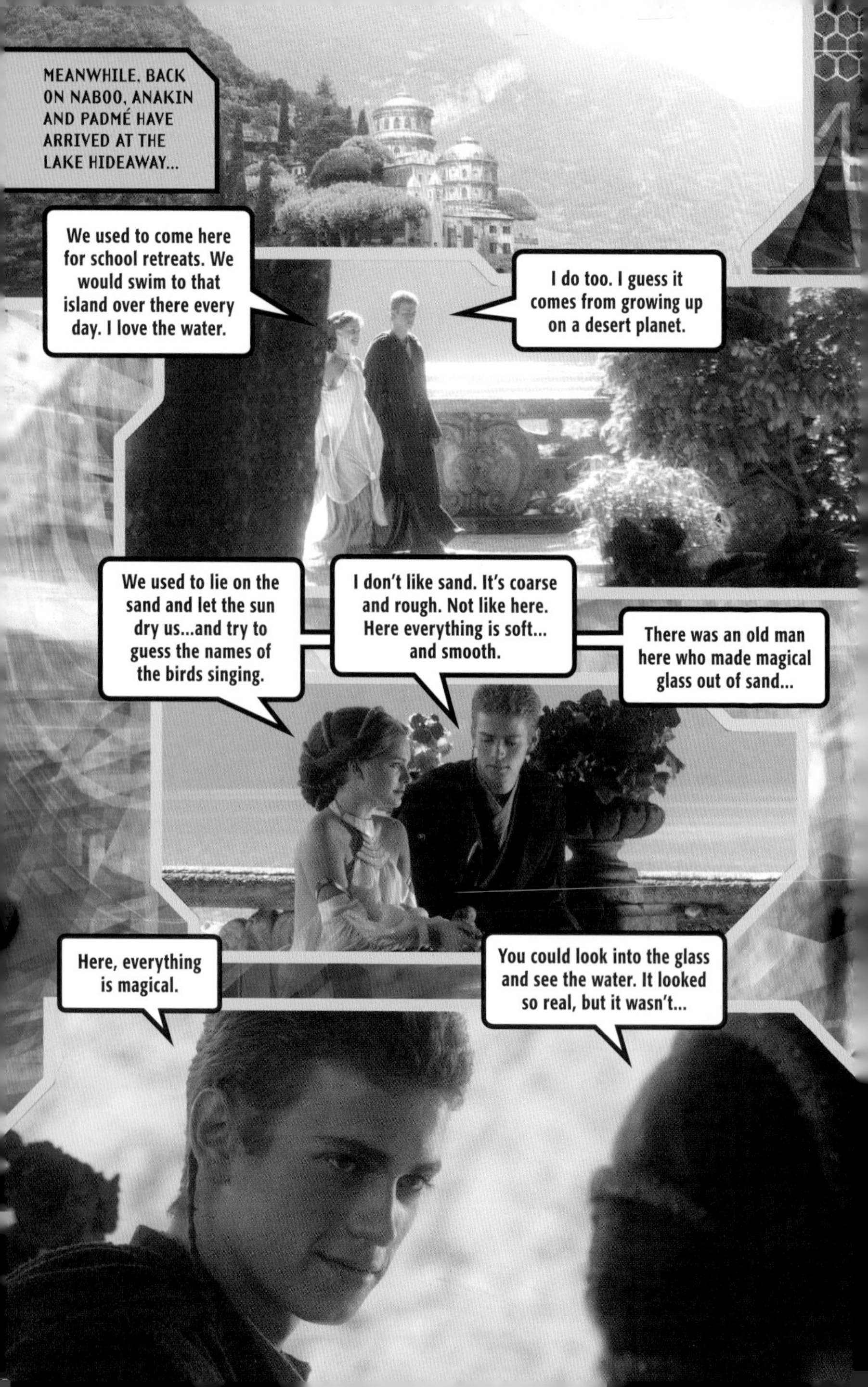
MEANWHILE, BACK ON NABOO, ANAKIN AND PADMÉ HAVE ARRIVED AT THE LAKE HIDEAWAY...
We used to come here for school retreats. We would swim to that island over there every day. I love the water.
I do too. I guess it comes from growing up on a desert planet.
We used to lie on the sand and let the sun dry us...and try to guess the names of the birds singing.
I don't like sand. It's coarse and rough. Not like here. Here everything is soft... and smooth.
There was an old man here who made magical glass out of sand...
Here, everything is magical.
You could look into the glass and see the water. It looked so real, but it wasn't...

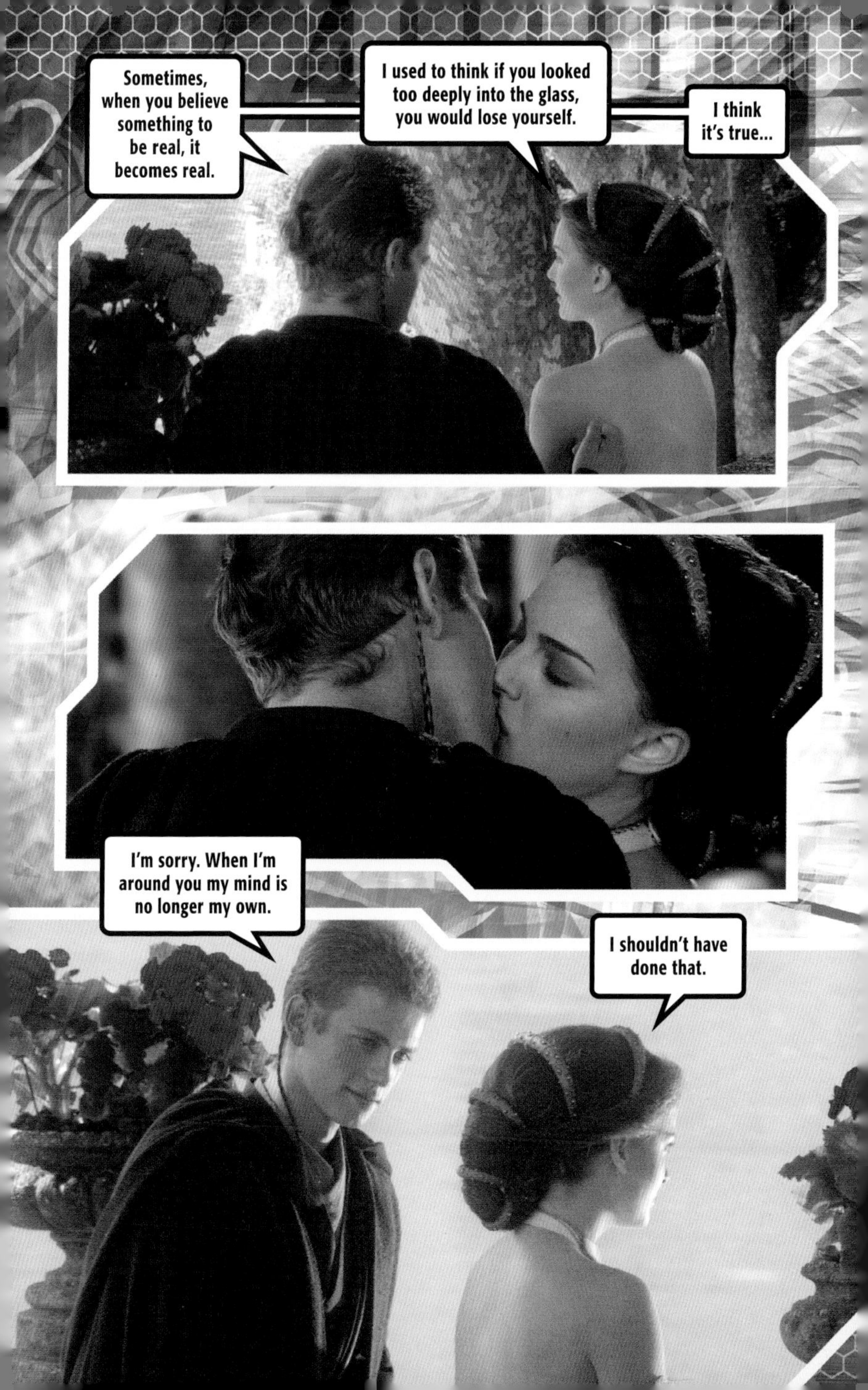
Sometimes, when you believe something to be real, it becomes real.
I used to think if you looked too deeply into the glass, you would lose yourself.
I think it's true...
I'm sorry. When I'm around you my mind is no longer my own.
I shouldn't have done that.

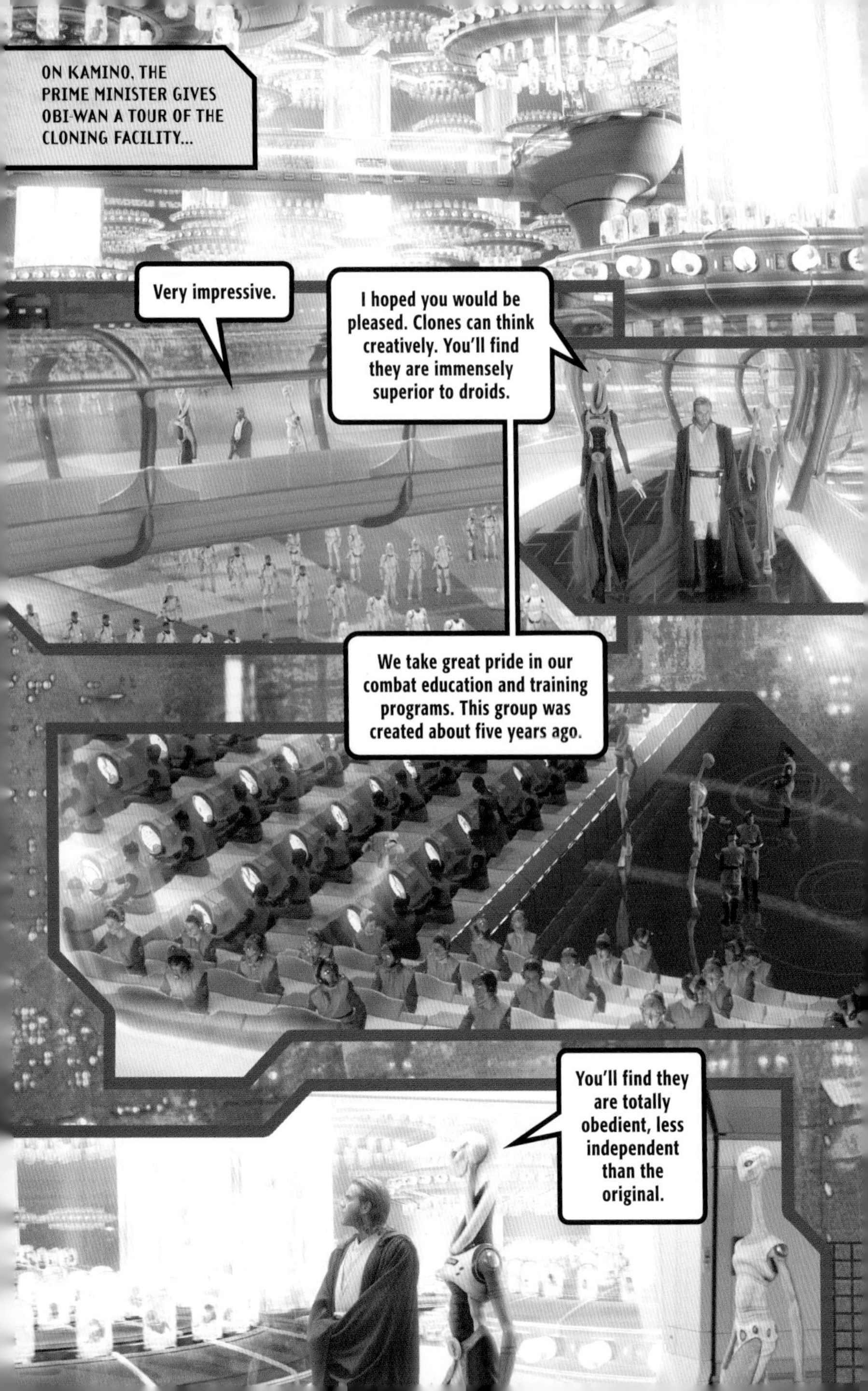

ON KAMINO, THE PRIME MINISTER GIVES OBI-WAN A TOUR OF THE CLONING FACILITY...
Very impressive.
I hoped you would be pleased. Clones can think creatively. You'll find they are immensely superior to droids.
We take great pride in our combat education and training programs. This group was created about five years ago.
You'll find they are totally obedient, less independent than the original.

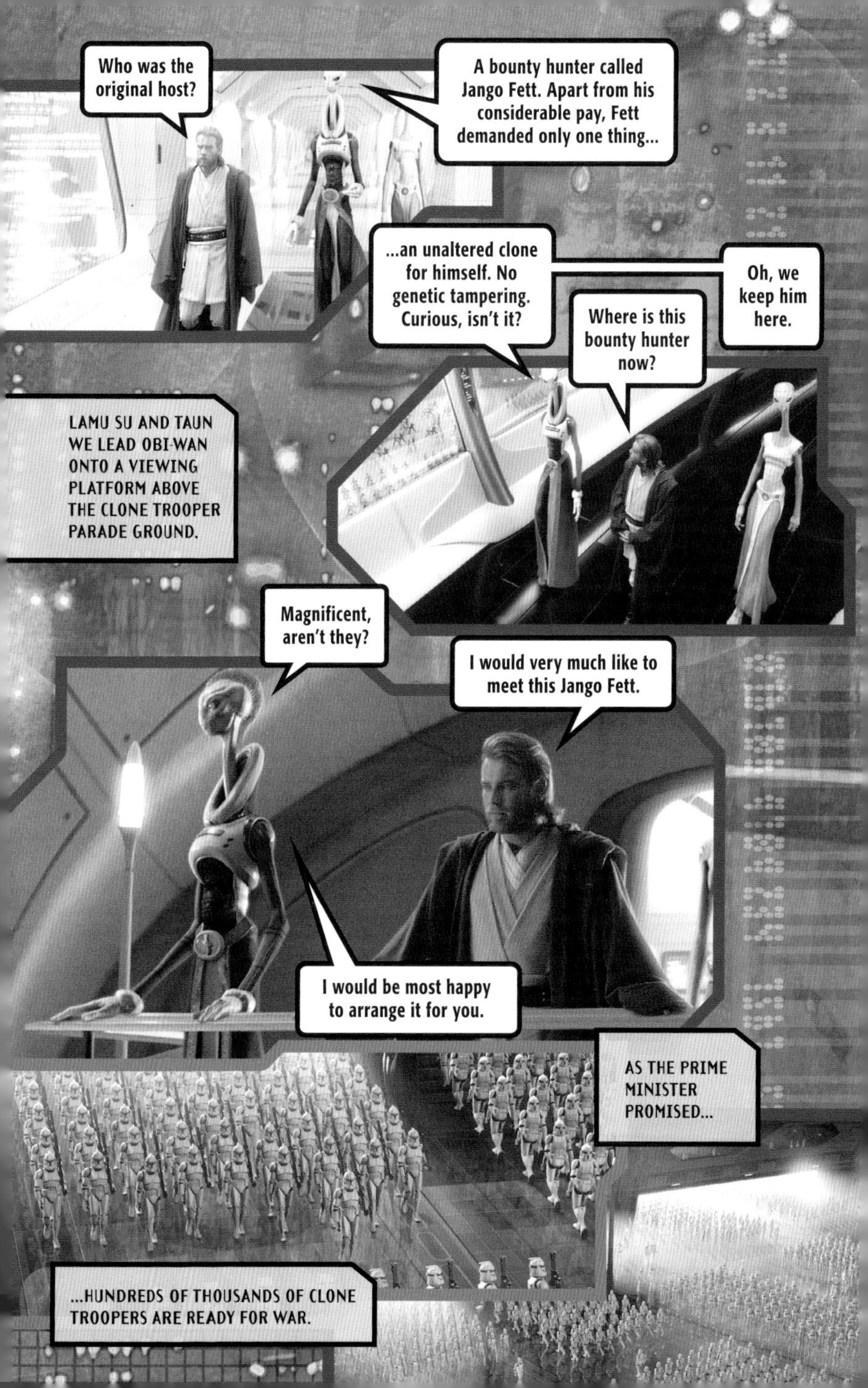
Who was the original host?
A bounty hunter called Jango Fett. Apart from his considerable pay, Fett demanded only one thing...
...an unaltered clone for himself. No genetic tampering. Curious, isn't it?
Where is this bounty hunter now?
Oh, we keep him here.
LAMU SU AND TAUN WE LEAD OBI-WAN ONTO A VIEWING PLATFORM ABOVE THE CLONE TROOPER PARADE GROUND.
Magnificent, aren't they?
I would very much like to meet this Jango Fett.
I would be most happy to arrange it for you.
AS THE PRIME MINISTER PROMISED...
...HUNDREDS OF THOUSANDS OF CLONE TROOPERS ARE READY FOR WAR.

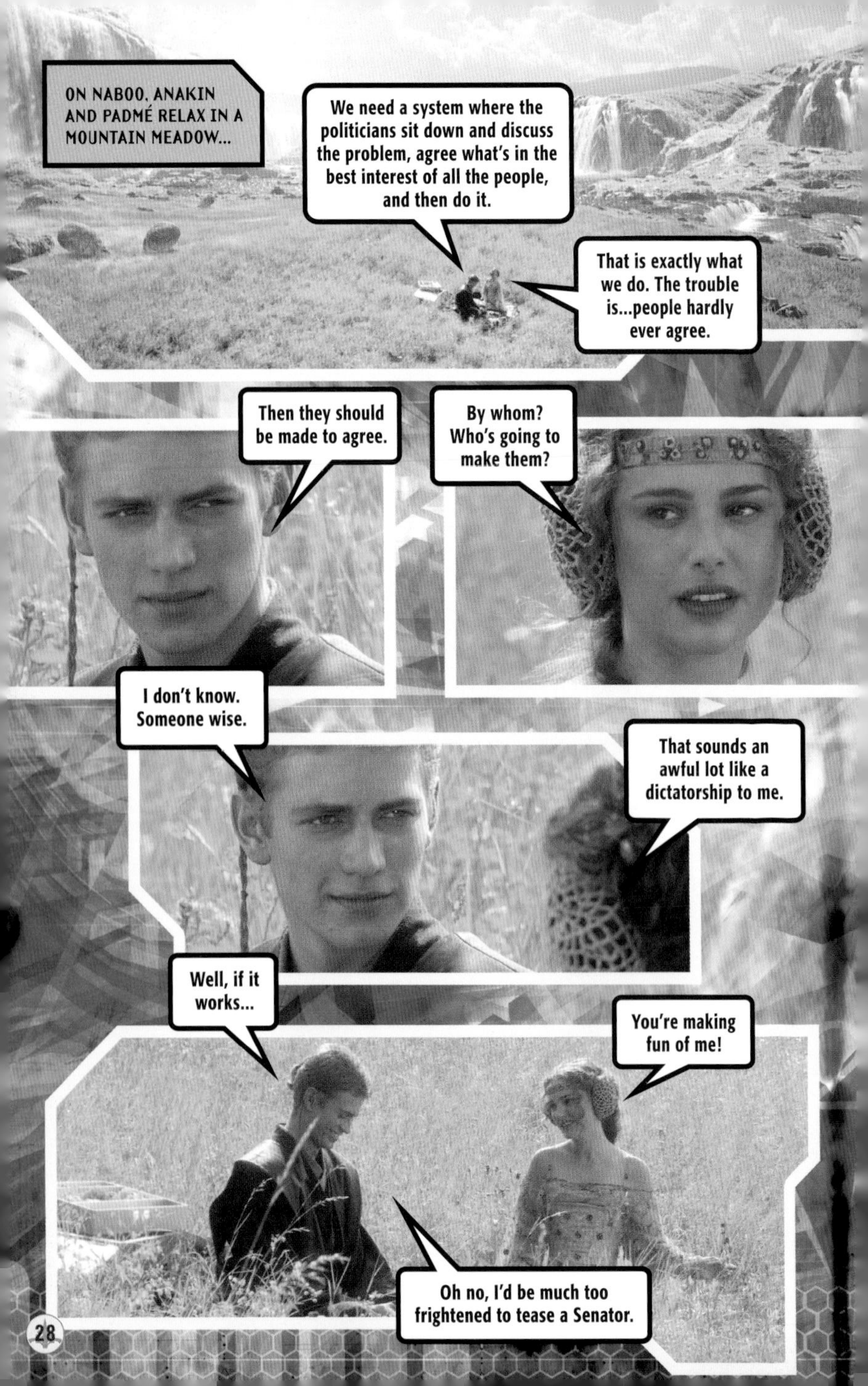
ON NABOO, ANAKIN AND PADMÉ RELAX IN A MOUNTAIN MEADOW...
We need a system where the politicians sit down and discuss the problem, agree what's in the best interest of all the people, and then do it.
That is exactly what we do. The trouble is...people hardly ever agree.
Then they should be made to agree.
By whom? Who's going to make them?
I don't know. Someone wise.
That sounds an awful lot like a dictatorship to me.
Well, if it works...
You're making fun of me!
Oh no, I'd be much too frightened to tease a Senator.

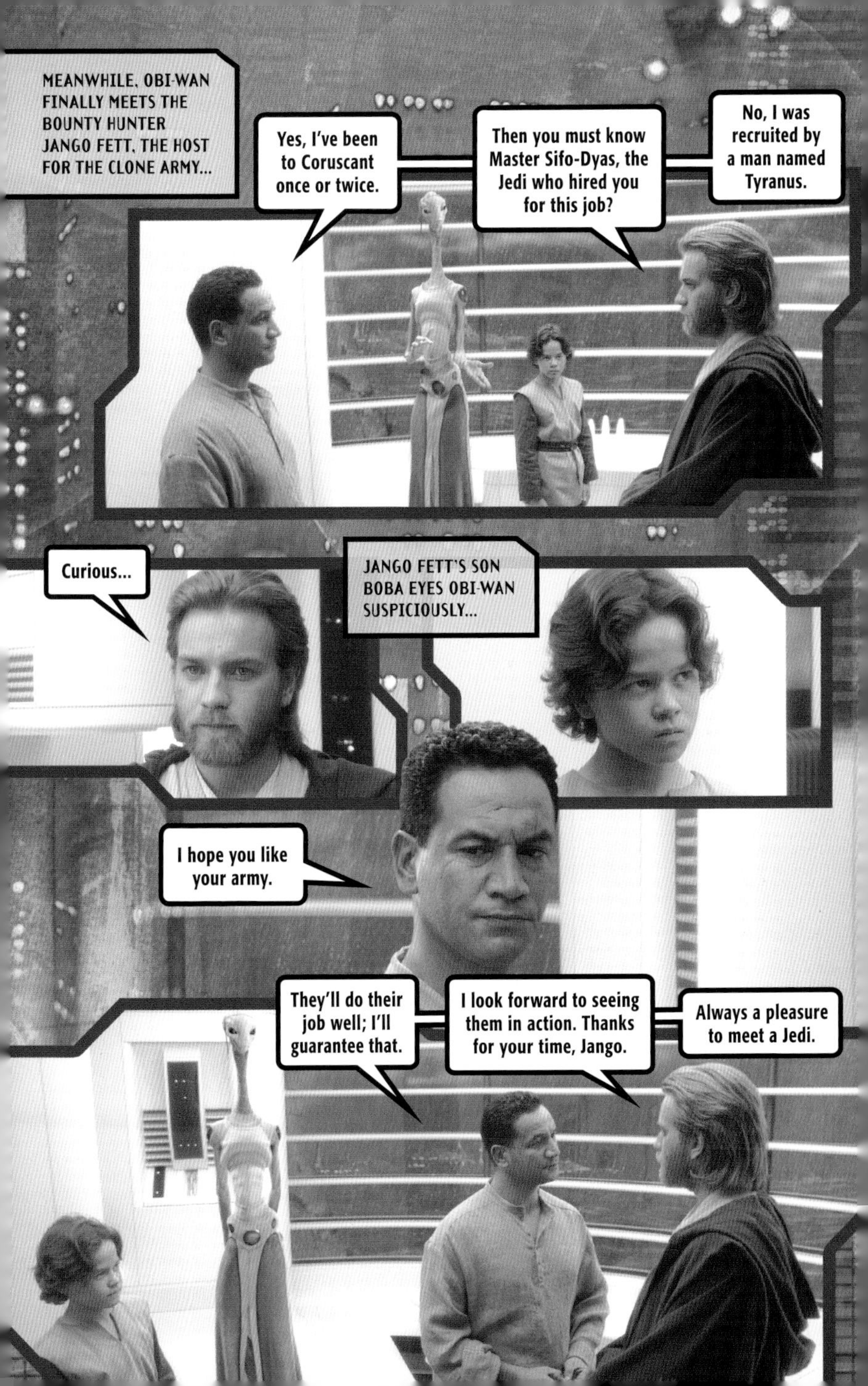
MEANWHILE, OBI-WAN FINALLY MEETS THE BOUNTY HUNTER JANGO FETT, THE HOST FOR THE CLONE ARMY...
Yes, I've been to Coruscant once or twice.
Then you must know Master Sifo-Dyas, the Jedi who hired you for this job?
No, I was recruited by a man named Tyranus.
Curious...
JANGO FETT'S SON BOBA EYES OBI-WAN SUSPICIOUSLY...
I hope you like your army.
They'll do their job well; I'll guarantee that.
I look forward to seeing them in action. Thanks for your time, Jango.
Always a pleasure to meet a Jedi.

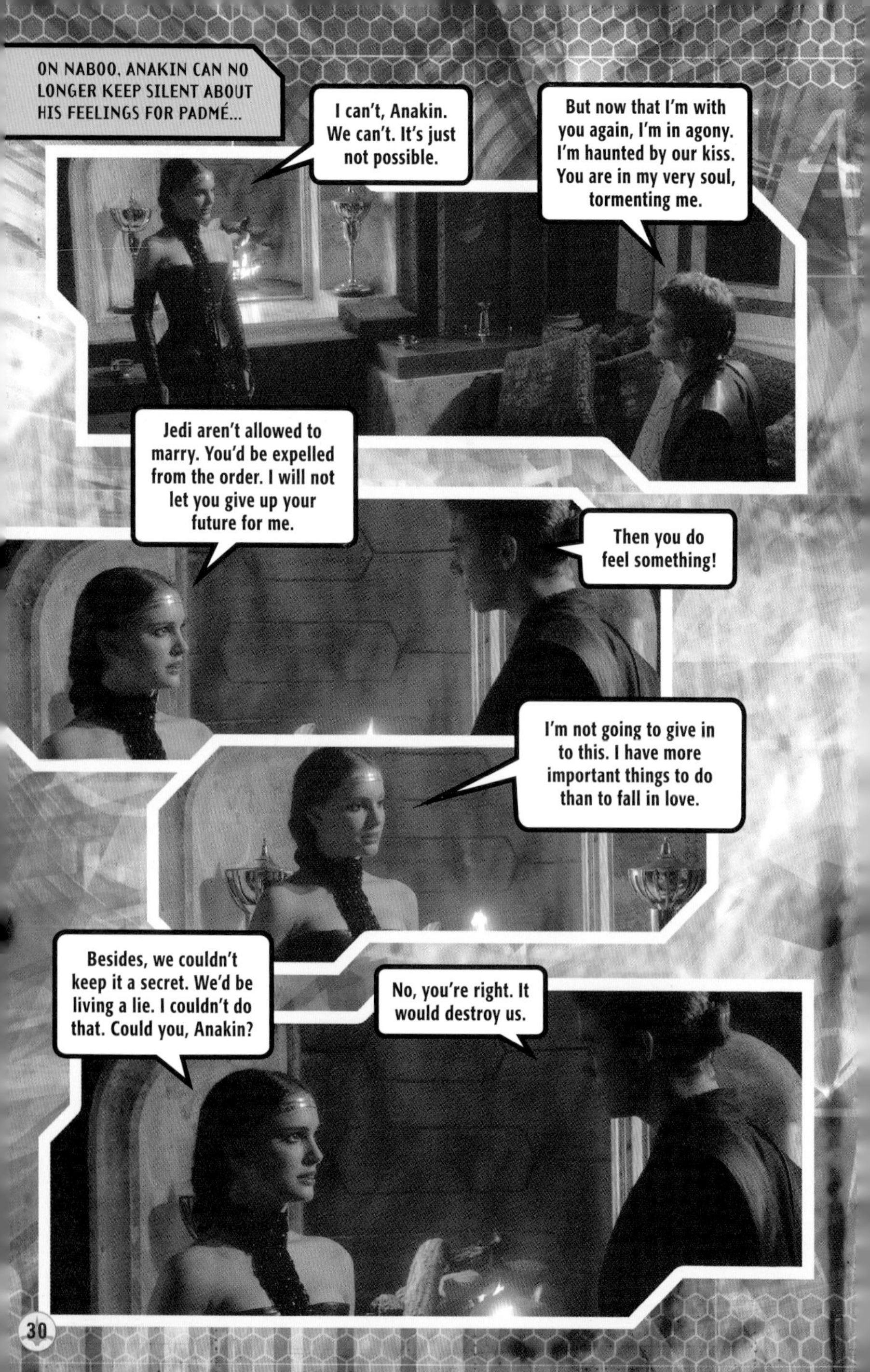
ON NABOO, ANAKIN CAN NO LONGER KEEP SILENT ABOUT HIS FEELINGS FOR PADMÉ...
I can't, Anakin. We can't. It's just not possible.
But now that I'm with you again, I'm in agony. I'm haunted by our kiss. You are in my very soul, tormenting me.
Jedi aren't allowed to marry. You'd be expelled from the order. I will not let you give up your future for me.
Then you do feel something!
I'm not going to give in to this. I have more important things to do than to fall in love.
Besides, we couldn't keep it a secret. We'd be living a lie. I couldn't do that. Could you, Anakin?
No, you're right. It would destroy us.

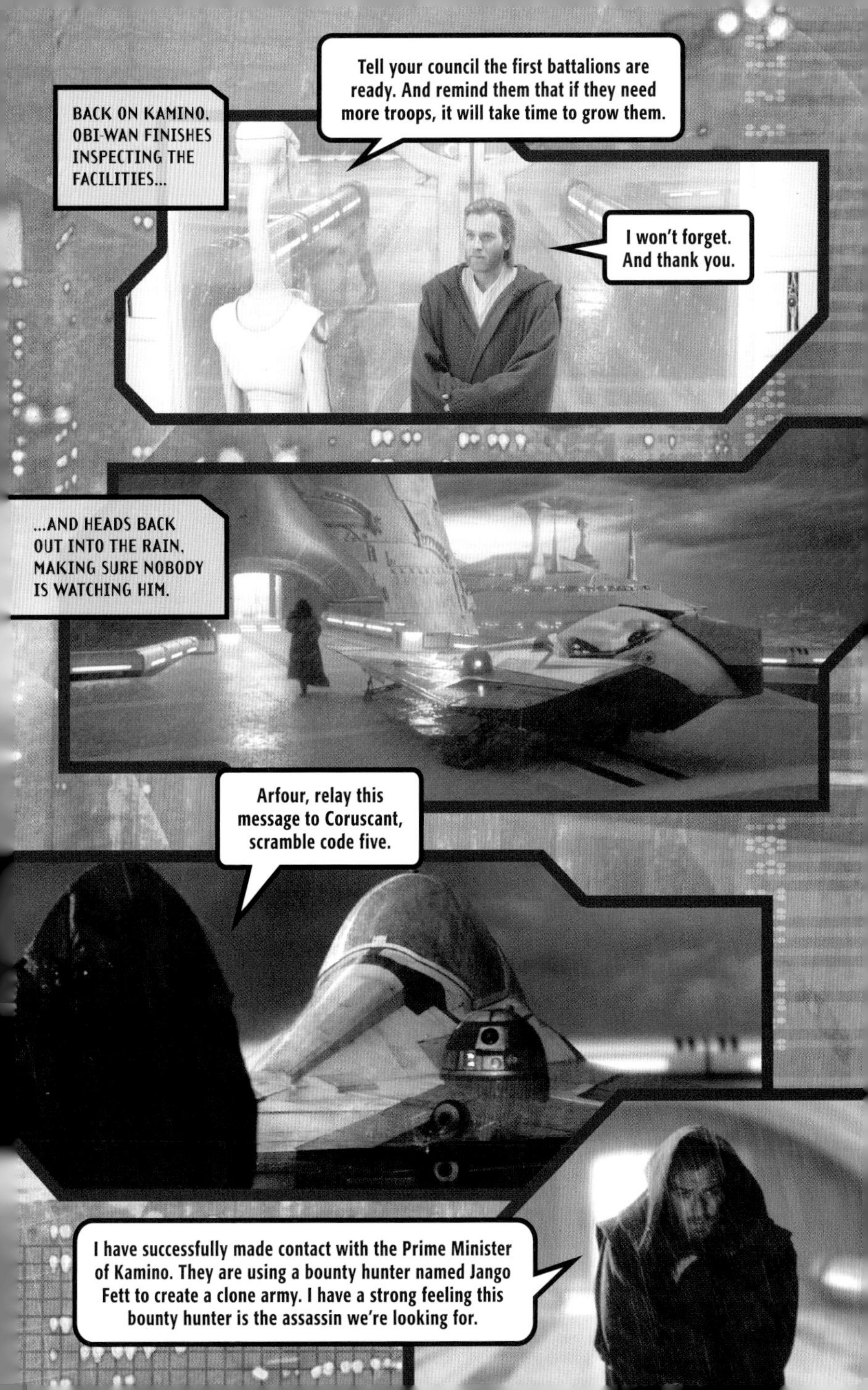
BACK ON KAMINO, OBI-WAN FINISHES INSPECTING THE FACILITIES...
Tell your council the first battalions are ready. And remind them that if they need more troops, it will take time to grow them.
I won't forget. And thank you.
...AND HEADS BACK OUT INTO THE RAIN, MAKING SURE NOBODY IS WATCHING HIM.
Arfour, relay this message to Coruscant, scramble code five.
I have successfully made contact with the Prime Minister of Kamino. They are using a bounty hunter named Jango Fett to create a clone army. I have a strong feeling this bounty hunter is the assassin we're looking for.

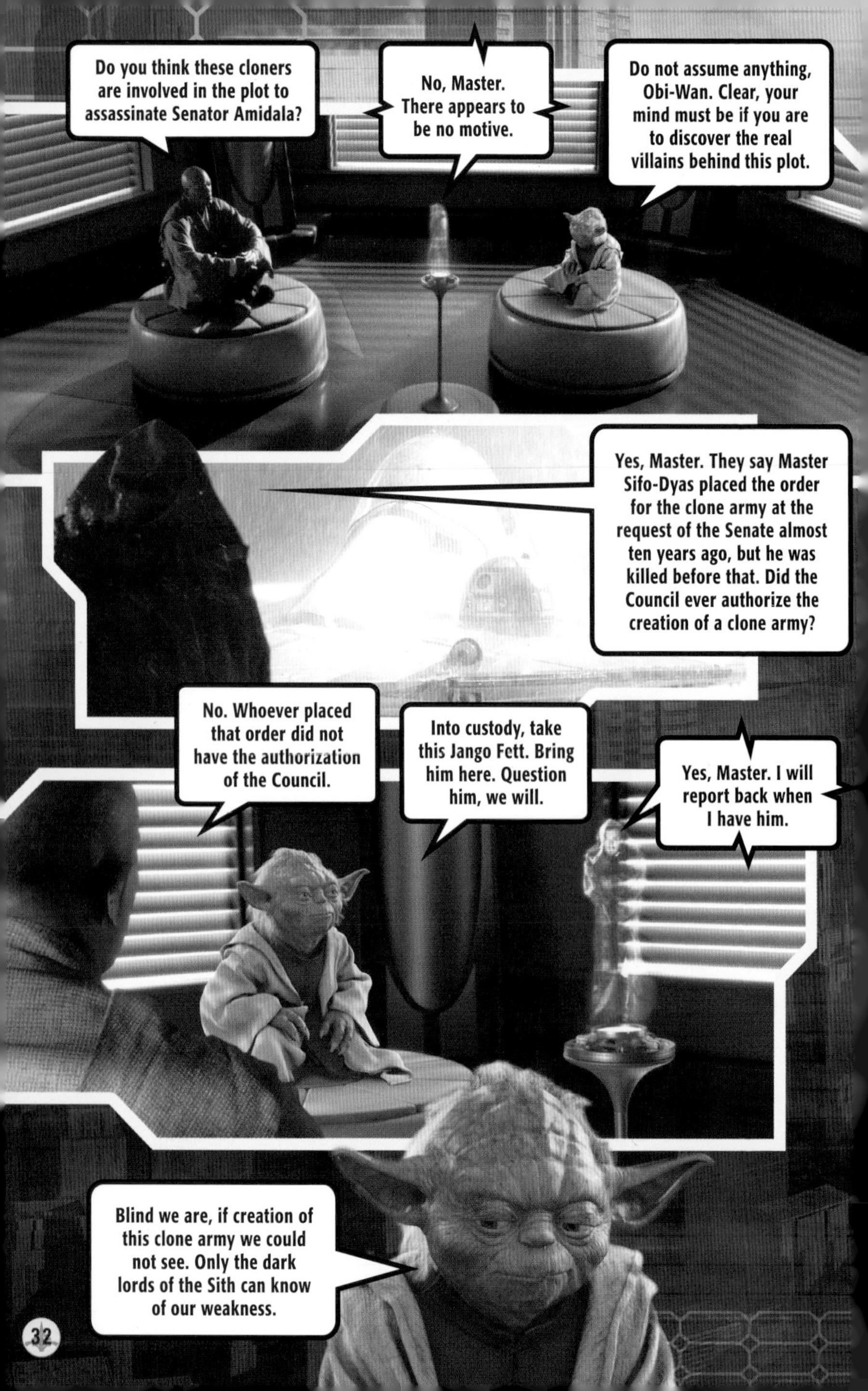
Do you think these cloners are involved in the plot to assassinate Senator Amidala?
No, Master. There appears to be no motive.
Do not assume anything, Obi-Wan. Clear, your mind must be if you are to discover the real villains behind this plot.
Yes, Master. They say Master Sifo-Dyas placed the order for the clone army at the request of the Senate almost ten years ago, but he was killed before that. Did the Council ever authorize the creation of a clone army?
No. Whoever placed that order did not have the authorization of the Council.
Into custody, take this Jango Fett. Bring him here. Question him, we will.
Yes, Master. I will report back when I have him.
Blind we are, if creation of this clone army we could not see. Only the dark lords of the Sith can know of our weakness.

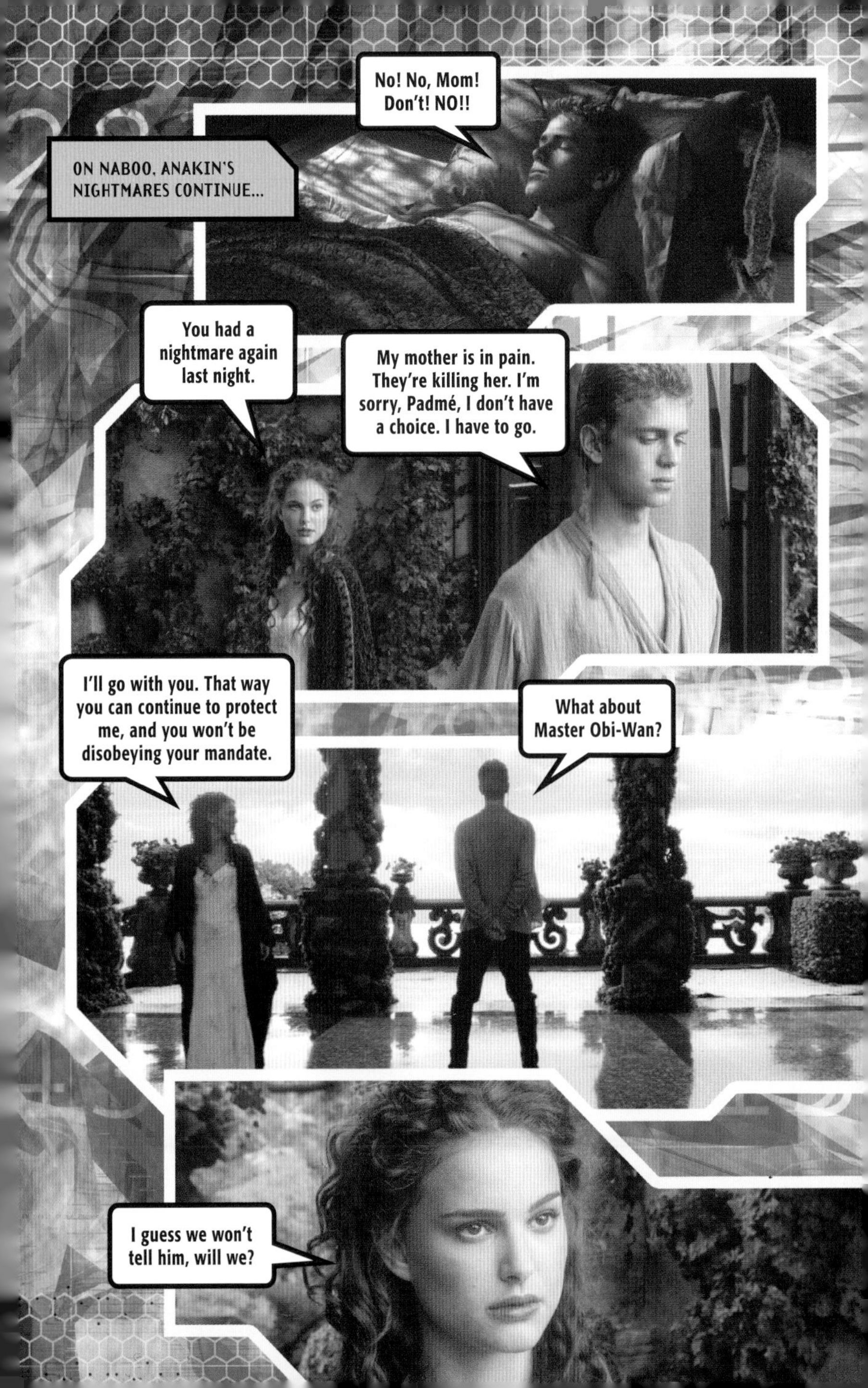
ON NABOO, ANAKIN'S NIGHTMARES CONTINUE...
No! No, Mom! Don't! NO!!
You had a nightmare again last night.
My mother is in pain. They're killing her. I'm sorry, Padmé, I don't have a choice. I have to go.
I'll go with you. That way you can continue to protect me, and you won't be disobeying your mandate.
What about Master Obi-Wan?
I guess we won't tell him, will we?

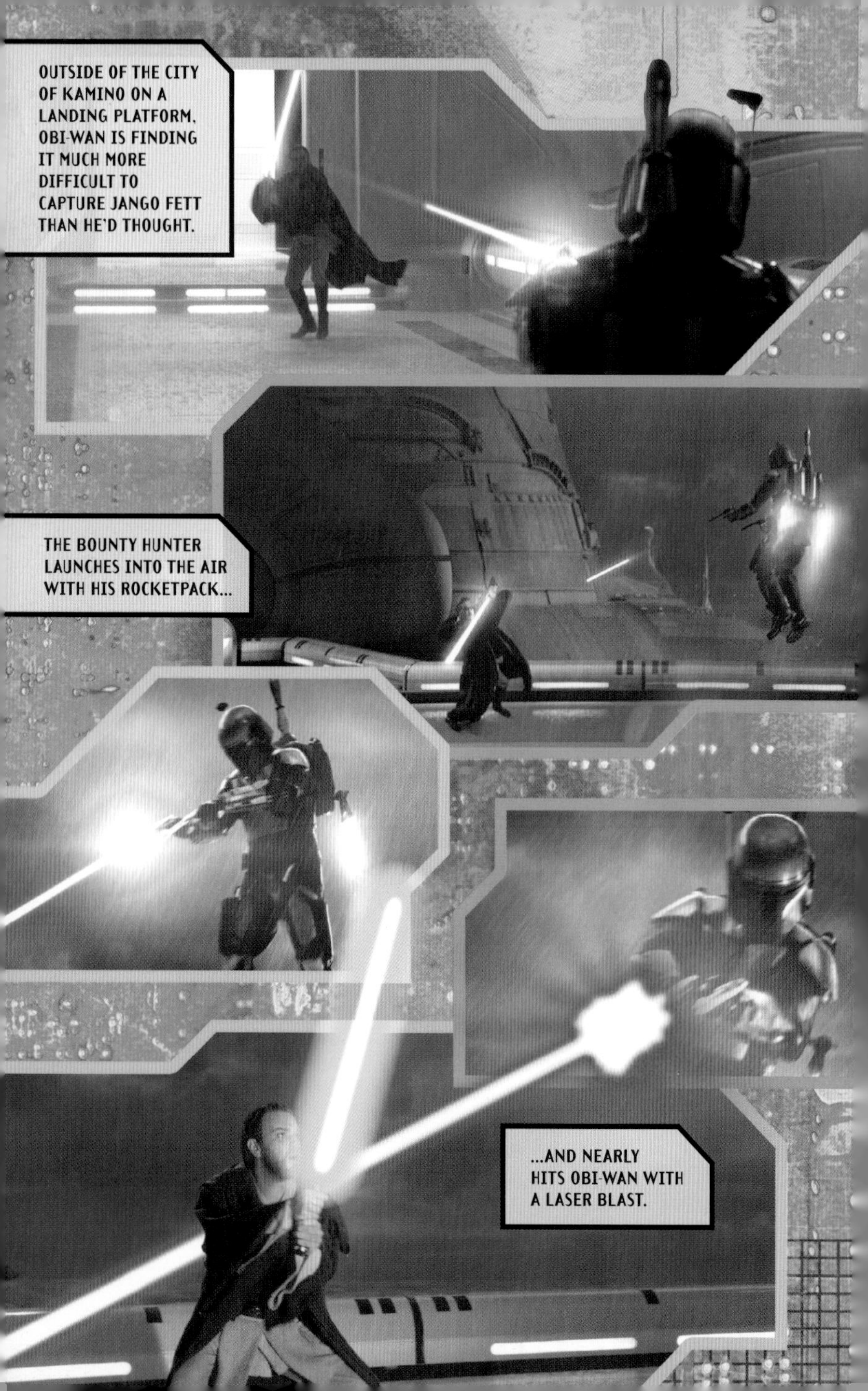
OUTSIDE OF THE CITY OF KAMINO ON A LANDING PLATFORM, OBI-WAN IS FINDING IT MUCH MORE DIFFICULT TO CAPTURE JANGO FETT THAN HE'D THOUGHT.
THE BOUNTY HUNTER LAUNCHES INTO THE AIR WITH HIS ROCKETPACK...
...AND NEARLY HITS OBI-WAN WITH A LASER BLAST.

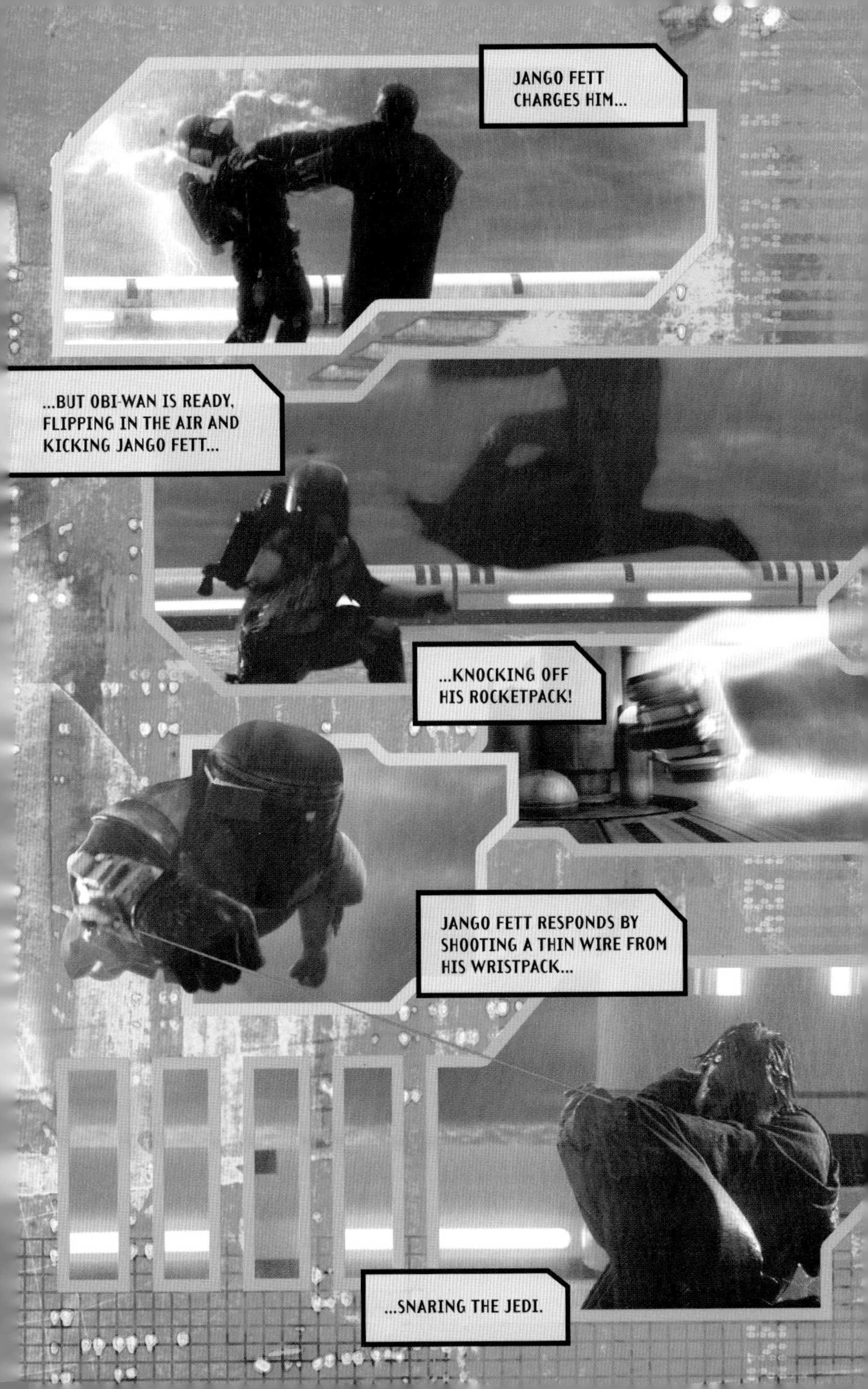
JANGO FETT CHARGES HIM...
...BUT OBI-WAN IS READY, FLIPPING IN THE AIR AND KICKING JANGO FETT...
...KNOCKING OFF HIS ROCKETPACK!
JANGO FETT RESPONDS BY SHOOTING A THIN WIRE FROM HIS WRISTPACK...
...SNARING THE JEDI.

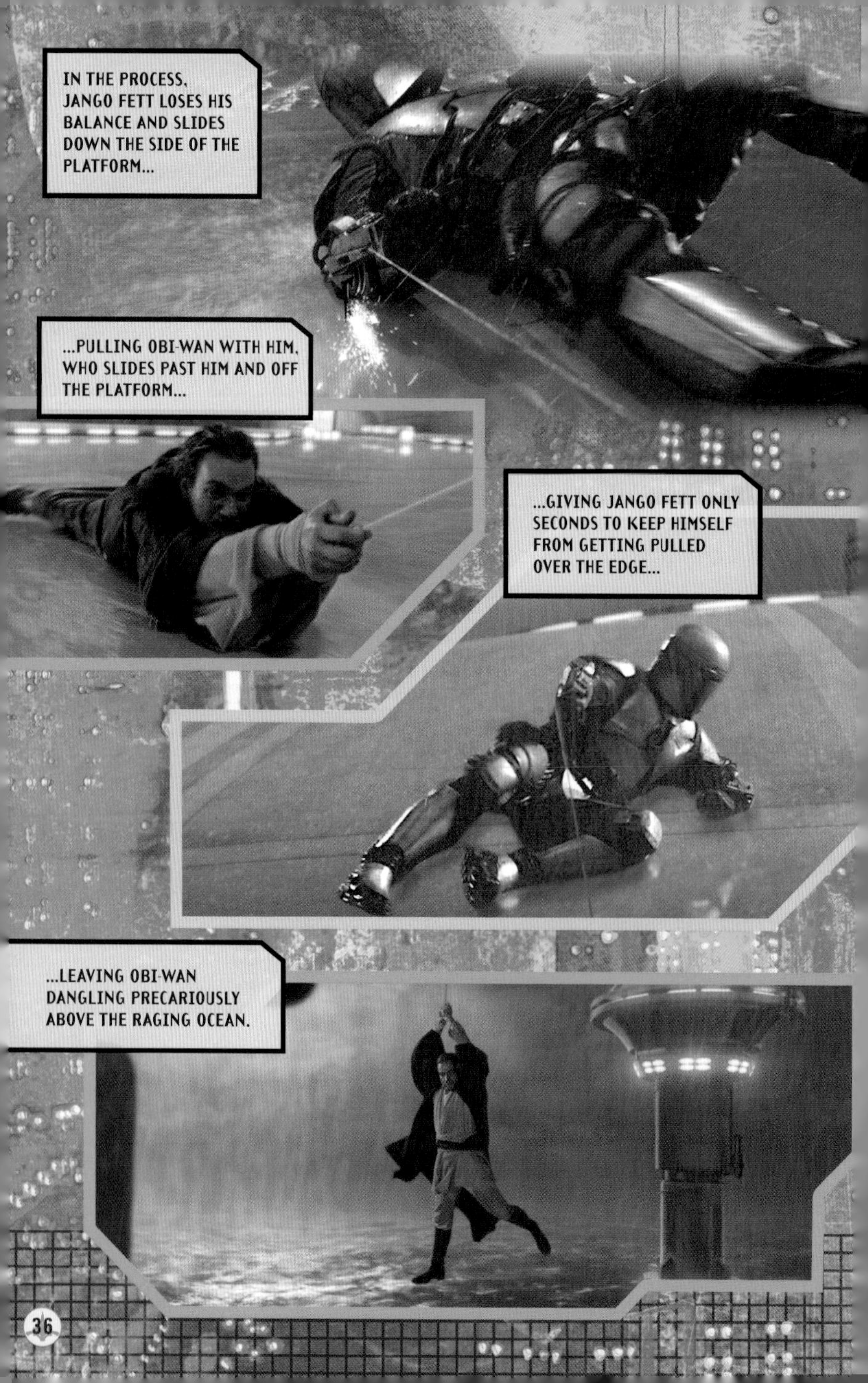
IN THE PROCESS, JANGO FETT LOSES HIS BALANCE AND SLIDES DOWN THE SIDE OF THE PLATFORM...
...PULLING OBI-WAN WITH HIM, WHO SLIDES PAST HIM AND OFF THE PLATFORM...
...GIVING JANGO FETT ONLY SECONDS TO KEEP HIMSELF FROM GETTING PULLED OVER THE EDGE...
...LEAVING OBI-WAN DANGLING PRECARIOUSLY ABOVE THE RAGING OCEAN.

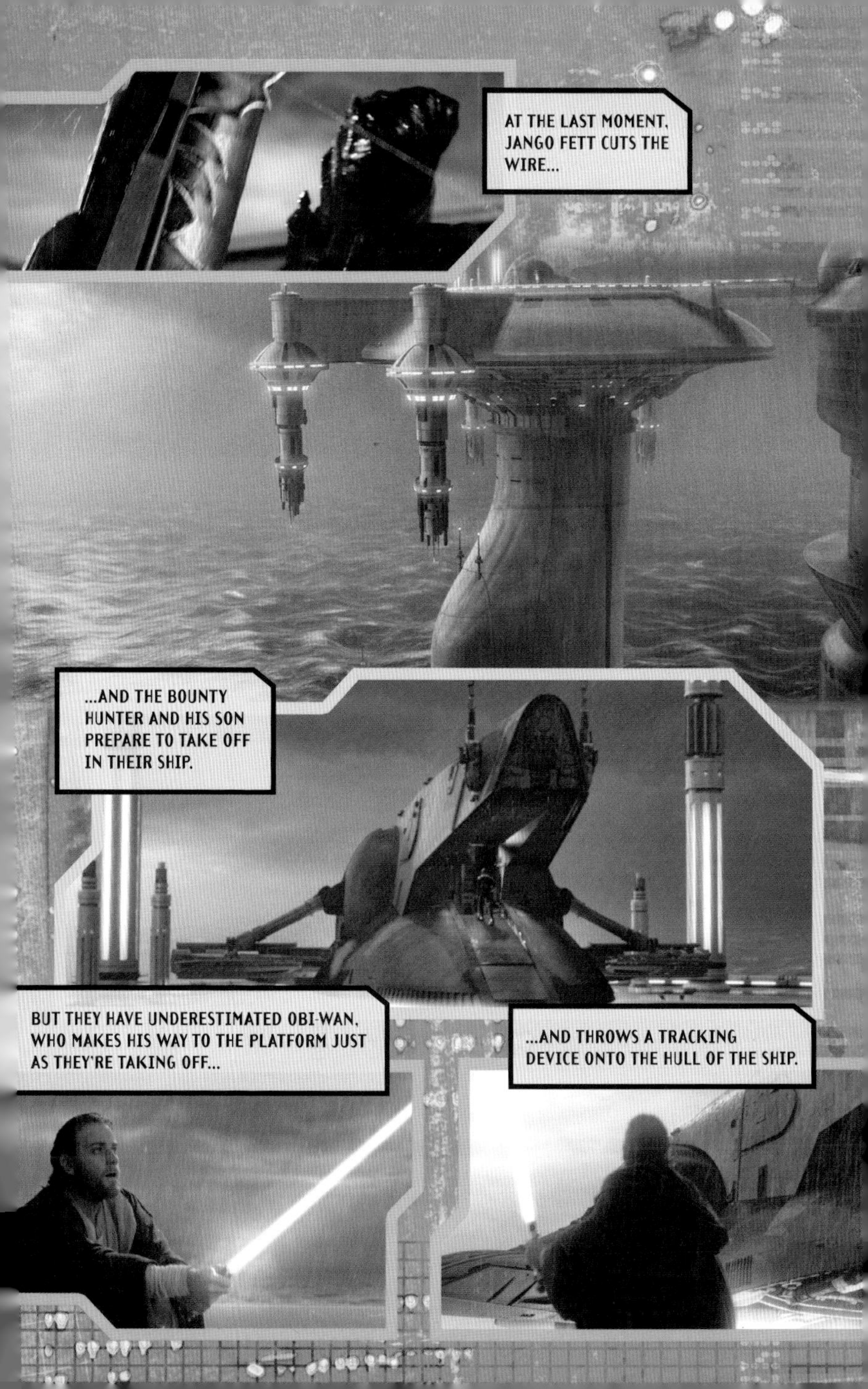
AT THE LAST MOMENT, JANGO FETT CUTS THE WIRE...
...AND THE BOUNTY HUNTER AND HIS SON PREPARE TO TAKE OFF IN THEIR SHIP.
BUT THEY HAVE UNDERESTIMATED OBI-WAN, WHO MAKES HIS WAY TO THE PLATFORM JUST AS THEY'RE TAKING OFF...
...AND THROWS A TRACKING DEVICE ONTO THE HULL OF THE SHIP.

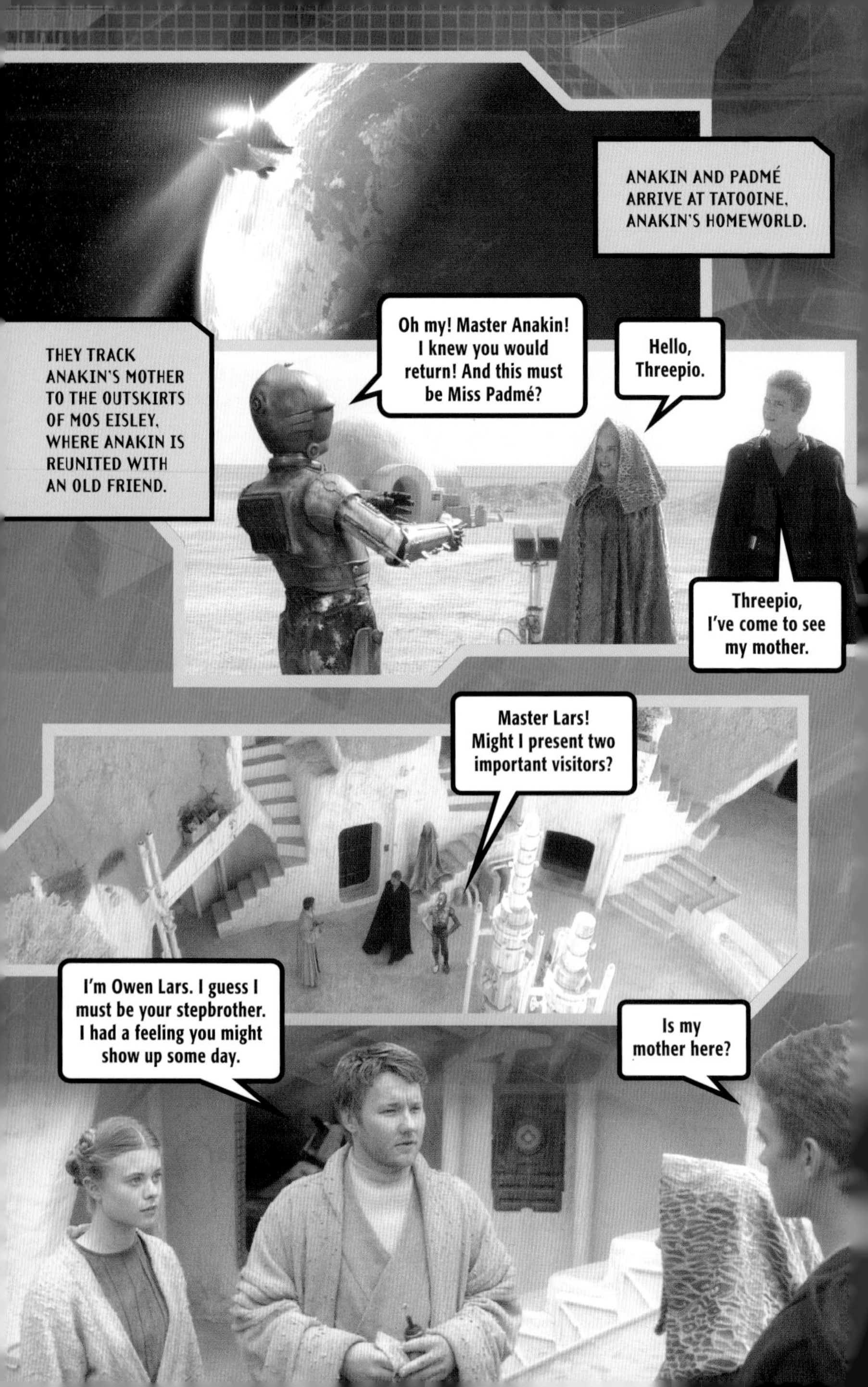

ANAKIN AND PADMÉ ARRIVE AT TATOOINE, ANAKIN'S HOMEWORLD.
THEY TRACK ANAKIN'S MOTHER TO THE OUTSKIRTS OF MOS EISLEY, WHERE ANAKIN IS REUNITED WITH AN OLD FRIEND.
Oh my! Master Anakin! I knew you would return! And this must be Miss Padmé?
Hello, Threepio.
Threepio, I've come to see my mother.
Master Lars! Might I present two important visitors?
I'm Owen Lars. I guess I must be your stepbrother. I had a feeling you might show up some day.
Is my mother here?

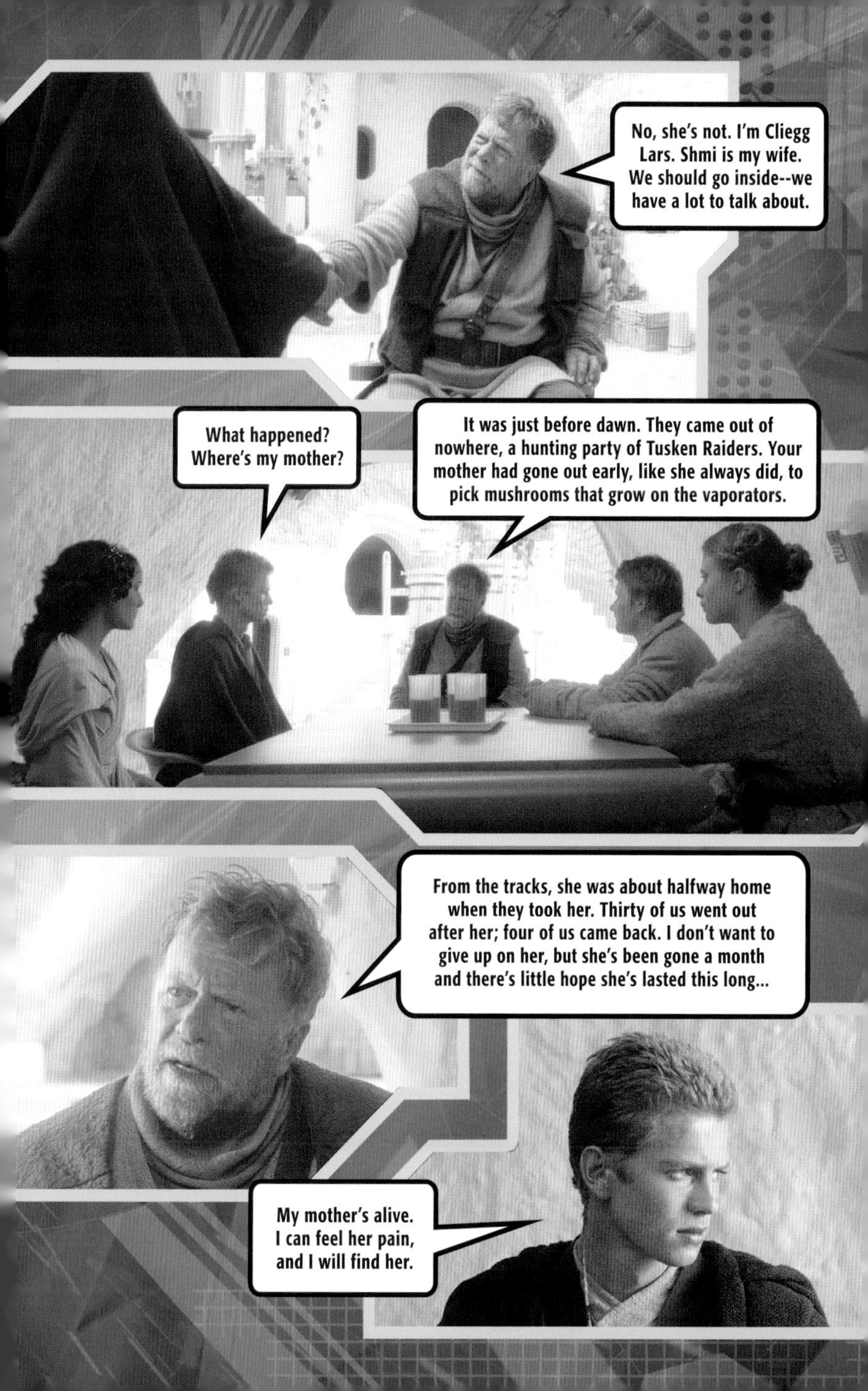
No, she's not. I'm Cliegg Lars. Shmi is my wife. We should go inside--we have a lot to talk about.
What happened? Where's my mother?
It was just before dawn. They came out of nowhere, a hunting party of Tusken Raiders. Your mother had gone out early, like she always did, to pick mushrooms that grow on the vaporators.
From the tracks, she was about halfway home when they took her. Thirty of us went out after her; four of us came back. I don't want to give up on her, but she's been gone a month and there's little hope she's lasted this long...
My mother's alive. I can feel her pain, and I will find her.

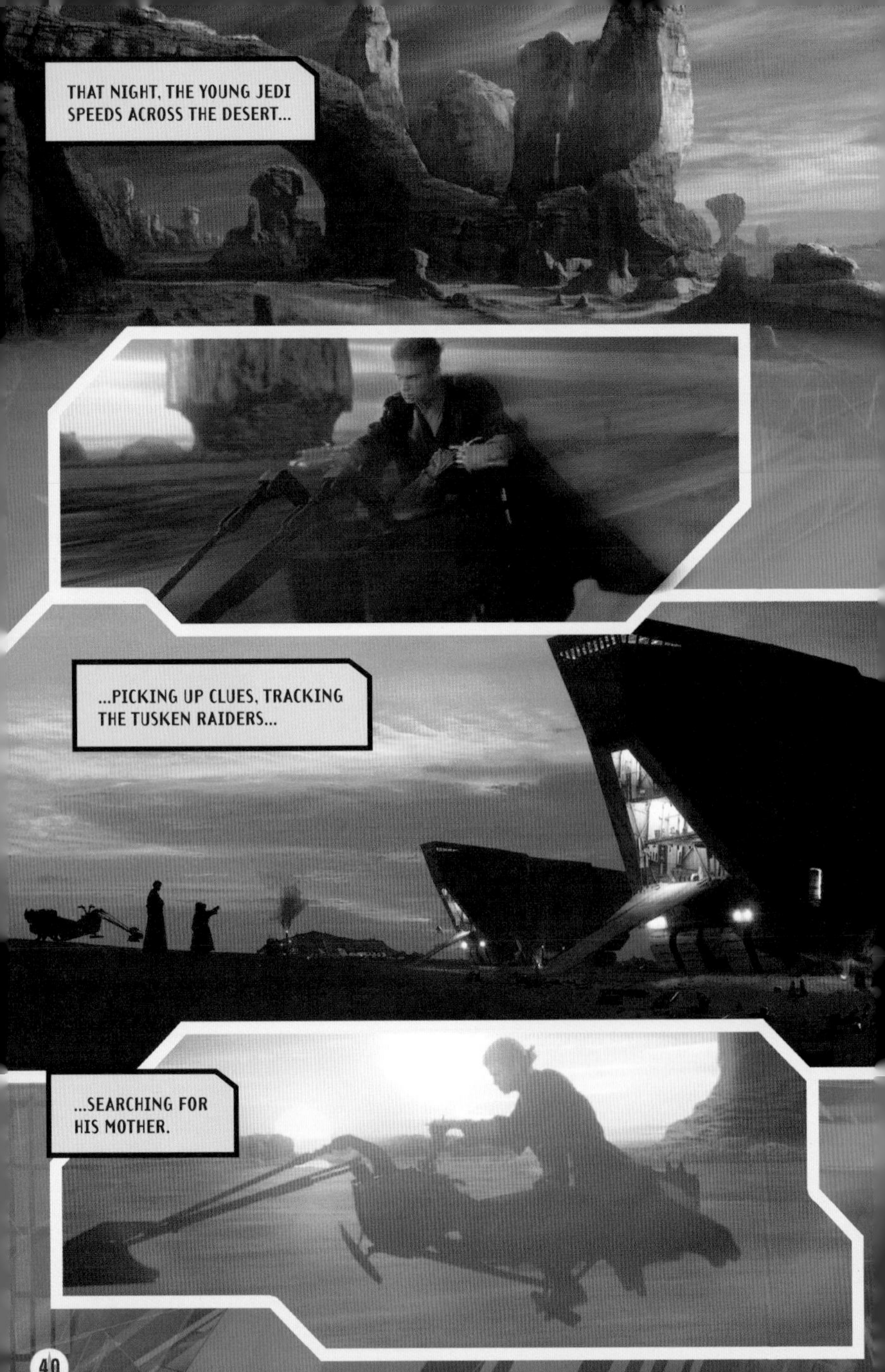
THAT NIGHT, THE YOUNG JEDI SPEEDS ACROSS THE DESERT...
...PICKING UP CLUES, TRACKING THE TUSKEN RAIDERS...
...SEARCHING FOR HIS MOTHER.

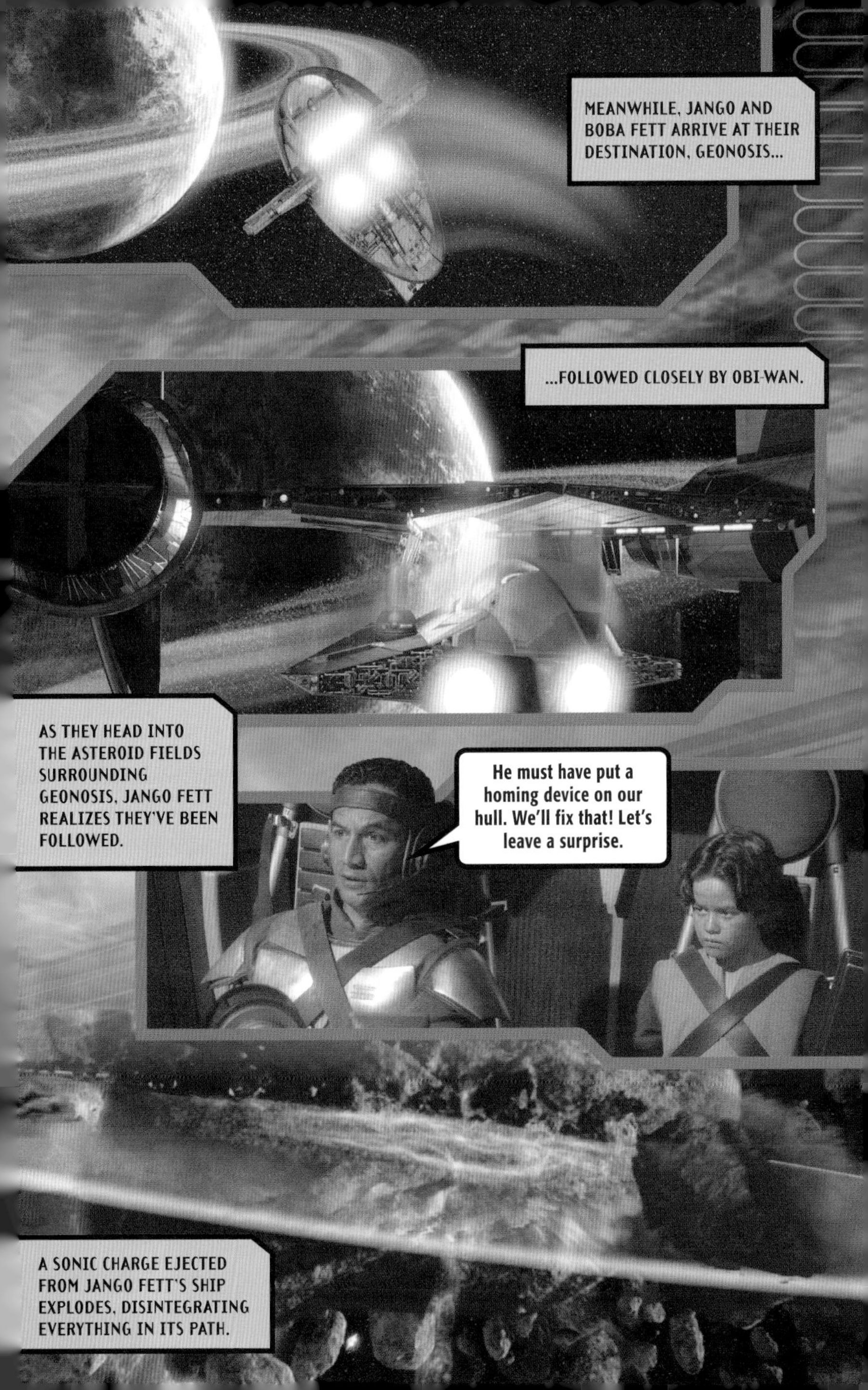
MEANWHILE, JANGO AND BOBA FETT ARRIVE AT THEIR DESTINATION, GEONOSIS...
...FOLLOWED CLOSELY BY OBI-WAN.
AS THEY HEAD INTO THE ASTEROID FIELDS SURROUNDING GEONOSIS, JANGO FETT REALIZES THEY'VE BEEN FOLLOWED.
He must have put a homing device on our hull. We'll fix that! Let's leave a surprise.
A SONIC CHARGE EJECTED FROM JANGO FETT'S SHIP EXPLODES, DISINTEGRATING EVERYTHING IN ITS PATH.

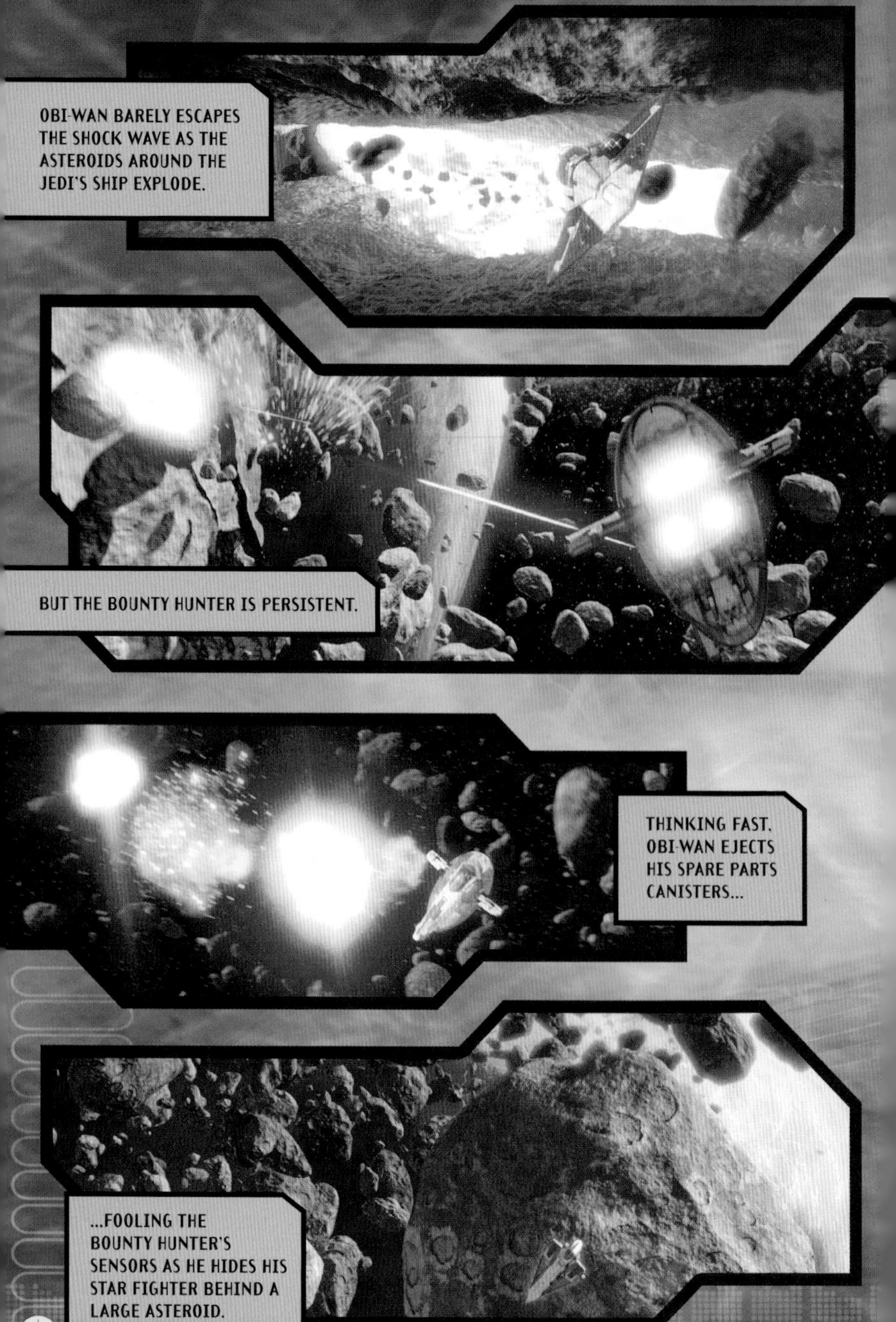
OBI-WAN BARELY ESCAPES THE SHOCK WAVE AS THE ASTEROIDS AROUND THE JEDI'S SHIP EXPLODE.
BUT THE BOUNTY HUNTER IS PERSISTENT.
THINKING FAST, OBI-WAN EJECTS HIS SPARE PARTS CANISTERS...
...FOOLING THE BOUNTY HUNTER'S SENSORS AS HE HIDES HIS STAR FIGHTER BEHIND A LARGE ASTEROID.

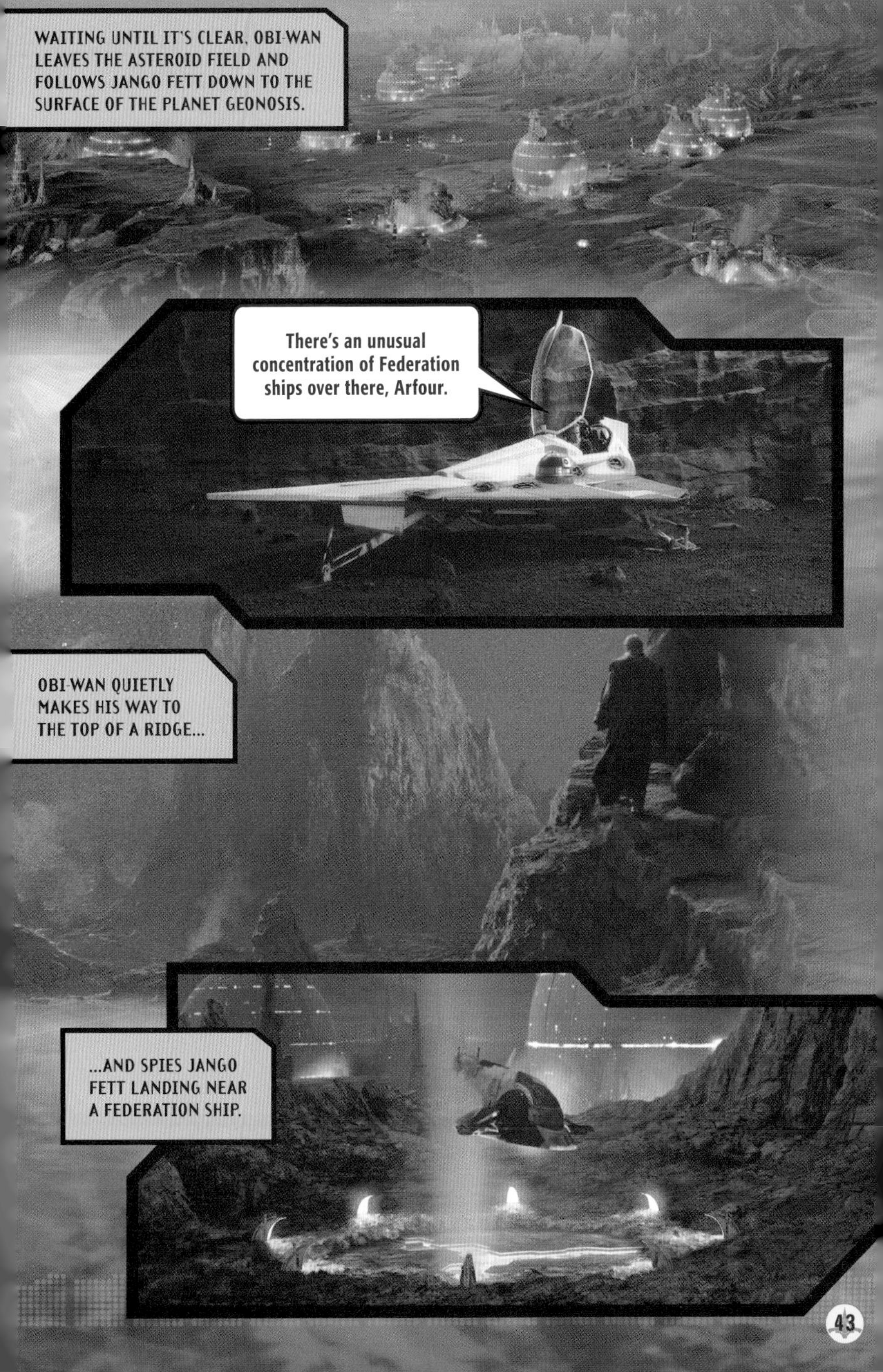
WAITING UNTIL IT'S CLEAR, OBI-WAN LEAVES THE ASTEROID FIELD AND FOLLOWS JANGO FETT DOWN TO THE SURFACE OF THE PLANET GEONOSIS.
There's an unusual concentration of Federation ships over there, Arfour.
OBI-WAN QUIETLY MAKES HIS WAY TO THE TOP OF A RIDGE...
...AND SPIES JANGO FETT LANDING NEAR A FEDERATION SHIP.

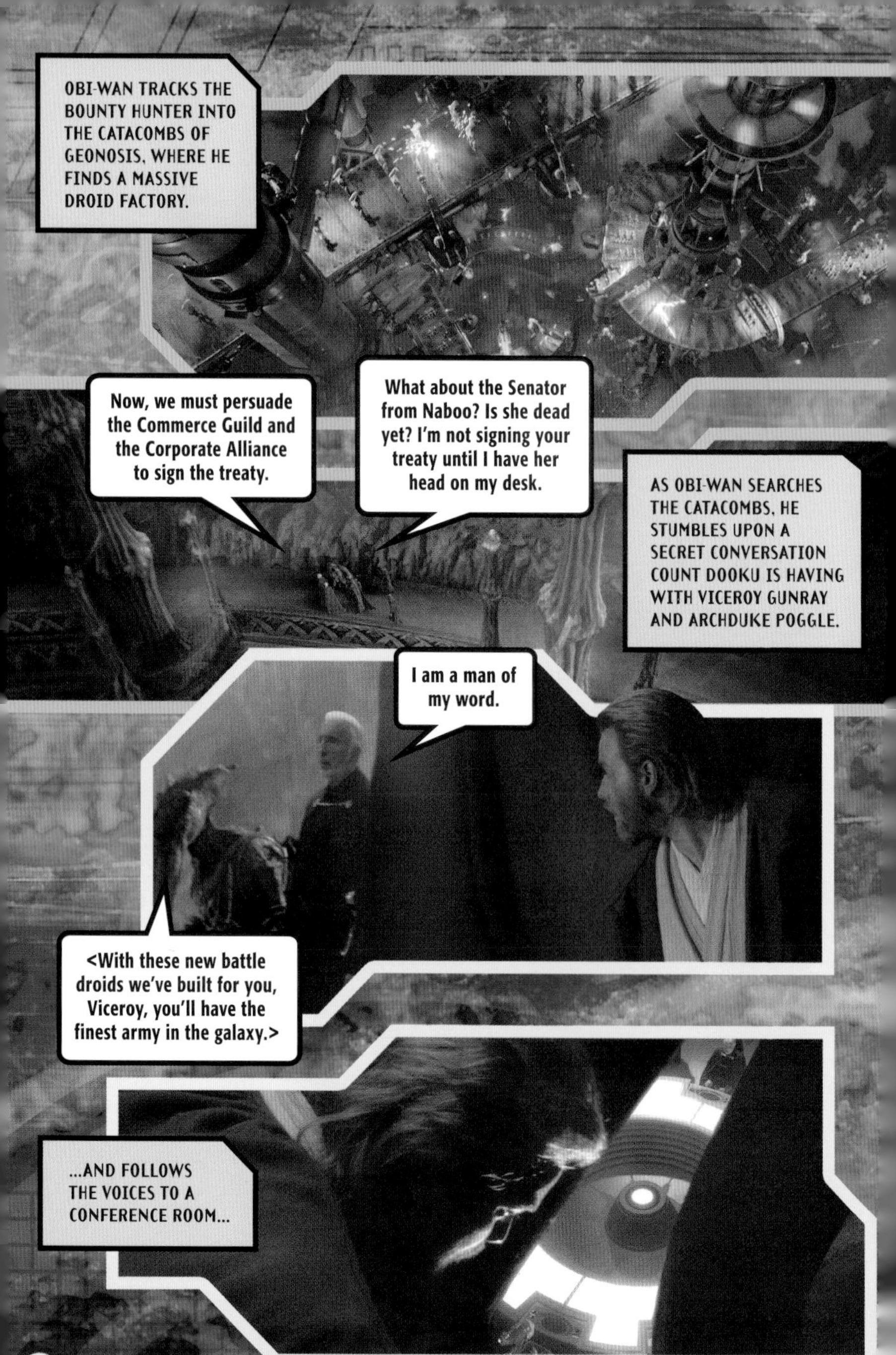
OBI-WAN TRACKS THE BOUNTY HUNTER INTO THE CATACOMBS OF GEONOSIS, WHERE HE FINDS A MASSIVE DROID FACTORY.
Now, we must persuade the Commerce Guild and the Corporate Alliance to sign the treaty.
What about the Senator from Naboo? Is she dead yet? I'm not signing your treaty until I have her head on my desk.
AS OBI-WAN SEARCHES THE CATACOMBS, HE STUMBLES UPON A SECRET CONVERSATION COUNT DOOKU IS HAVING WITH VICEROY GUNRAY AND ARCHDUKE POGGLE.
I am a man of my word.
<With these new battle droids we've built for you, Viceroy, you'll have the finest army in the galaxy.>
...AND FOLLOWS THE VOICES TO A CONFERENCE ROOM...

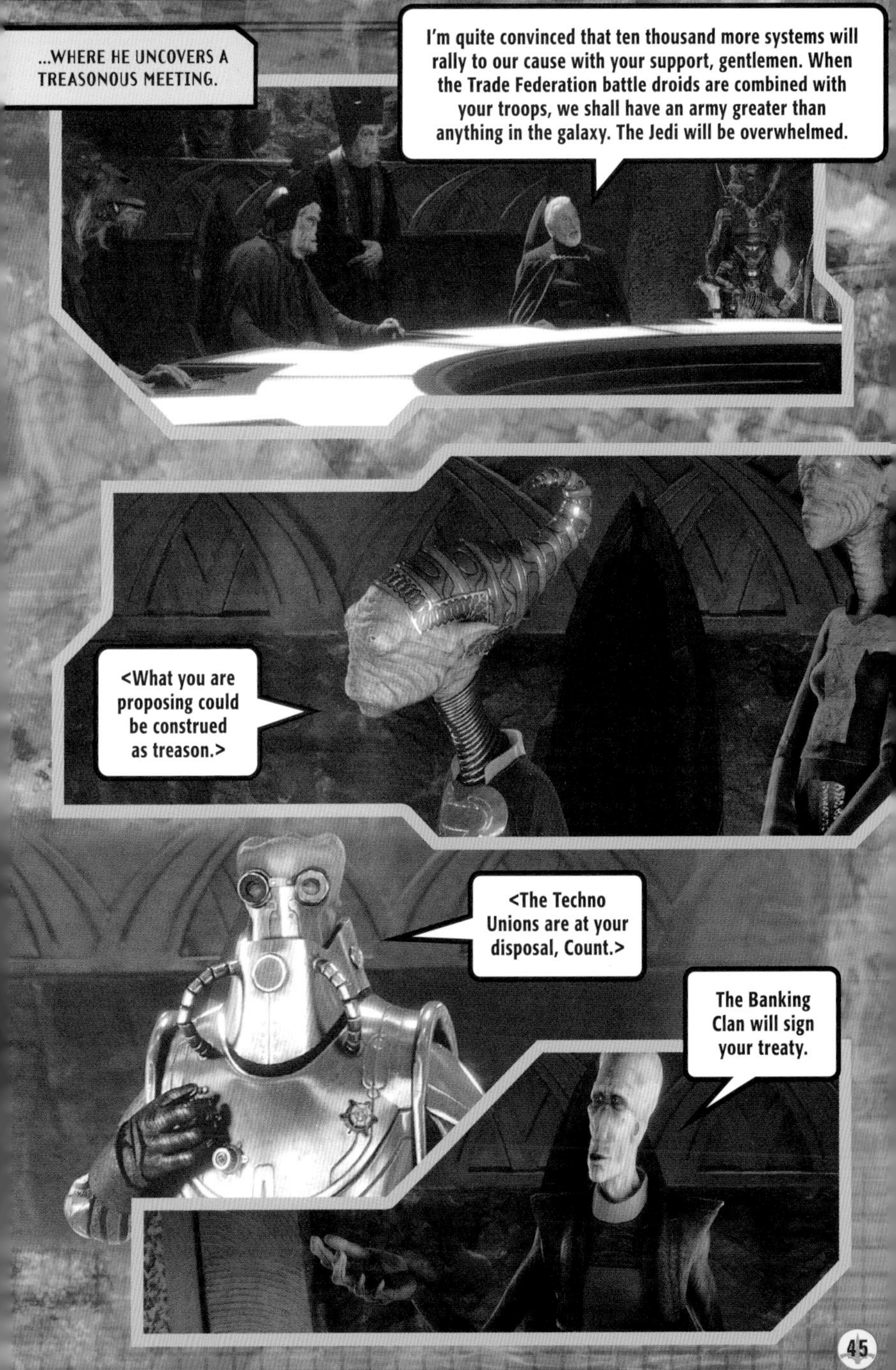
...WHERE HE UNCOVERS A TREASONOUS MEETING.
I'm quite convinced that ten thousand more systems will rally to our cause with your support, gentlemen. When the Trade Federation battle droids are combined with your troops, we shall have an army greater than anything in the galaxy. The Jedi will be overwhelmed.
<What you are proposing could be construed as treason.>
<The Techno Unions are at your disposal, Count.>
The Banking Clan will sign your treaty.

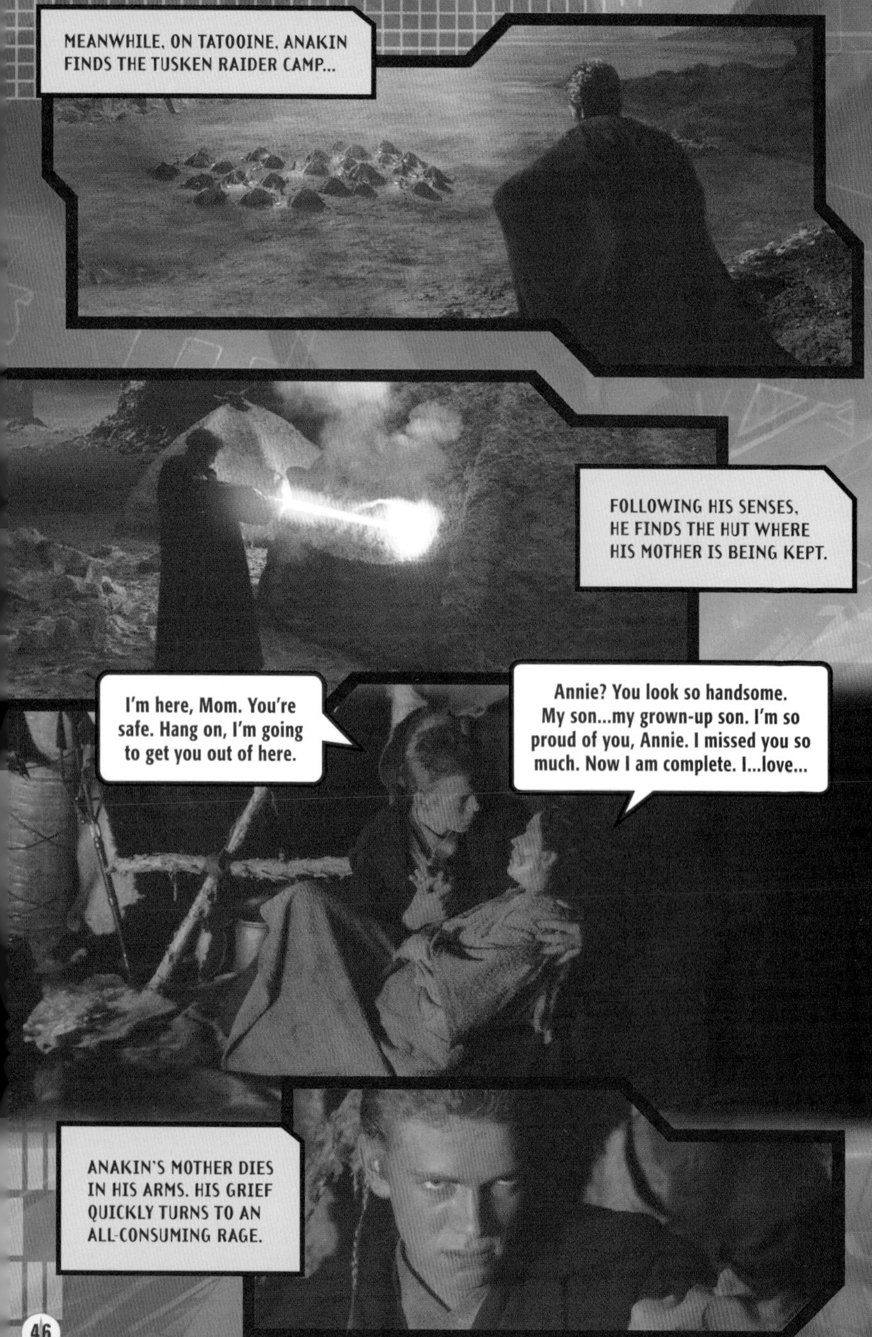

MEANWHILE, ON TATOOINE, ANAKIN FINDS THE TUSKEN RAIDER CAMP...
FOLLOWING HIS SENSES, HE FINDS THE HUT WHERE HIS MOTHER IS BEING KEPT.
I'm here, Mom. You're safe. Hang on, I'm going to get you out of here.
Annie? You look so handsome. My son...my grown-up son. I'm so proud of you, Annie. I missed you so much. Now I am complete. I...love...
ANAKIN'S MOTHER DIES IN HIS ARMS. HIS GRIEF QUICKLY TURNS TO AN ALL-CONSUMING RAGE.

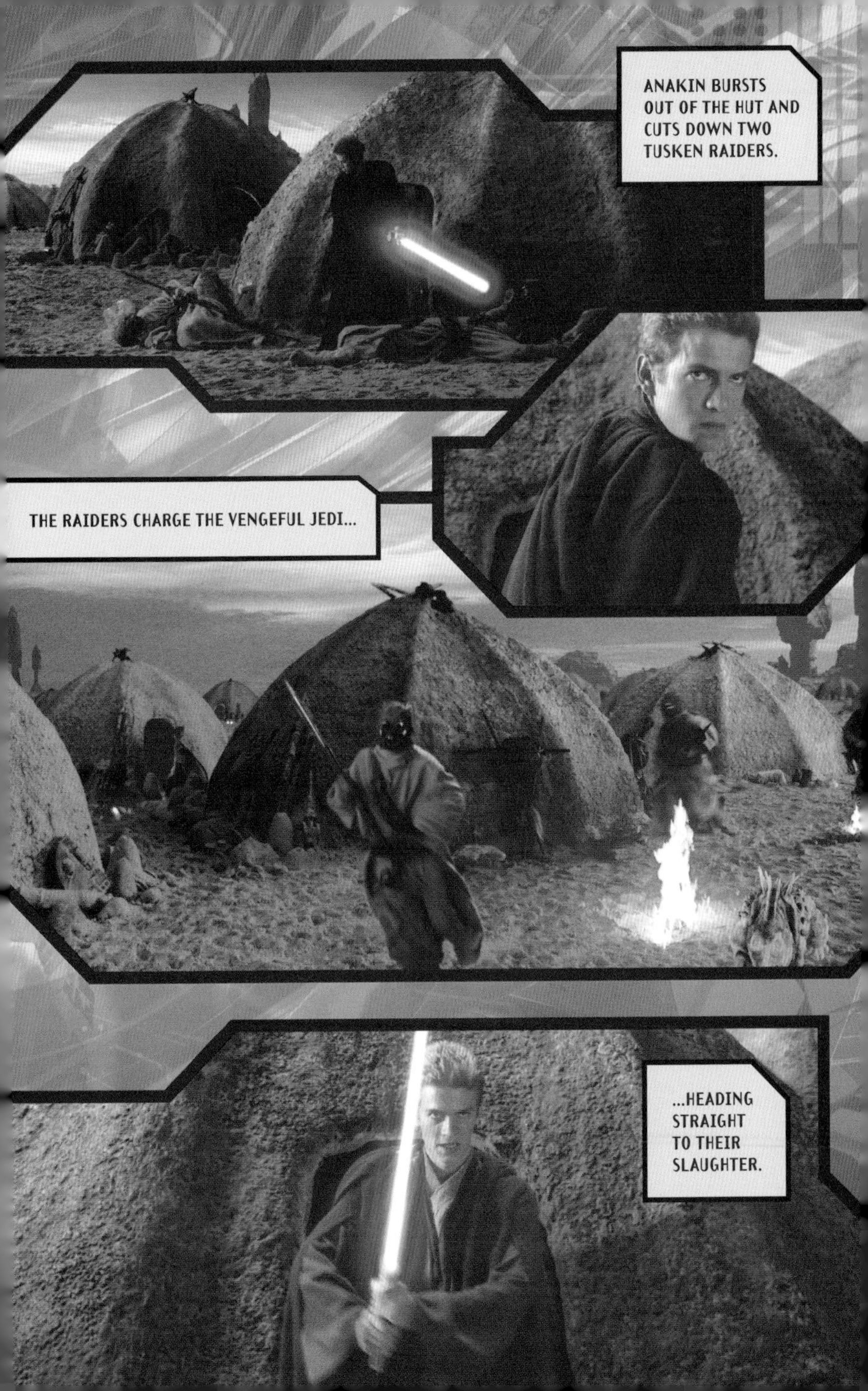
ANAKIN BURSTS OUT OF THE HUT AND CUTS DOWN TWO TUSKEN RAIDERS.
THE RAIDERS CHARGE THE VENGEFUL JEDI...
...HEADING STRAIGHT TO THEIR SLAUGHTER.

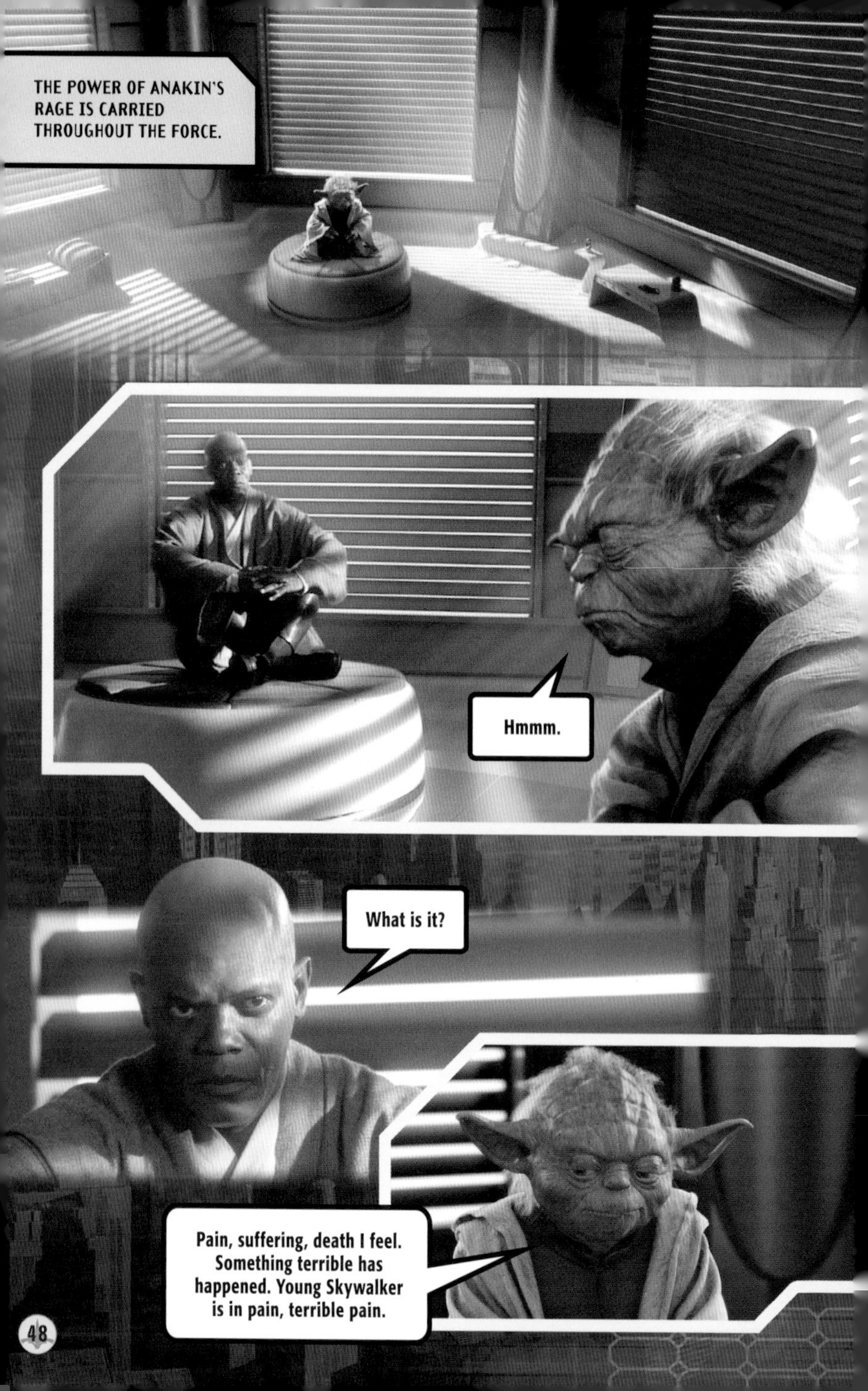
THE POWER OF ANAKIN'S RAGE IS CARRIED THROUGHOUT THE FORCE.
Hmmm.
What is it?
Pain, suffering, death I feel. Something terrible has happened. Young Skywalker is in pain, terrible pain.

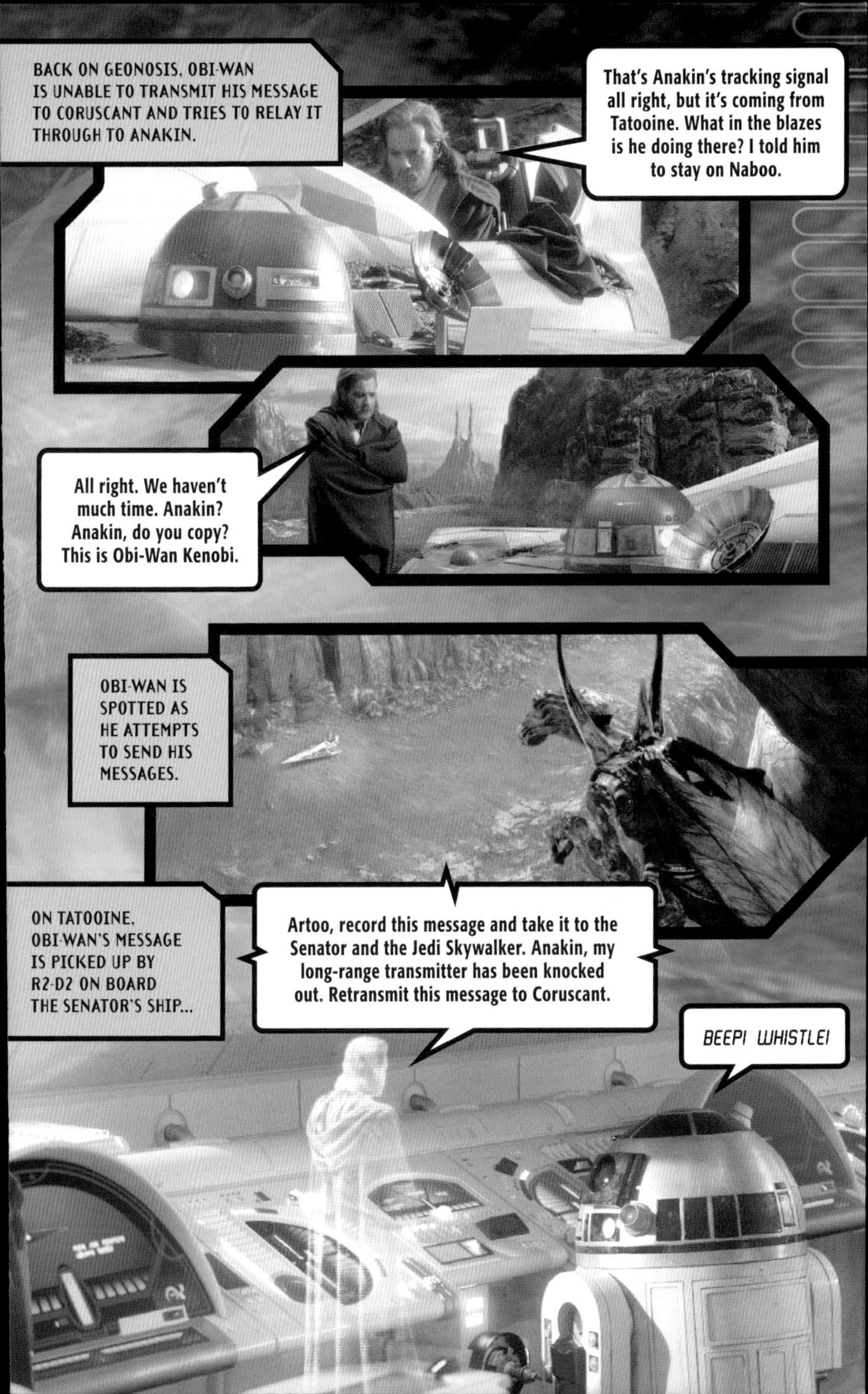
BACK ON GEONOSIS, OBI-WAN IS UNABLE TO TRANSMIT HIS MESSAGE TO CORUSCANT AND TRIES TO RELAY IT THROUGH TO ANAKIN.
That's Anakin's tracking signal all right, but it's coming from Tatooine. What in the blazes is he doing there? I told him to stay on Naboo.
All right. We haven't much time. Anakin? Anakin, do you copy? This is Obi-Wan Kenobi.
OBI-WAN IS SPOTTED AS HE ATTEMPTS TO SEND HIS MESSAGES.
ON TATOOINE, OBI-WAN'S MESSAGE IS PICKED UP BY R2-D2 ON BOARD THE SENATOR'S SHIP...
Artoo, record this message and take it to the Senator and the Jedi Skywalker. Anakin, my long-range transmitter has been knocked out. Retransmit this message to Coruscant.
BEEP! WHISTLE!

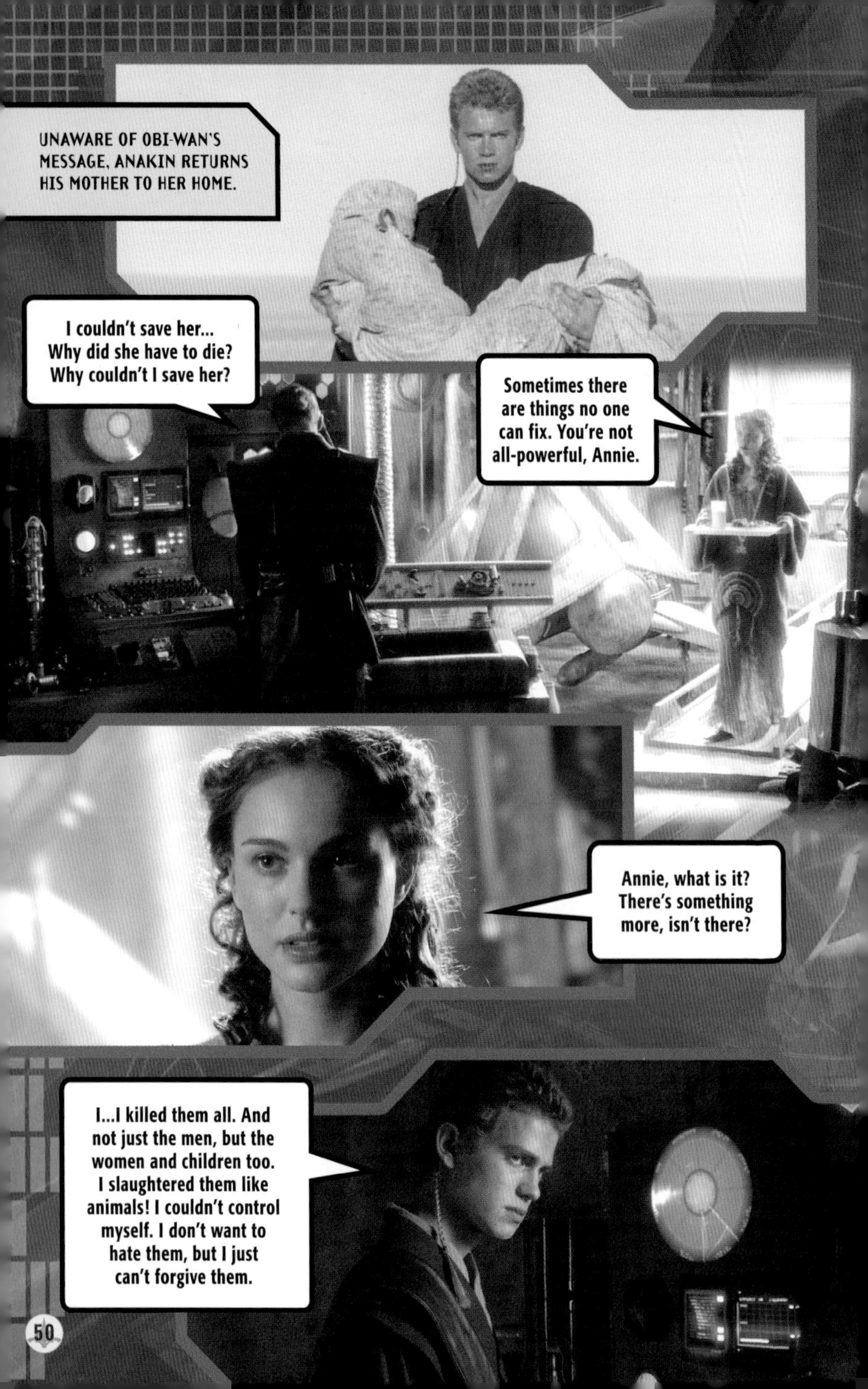
UNAWARE OF OBI-WAN'S MESSAGE, ANAKIN RETURNS HIS MOTHER TO HER HOME.
I couldn't save her... Why did she have to die? Why couldn't I save her?
Sometimes there are things no one can fix. You're not all-powerful, Annie.
Annie, what is it? There's something more, isn't there?
I...I killed them all. And not just the men, but the women and children too. I slaughtered them like animals! I couldn't control myself. I don't want to hate them, but I just can't forgive them.

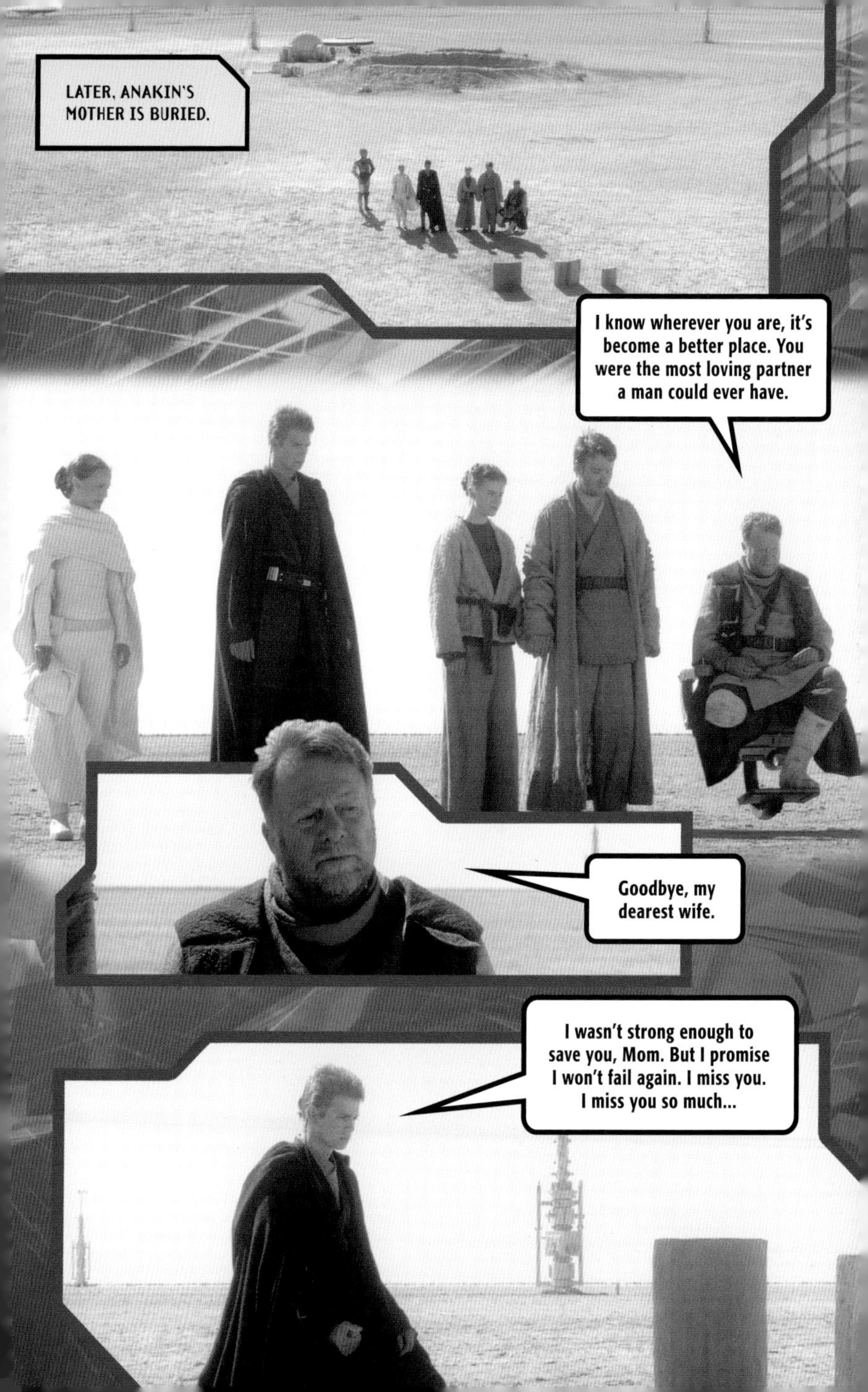
LATER, ANAKIN'S MOTHER IS BURIED.
I know wherever you are, it's become a better place. You were the most loving partner a man could ever have.
Goodbye, my dearest wife.
I wasn't strong enough to save you, Mom. But I promise I won't fail again. I miss you. I miss you so much...

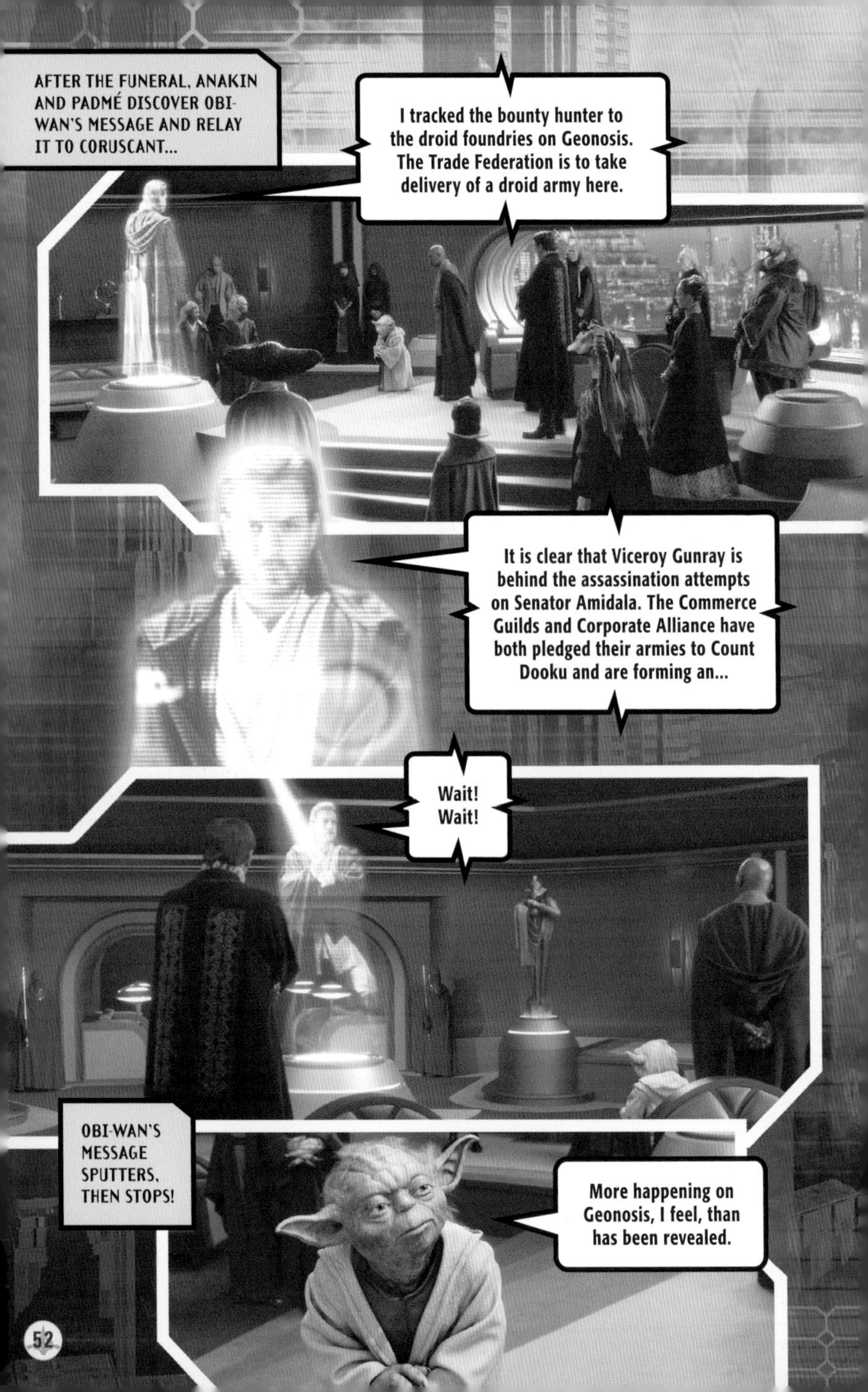
AFTER THE FUNERAL, ANAKIN AND PADMÉ DISCOVER OBI-WAN'S MESSAGE AND RELAY IT TO CORUSCANT...
I tracked the bounty hunter to the droid foundries on Geonosis. The Trade Federation is to take delivery of a droid army here.
It is clear that Viceroy Gunray is behind the assassination attempts on Senator Amidala. The Commerce Guilds and Corporate Alliance have both pledged their armies to Count Dooku and are forming an...
Wait! Wait!
OBI-WAN'S MESSAGE SPUTTERS, THEN STOPS!
More happening on Geonosis, I feel, than has been revealed.

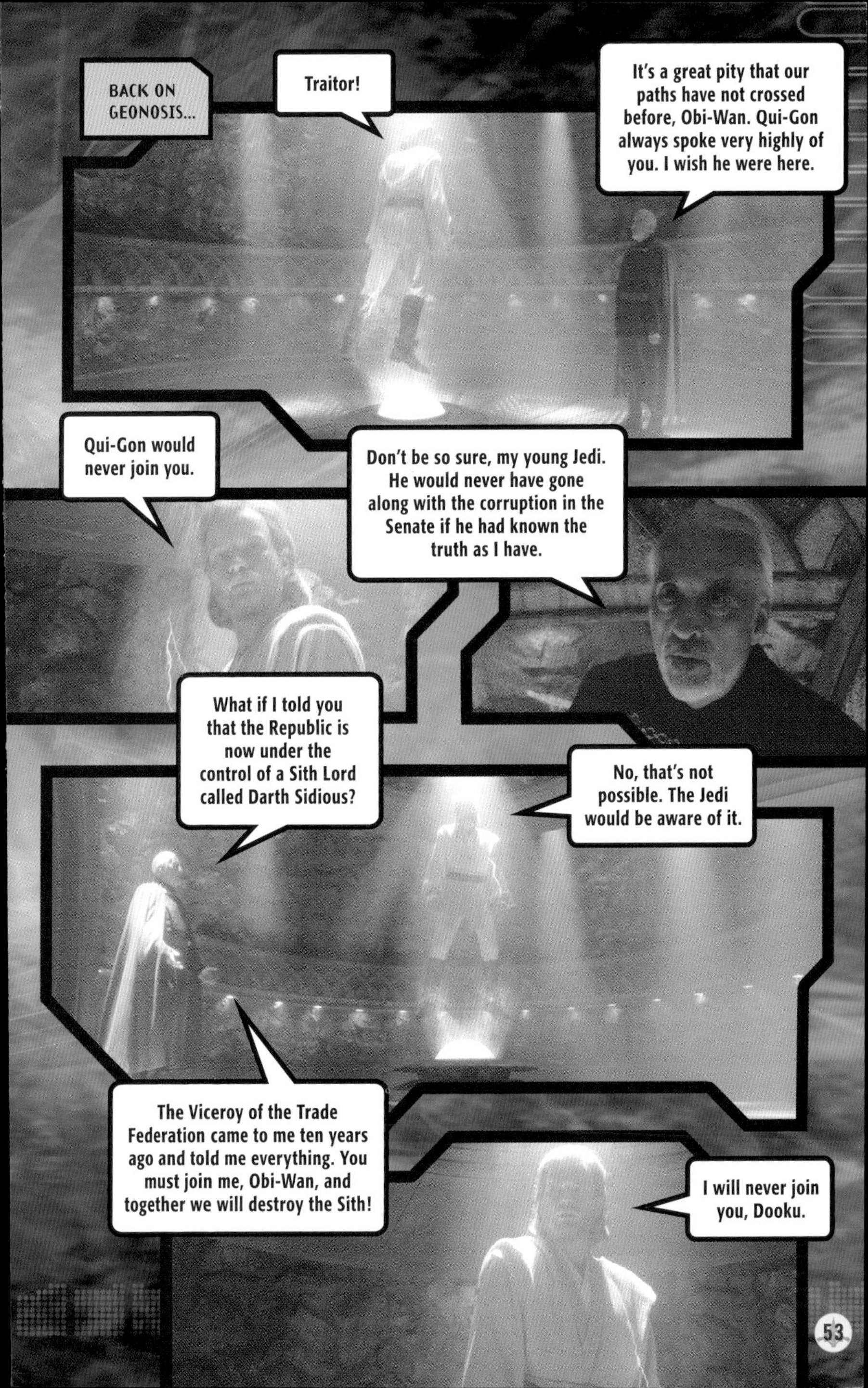
BACK ON GEONOSIS...
Traitor!
It's a great pity that our paths have not crossed before, Obi-Wan. Qui-Gon always spoke very highly of you. I wish he were here.
Qui-Gon would never join you.
Don't be so sure, my young Jedi. He would never have gone along with the corruption in the Senate if he had known the truth as I have.
What if I told you that the Republic is now under the control of a Sith Lord called Darth Sidious?
No, that's not possible. The Jedi would be aware of it.
The Viceroy of the Trade Federation came to me ten years ago and told me everything. You must join me, Obi-Wan, and together we will destroy the Sith!
I will never join you, Dooku.

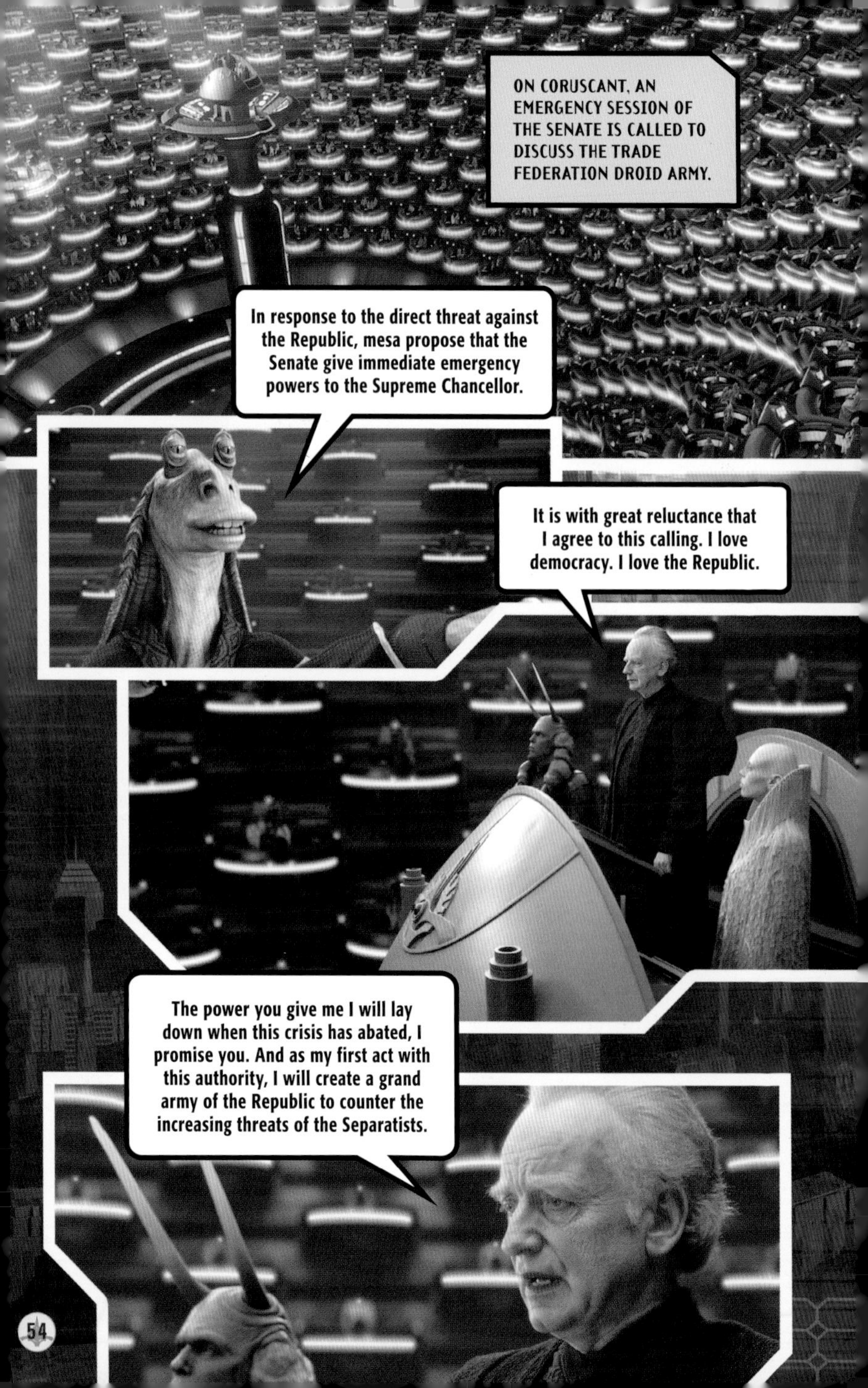
ON CORUSCANT, AN EMERGENCY SESSION OF THE SENATE IS CALLED TO DISCUSS THE TRADE FEDERATION DROID ARMY.
In response to the direct threat against the Republic, mesa propose that the Senate give immediate emergency powers to the Supreme Chancellor.
It is with great reluctance that I agree to this calling. I love democracy. I love the Republic.
The power you give me I will lay down when this crisis has abated, I promise you. And as my first act with this authority, I will create a grand army of the Republic to counter the increasing threats of the Separatists.

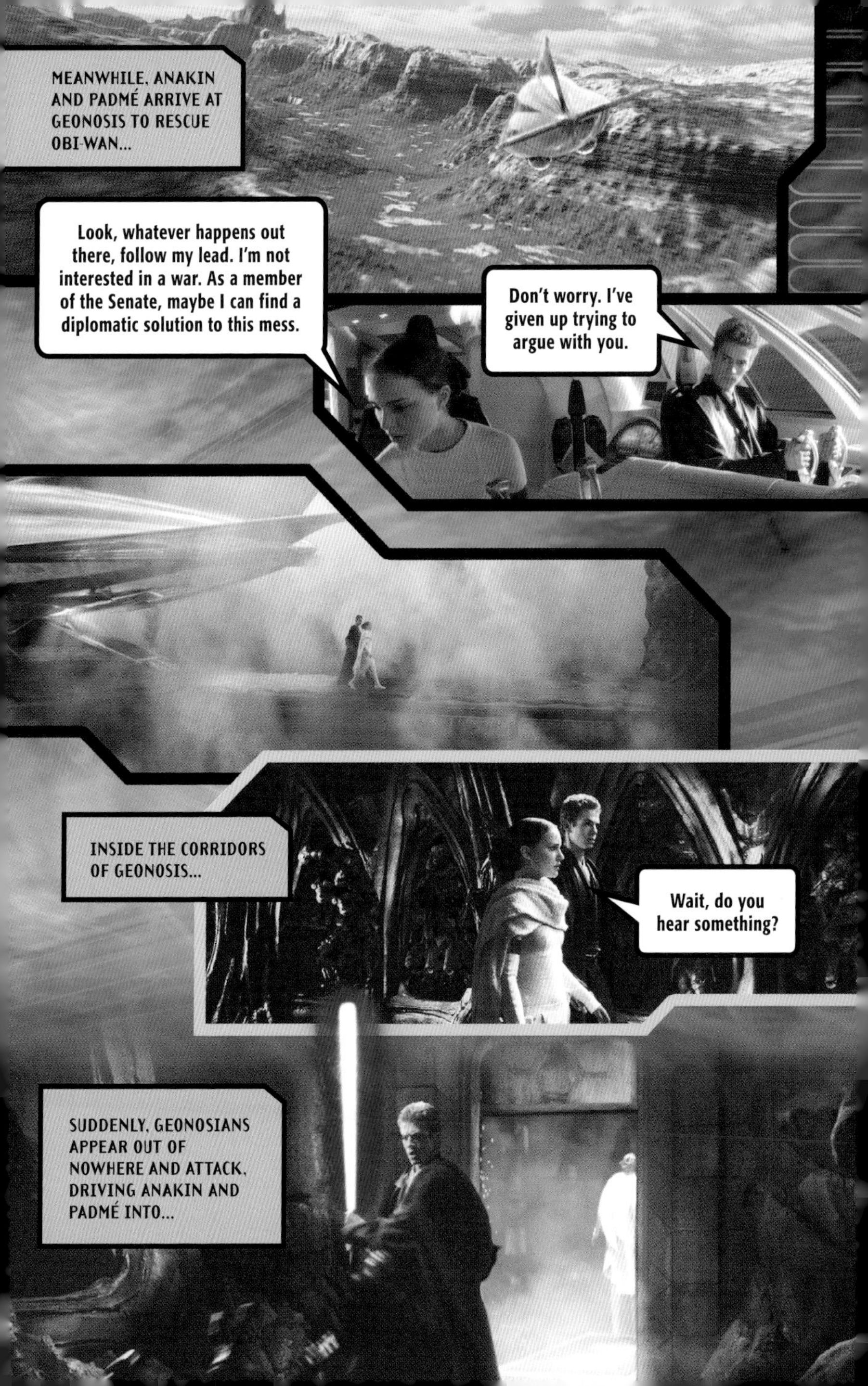
MEANWHILE, ANAKIN AND PADMÉ ARRIVE AT GEONOSIS TO RESCUE OBI-WAN...
Look, whatever happens out there, follow my lead. I'm not interested in a war. As a member of the Senate, maybe I can find a diplomatic solution to this mess.
Don't worry. I've given up trying to argue with you.
INSIDE THE CORRIDORS OF GEONOSIS...
Wait, do you hear something?
SUDDENLY, GEONOSIANS APPEAR OUT OF NOWHERE AND ATTACK, DRIVING ANAKIN AND PADMÉ INTO...

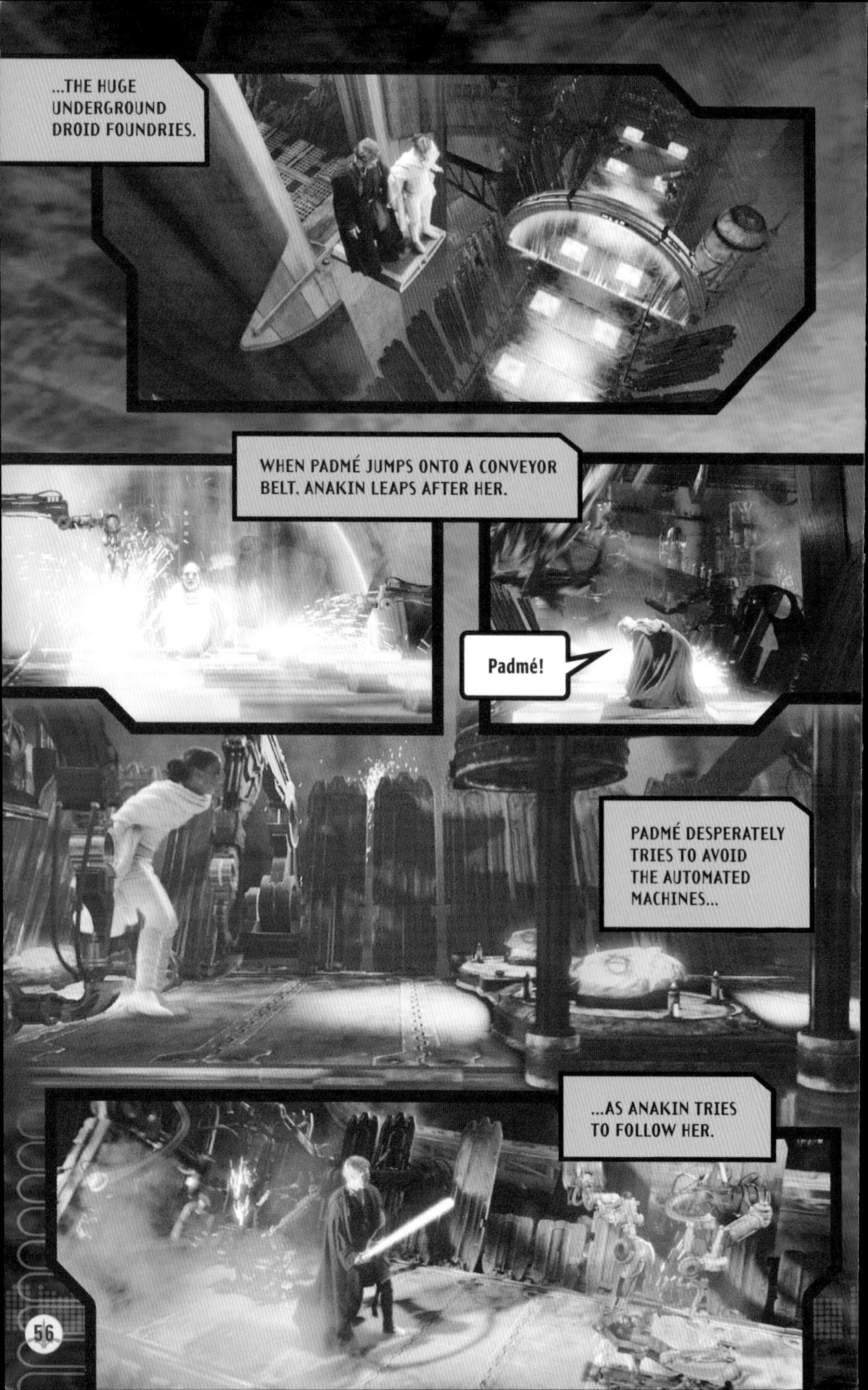
...THE HUGE UNDERGROUND DROID FOUNDRIES.
WHEN PADMÉ JUMPS ONTO A CONVEYOR BELT, ANAKIN LEAPS AFTER HER.
Padmé!
PADMÉ DESPERATELY TRIES TO AVOID THE AUTOMATED MACHINES...
...AS ANAKIN TRIES TO FOLLOW HER.

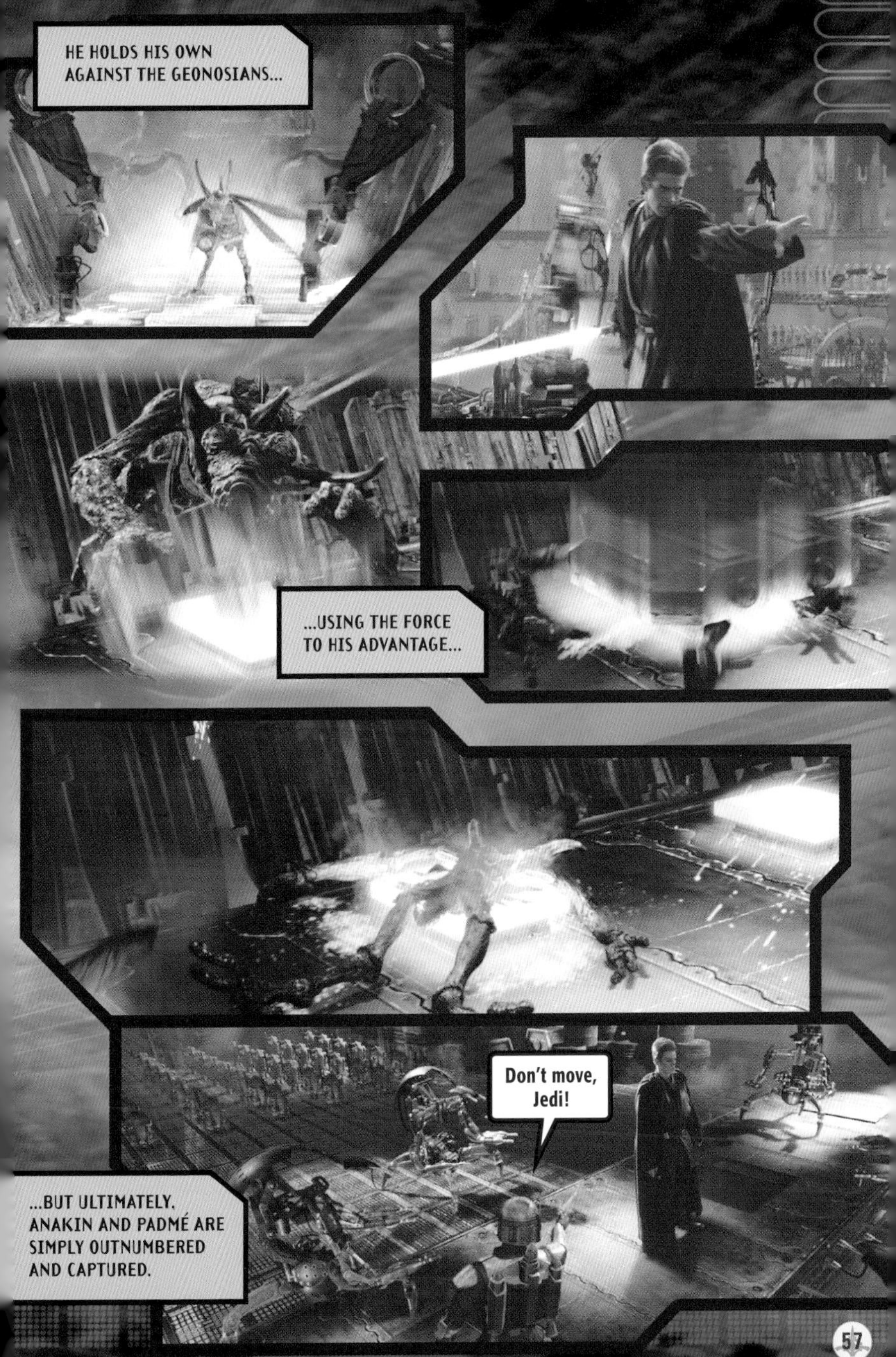
HE HOLDS HIS OWN AGAINST THE GEONOSIANS...
...USING THE FORCE TO HIS ADVANTAGE...
Don't move, Jedi!
...BUT ULTIMATELY, ANAKIN AND PADMÉ ARE SIMPLY OUTNUMBERED AND CAPTURED.

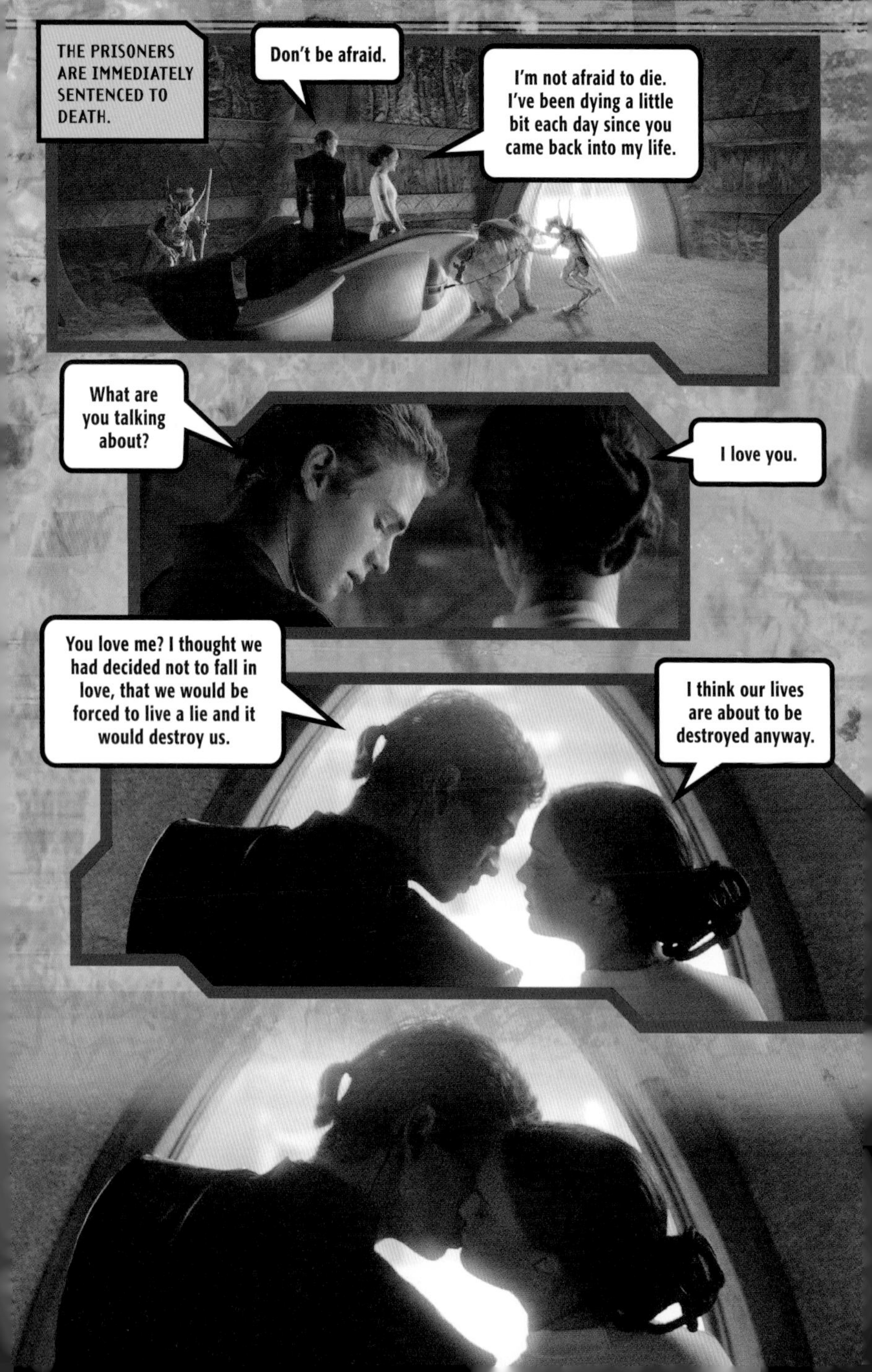
THE PRISONERS ARE IMMEDIATELY SENTENCED TO DEATH.
Don't be afraid.
I'm not afraid to die. I've been dying a little bit each day since you came back into my life.
What are you talking about?
I love you.
You love me? I thought we had decided not to fall in love, that we would be forced to live a lie and it would destroy us.
I think our lives are about to be destroyed anyway.

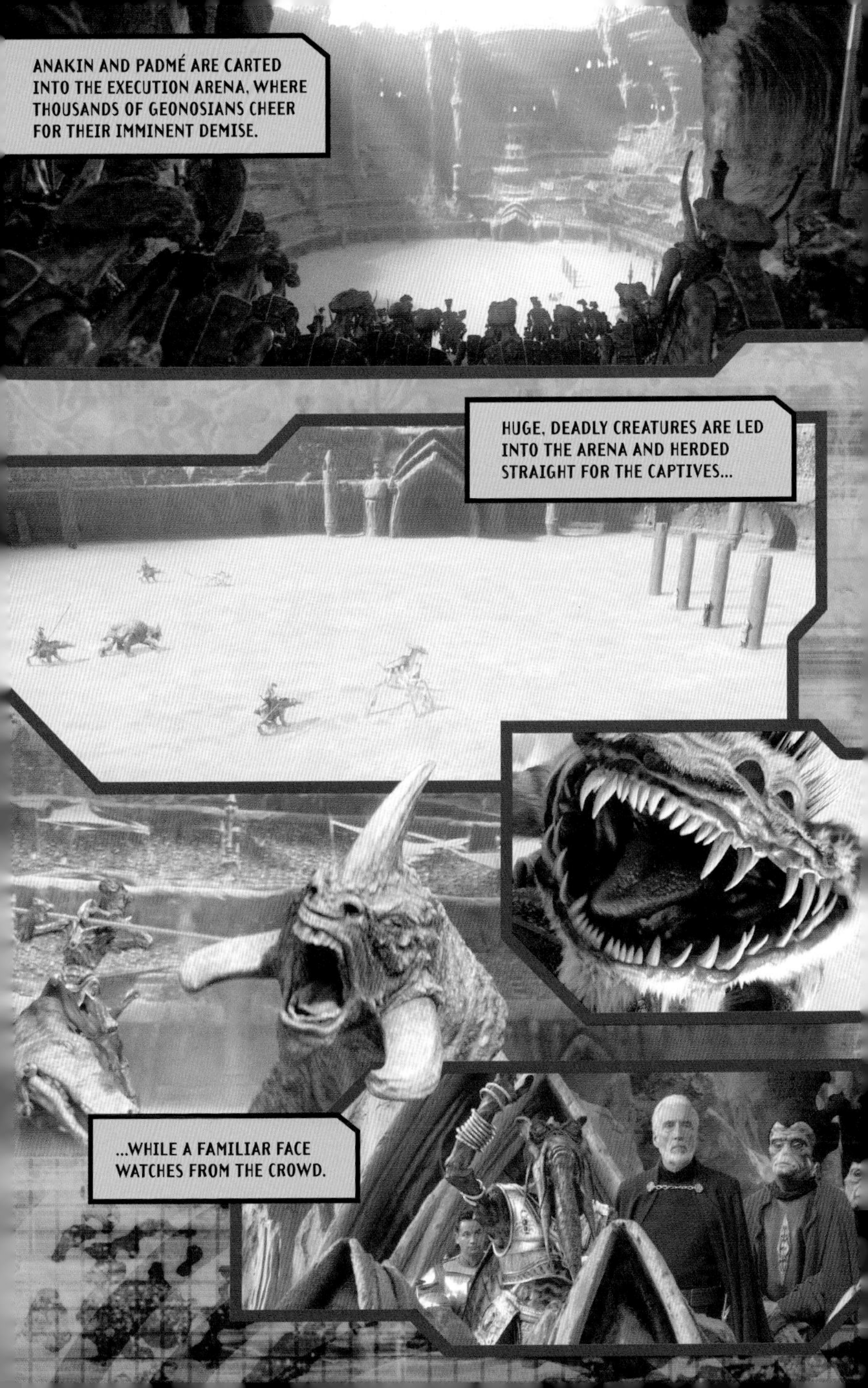
ANAKIN AND PADMÉ ARE CARTED INTO THE EXECUTION ARENA, WHERE THOUSANDS OF GEONOSIANS CHEER FOR THEIR IMMINENT DEMISE.
HUGE, DEADLY CREATURES ARE LED INTO THE ARENA AND HERDED STRAIGHT FOR THE CAPTIVES...
...WHILE A FAMILIAR FACE WATCHES FROM THE CROWD.

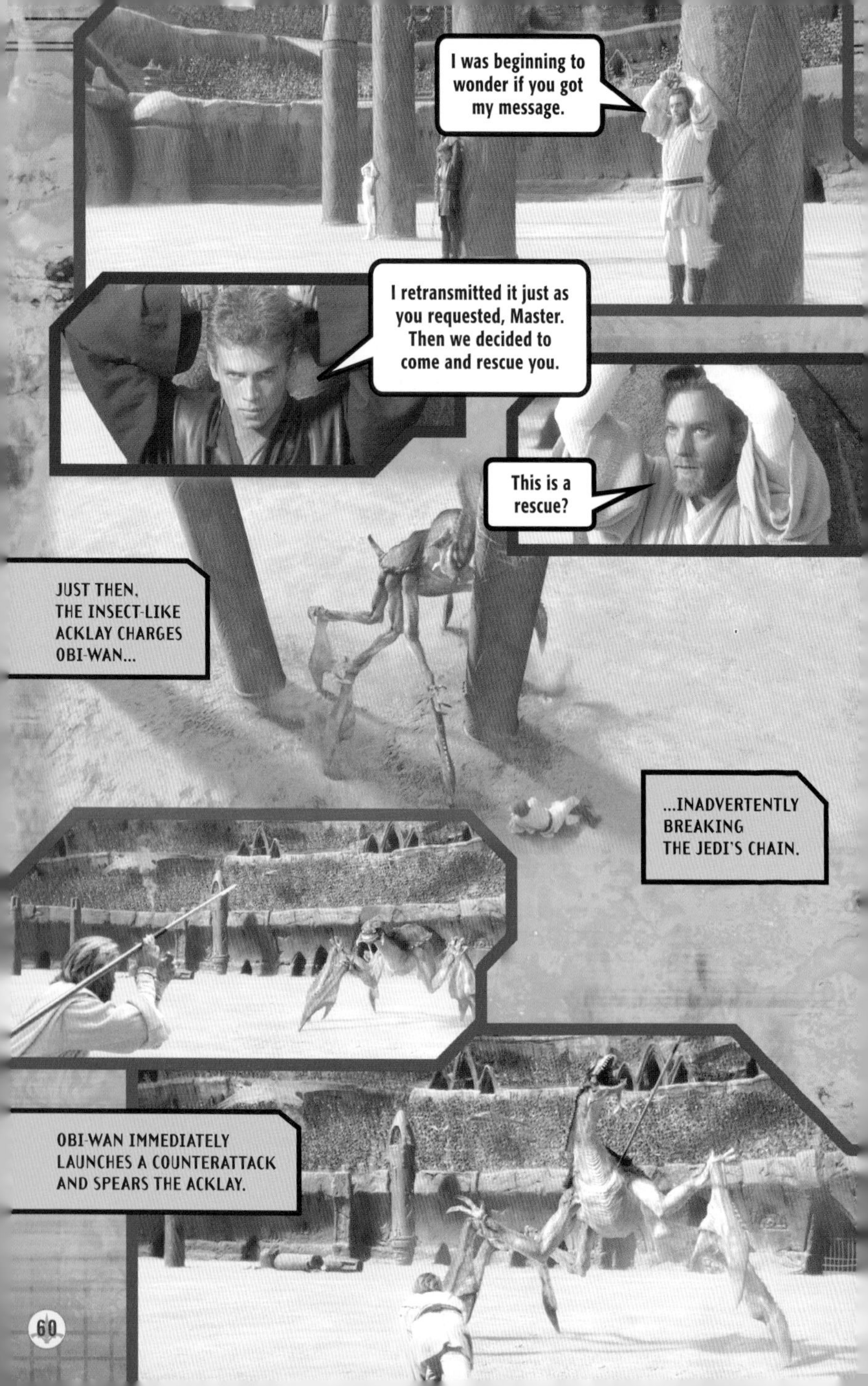
I was beginning to wonder if you got my message.
I retransmitted it just as you requested, Master. Then we decided to come and rescue you.
This is a rescue?
JUST THEN, THE INSECT-LIKE ACKLAY CHARGES OBI-WAN...
...INADVERTENTLY BREAKING THE JEDI'S CHAIN.
OBI-WAN IMMEDIATELY LAUNCHES A COUNTERATTACK AND SPEARS THE ACKLAY.

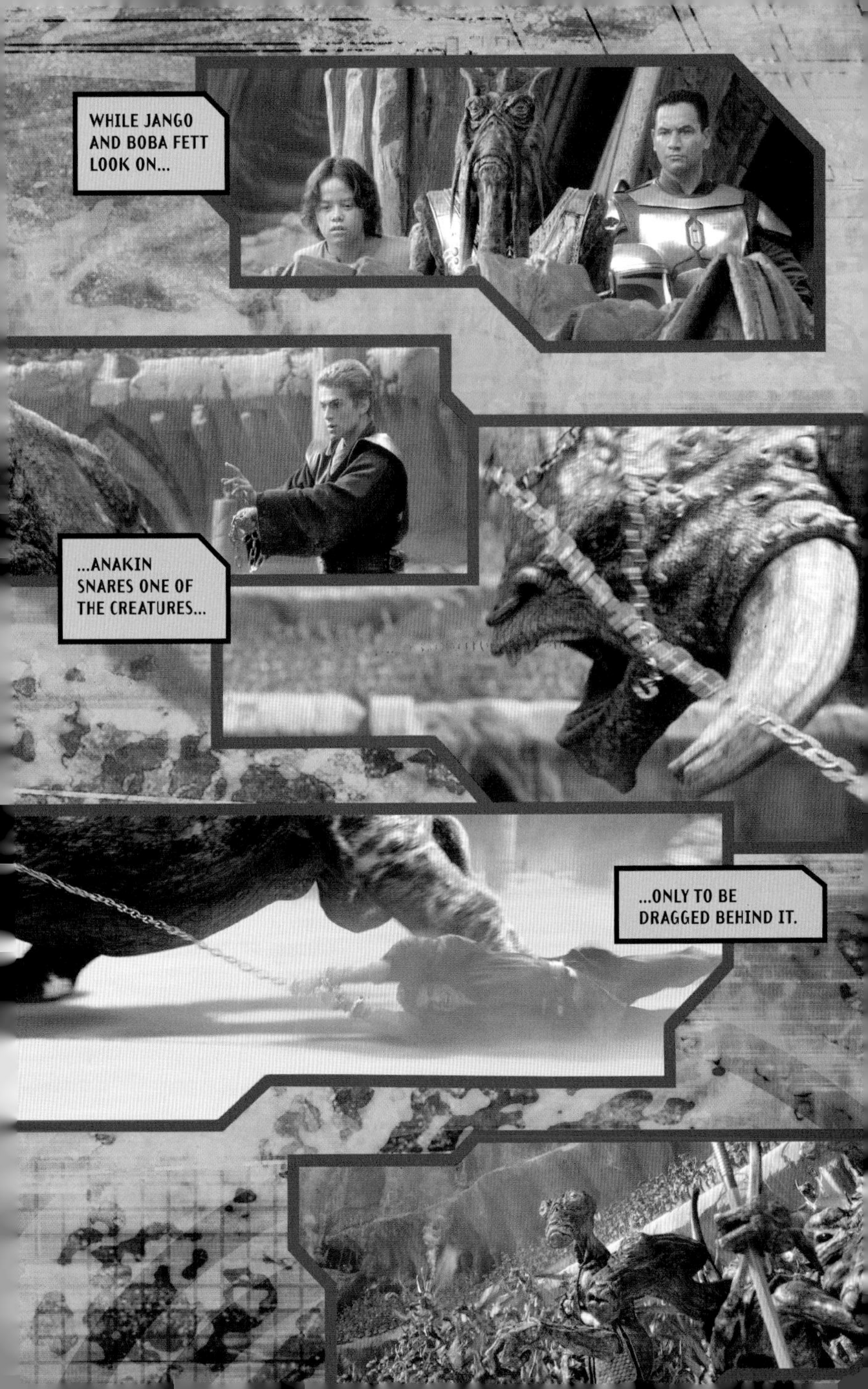
WHILE JANGO AND BOBA FETT LOOK ON...
...ANAKIN SNARES ONE OF THE CREATURES...
...ONLY TO BE DRAGGED BEHIND IT.

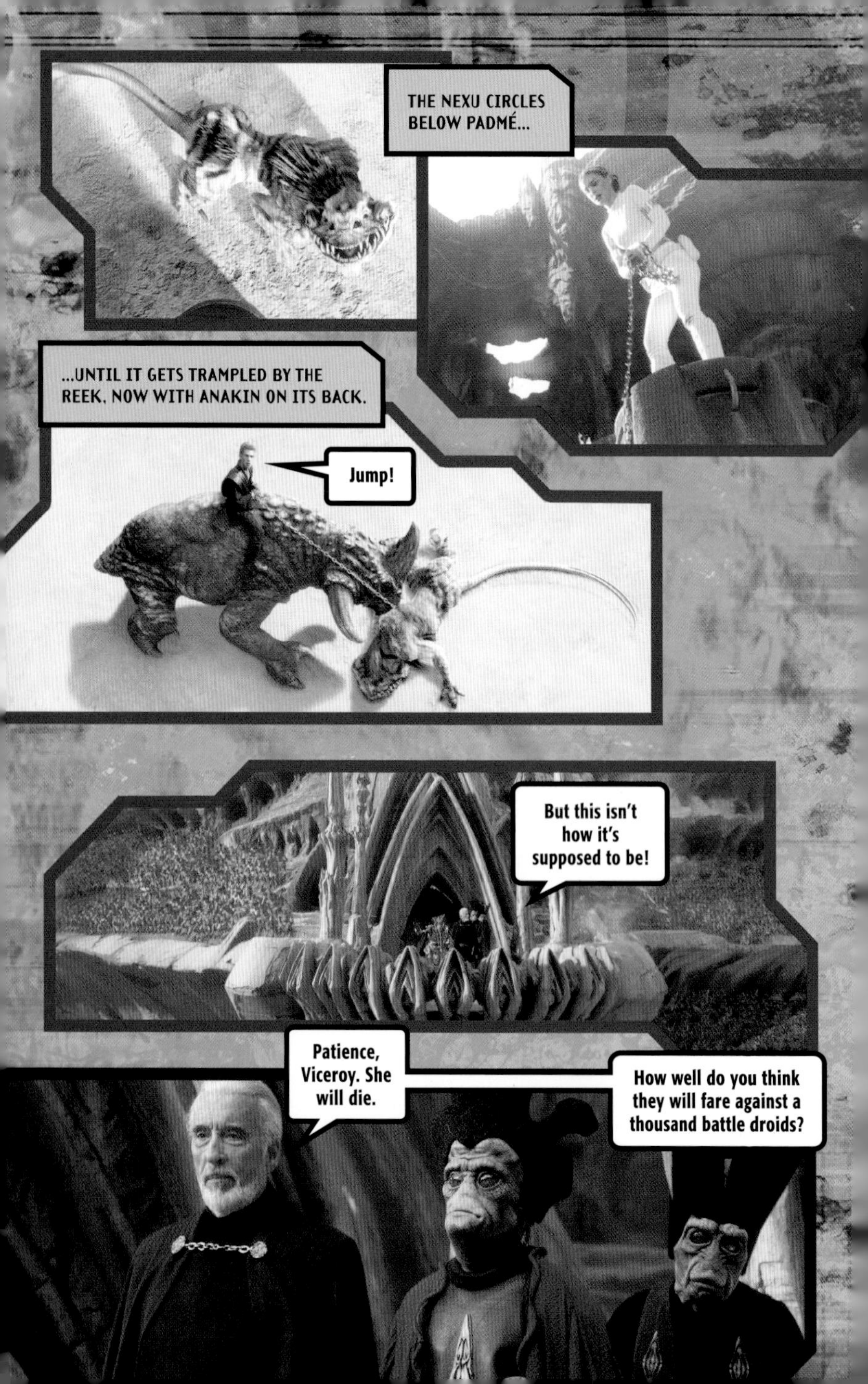
THE NEXU CIRCLES BELOW PADMÉ...
...UNTIL IT GETS TRAMPLED BY THE REEK, NOW WITH ANAKIN ON ITS BACK.
Jump!
But this isn't how it's supposed to be!
Patience, Viceroy. She will die.
How well do you think they will fare against a thousand battle droids?

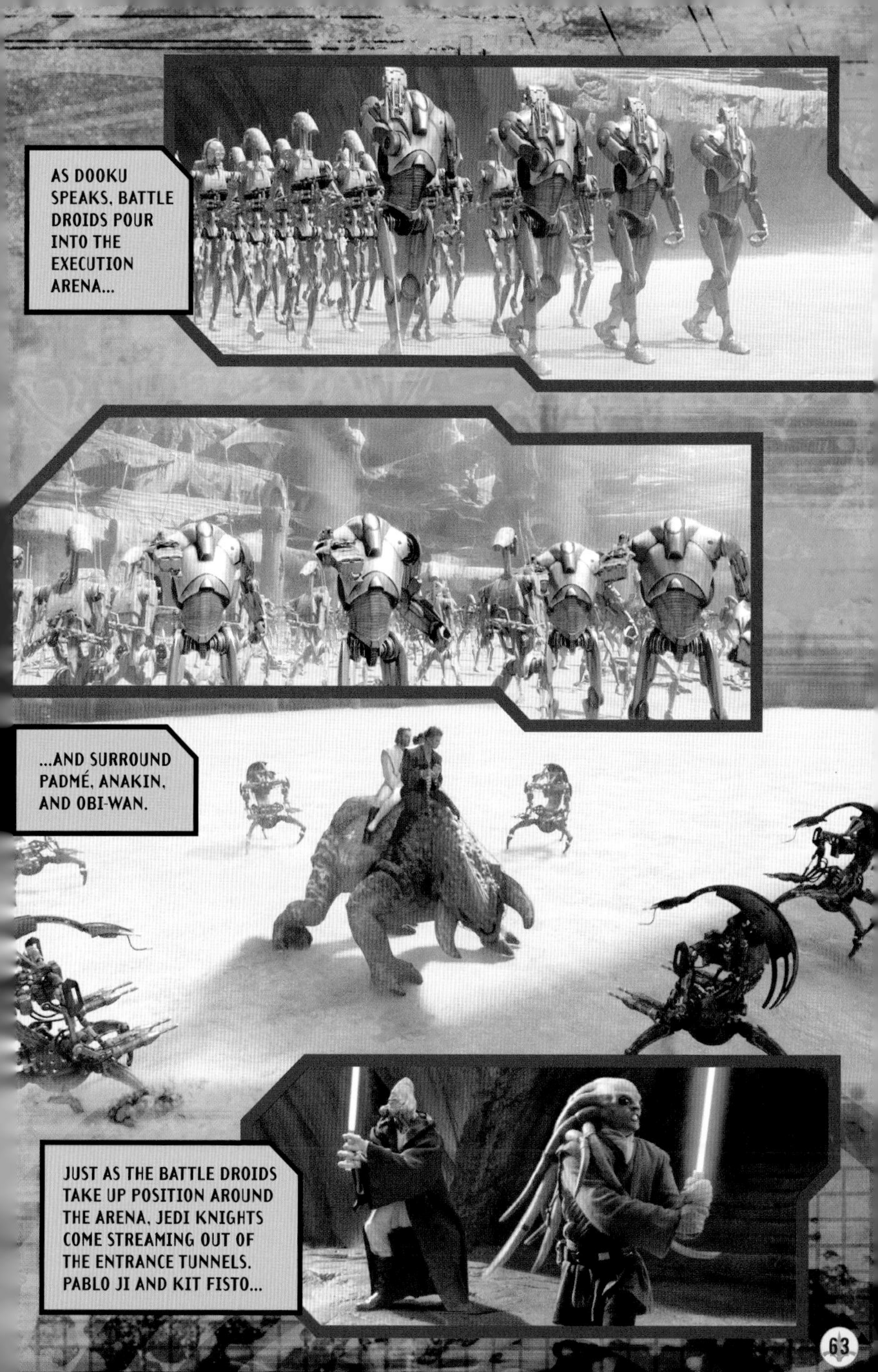
AS DOOKU SPEAKS, BATTLE DROIDS POUR INTO THE EXECUTION ARENA...
...AND SURROUND PADMÉ, ANAKIN, AND OBI-WAN.
JUST AS THE BATTLE DROIDS TAKE UP POSITION AROUND THE ARENA, JEDI KNIGHTS COME STREAMING OUT OF THE ENTRANCE TUNNELS. PABLO JI AND KIT FISTO...

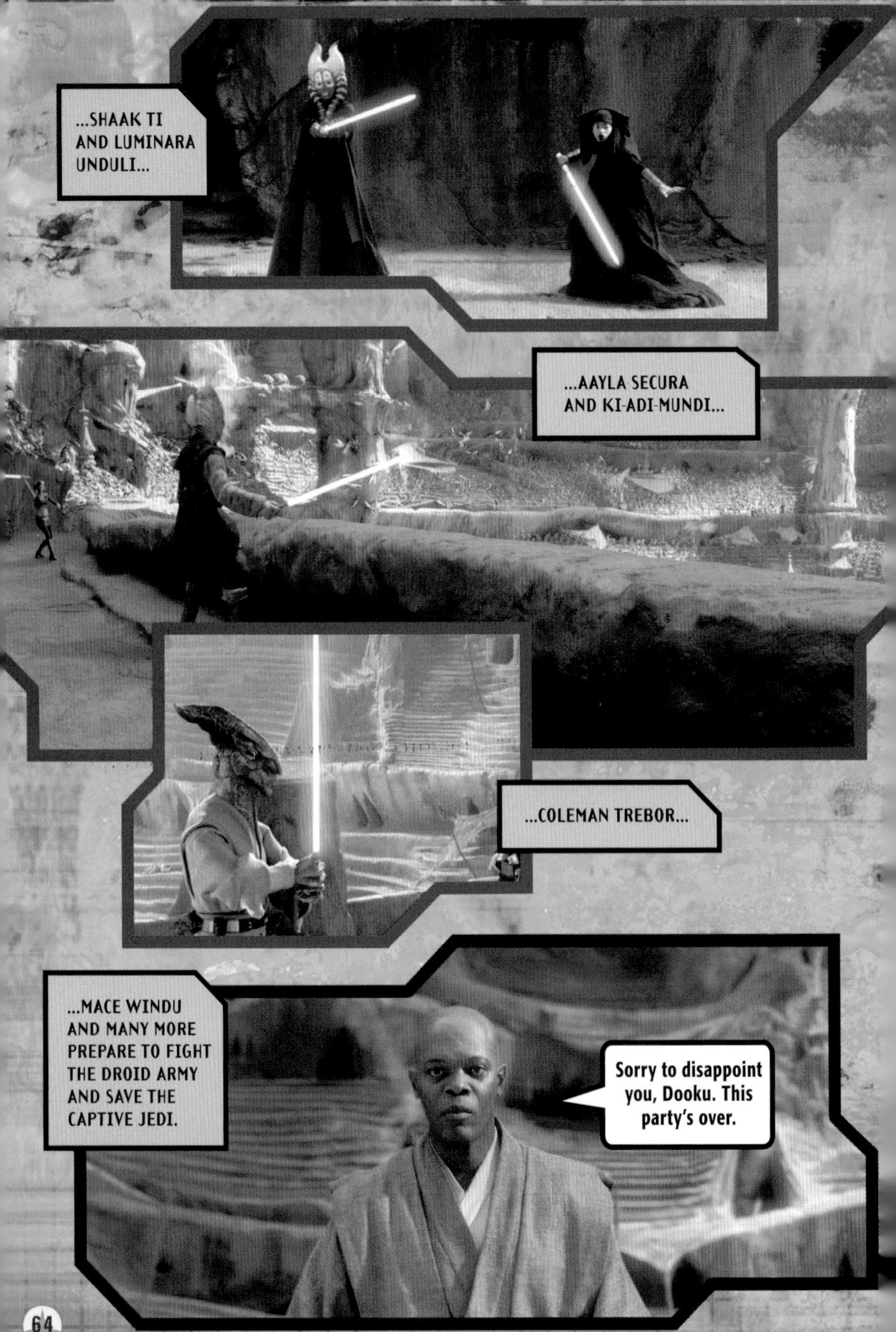
...SHAAK TI AND LUMINARA UNDULI...
...AAYLA SECURA AND KI-ADI-MUNDI...
...COLEMAN TREBOR...
...MACE WINDU AND MANY MORE PREPARE TO FIGHT THE DROID ARMY AND SAVE THE CAPTIVE JEDI.
Sorry to disappoint you, Dooku. This party's over.

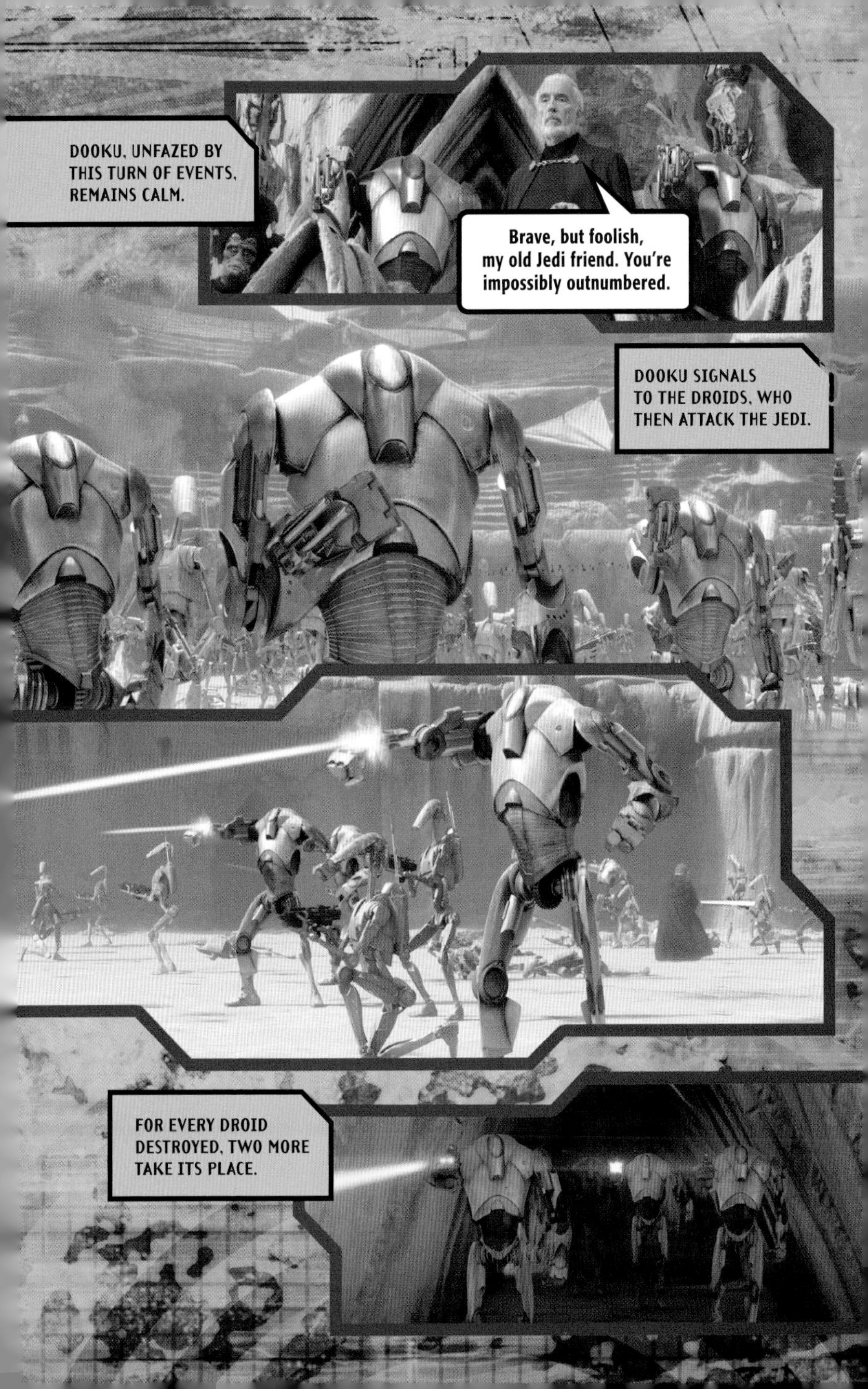

DOOKU, UNFAZED BY THIS TURN OF EVENTS, REMAINS CALM.
Brave, but foolish, my old Jedi friend. You're impossibly outnumbered.
DOOKU SIGNALS TO THE DROIDS, WHO THEN ATTACK THE JEDI.
FOR EVERY DROID DESTROYED, TWO MORE TAKE ITS PLACE.

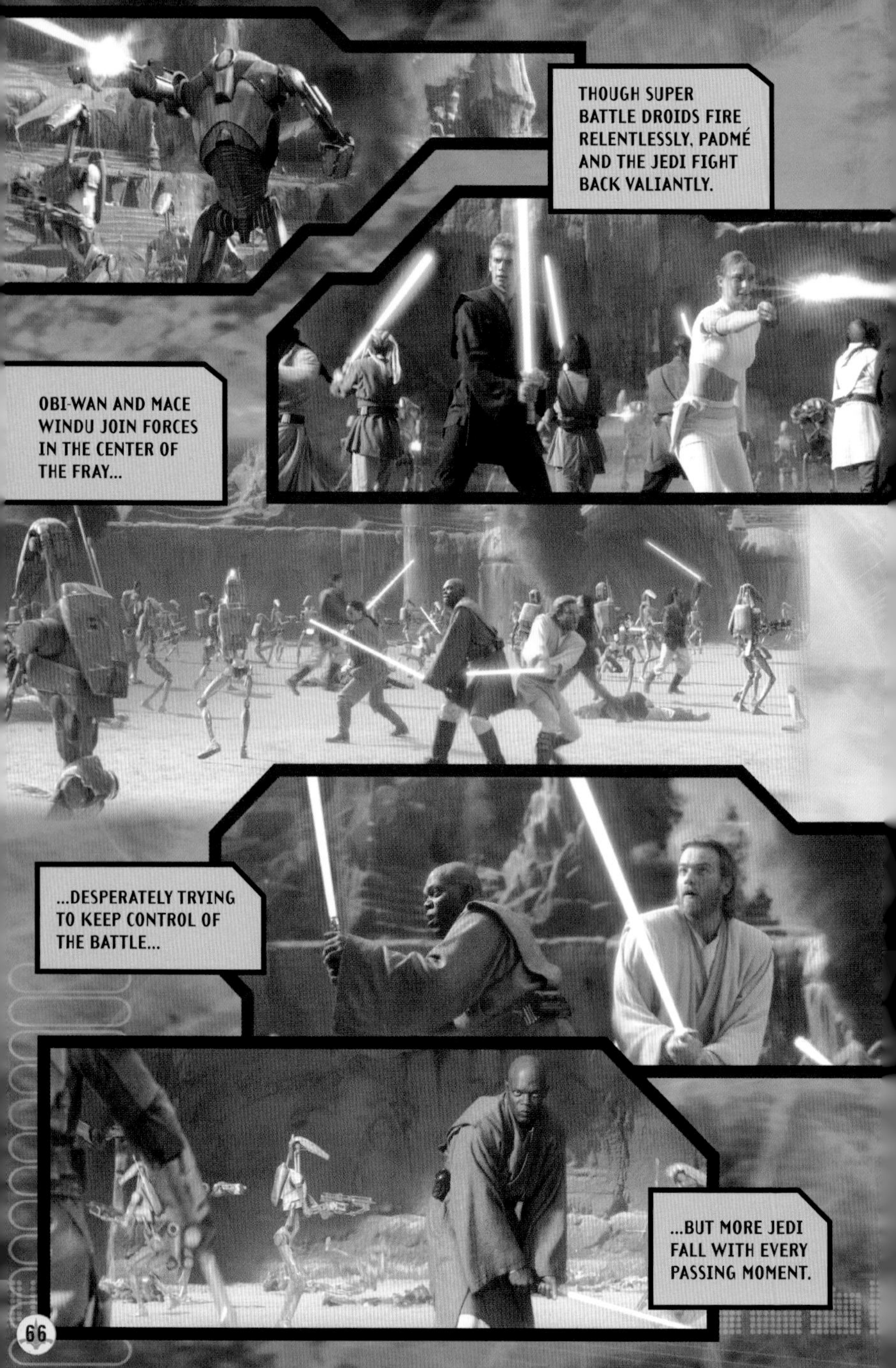
THOUGH SUPER BATTLE DROIDS FIRE RELENTLESSLY, PADMÉ AND THE JEDI FIGHT BACK VALIANTLY.
OBI-WAN AND MACE WINDU JOIN FORCES IN THE CENTER OF THE FRAY...
...DESPERATELY TRYING TO KEEP CONTROL OF THE BATTLE...
...BUT MORE JEDI FALL WITH EVERY PASSING MOMENT.

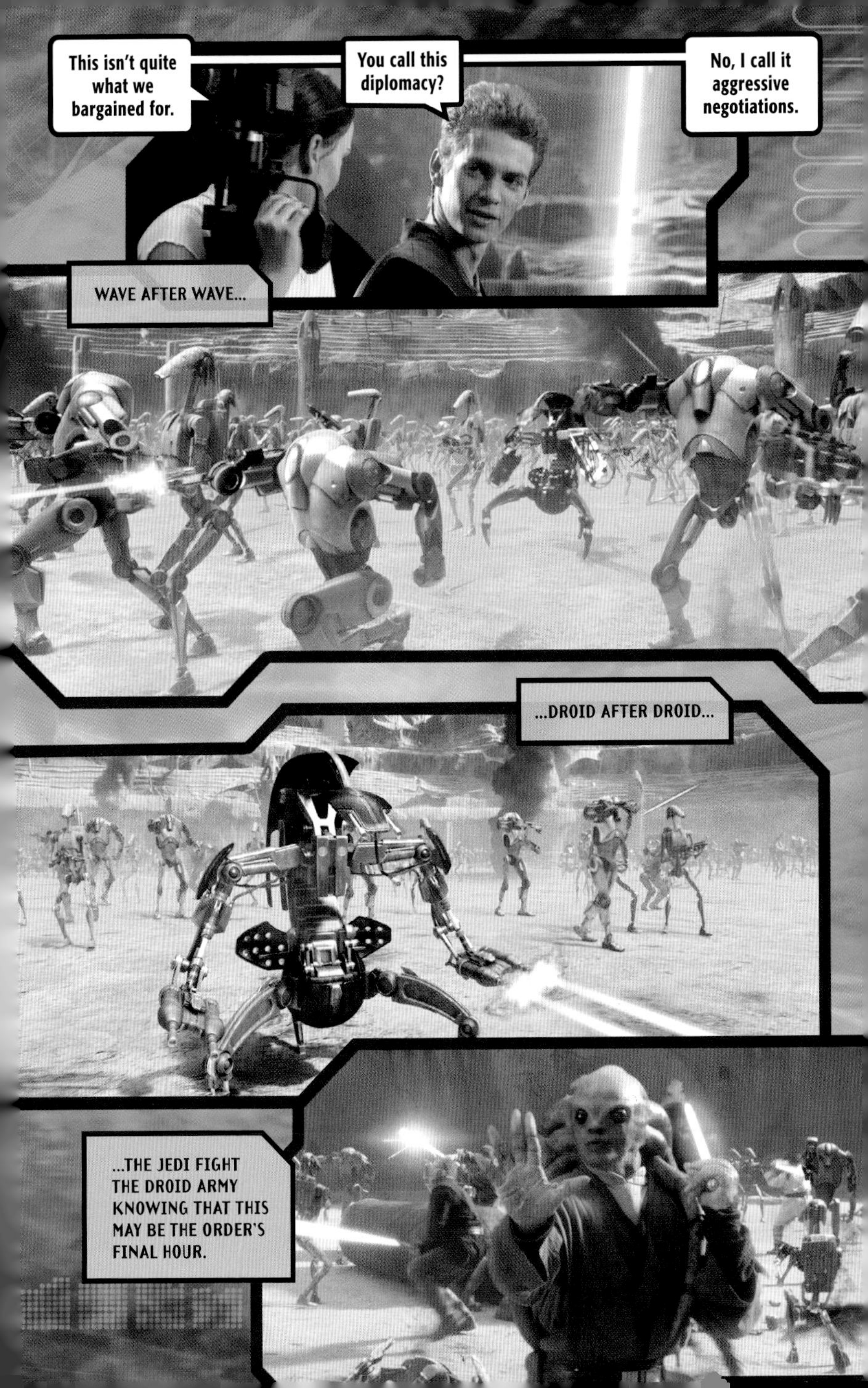
This isn't quite what we bargained for.
You call this diplomacy?
No, I call it aggressive negotiations.
WAVE AFTER WAVE...
...DROID AFTER DROID...
...THE JEDI FIGHT THE DROID ARMY KNOWING THAT THIS MAY BE THE ORDER'S FINAL HOUR.

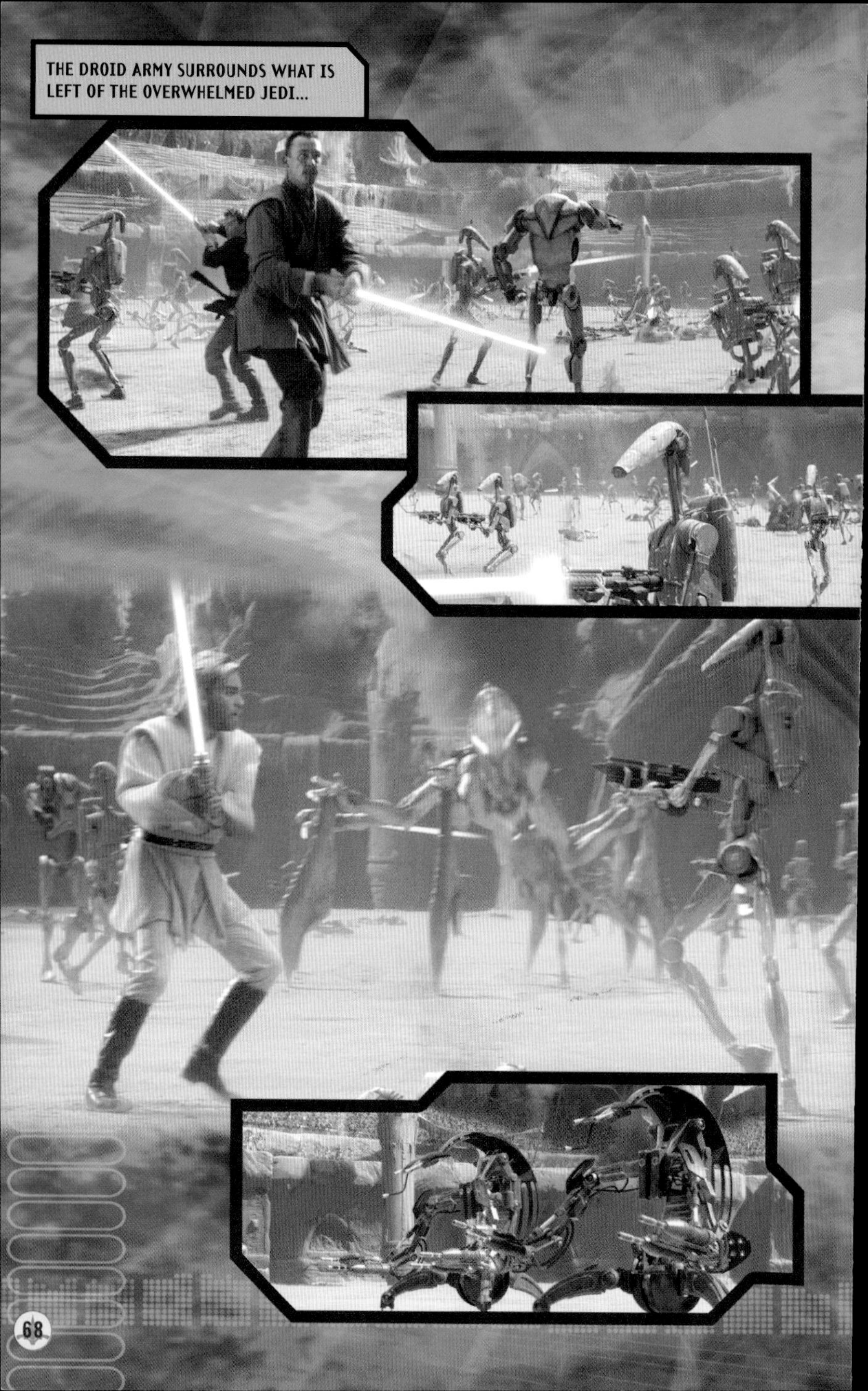
THE DROID ARMY SURROUNDS WHAT IS LEFT OF THE OVERWHELMED JEDI...

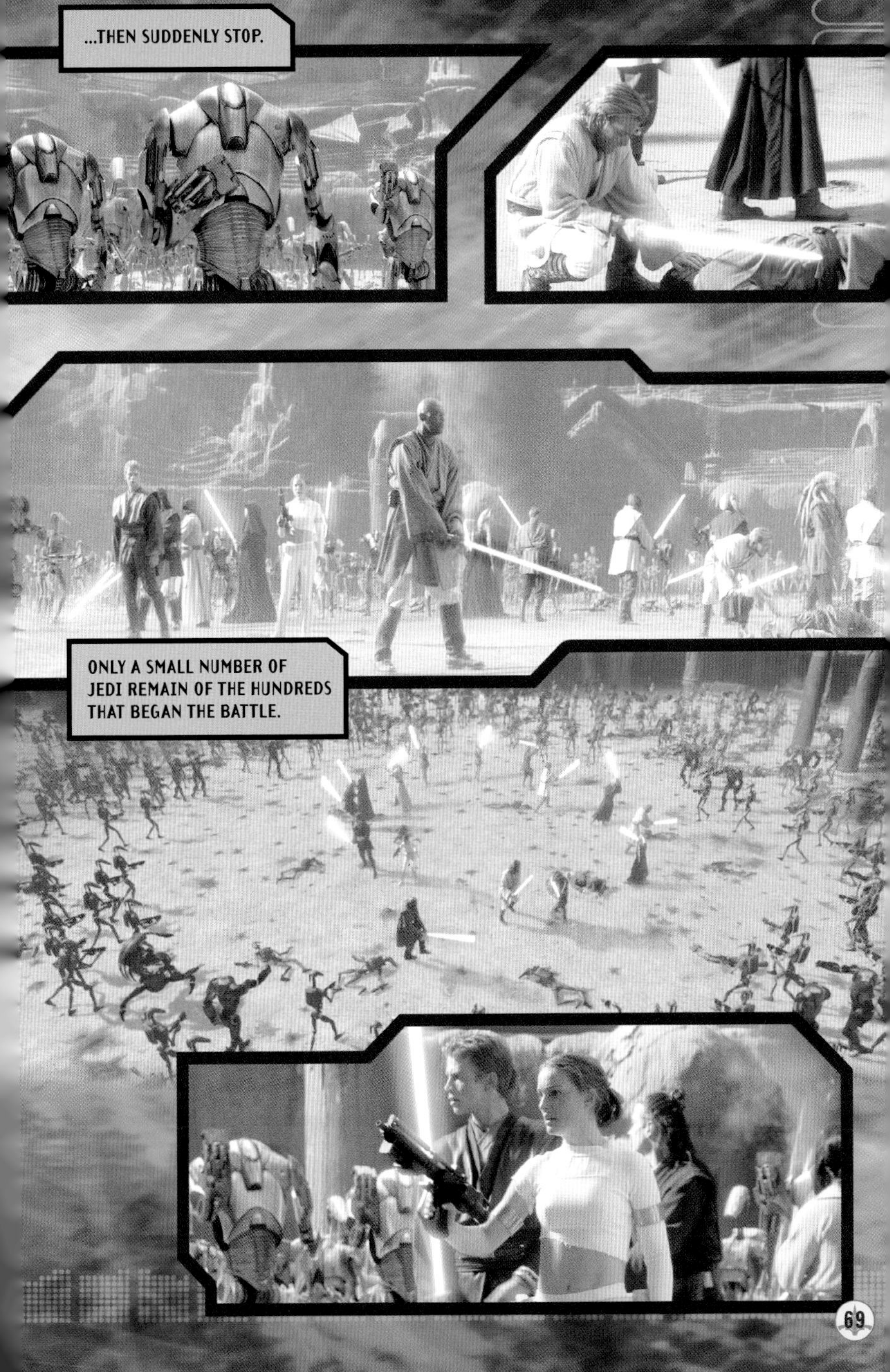
...THEN SUDDENLY STOP.
ONLY A SMALL NUMBER OF JEDI REMAIN OF THE HUNDREDS THAT BEGAN THE BATTLE.

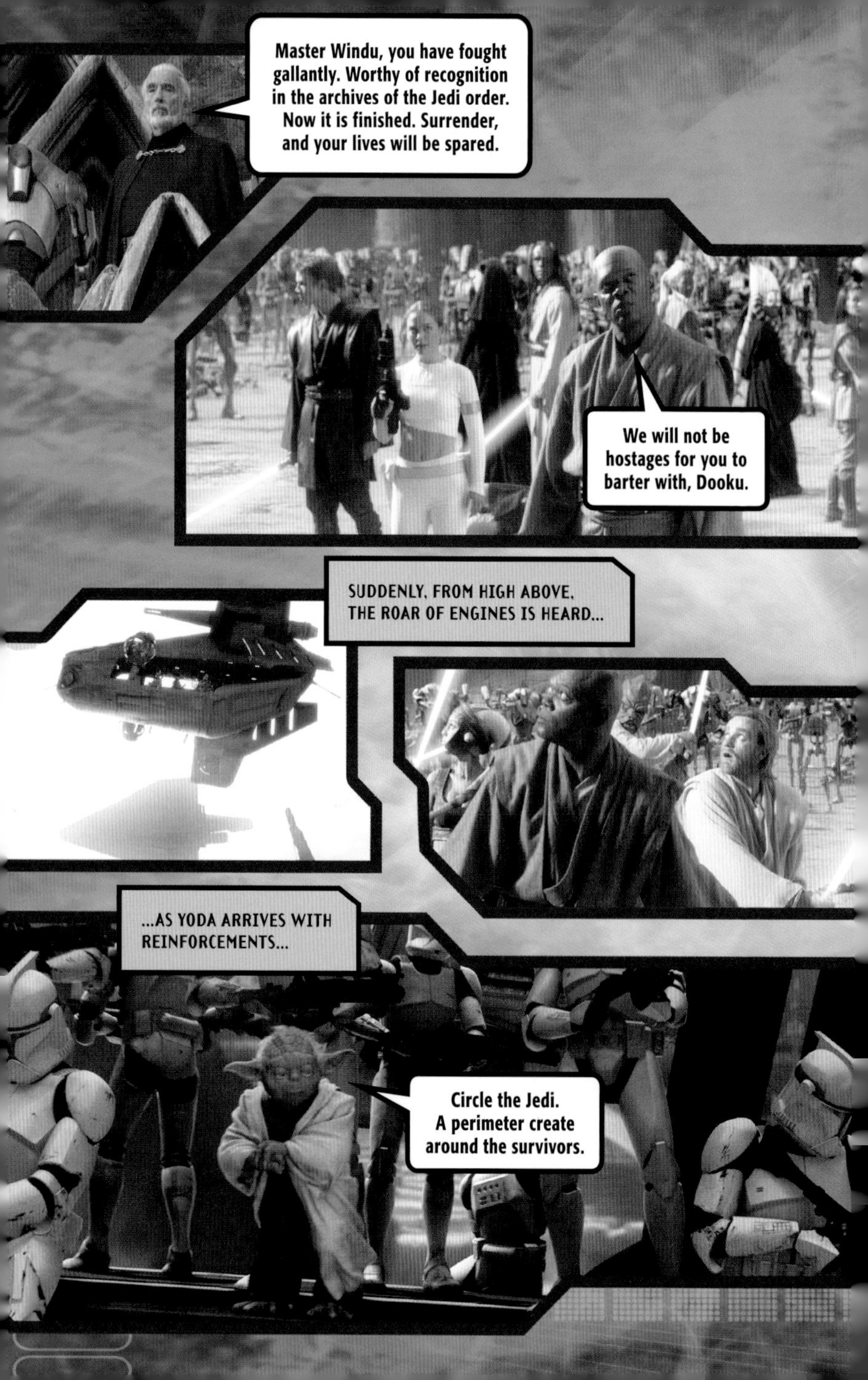

Master Windu, you have fought gallantly. Worthy of recognition in the archives of the Jedi order. Now it is finished. Surrender, and your lives will be spared.
We will not be hostages for you to barter with, Dooku.
SUDDENLY, FROM HIGH ABOVE, THE ROAR OF ENGINES IS HEARD...
...AS YODA ARRIVES WITH REINFORCEMENTS...
Circle the Jedi. A perimeter create around the survivors.

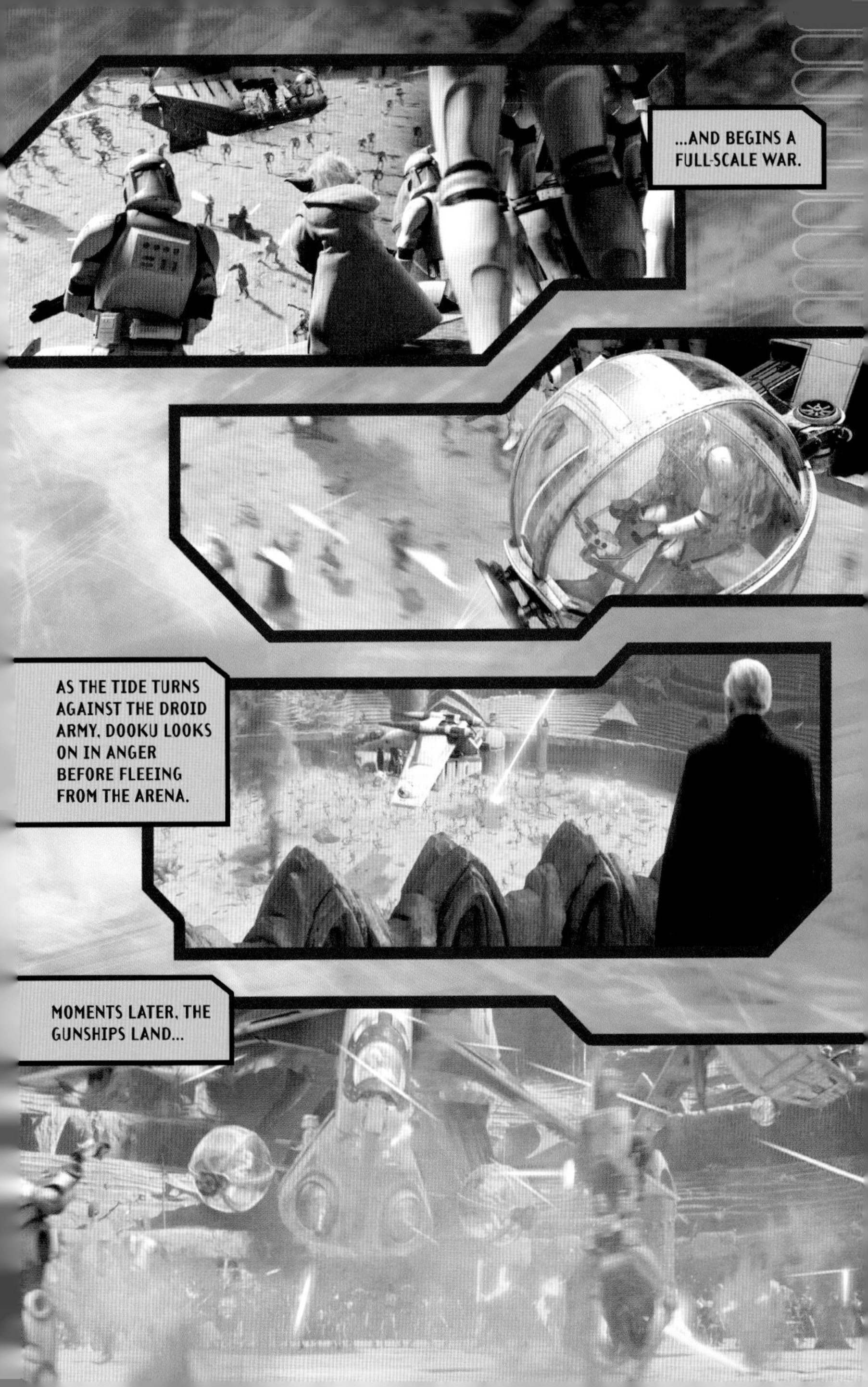
...AND BEGINS A FULL-SCALE WAR.
AS THE TIDE TURNS AGAINST THE DROID ARMY, DOOKU LOOKS ON IN ANGER BEFORE FLEEING FROM THE ARENA.
MOMENTS LATER, THE GUNSHIPS LAND...

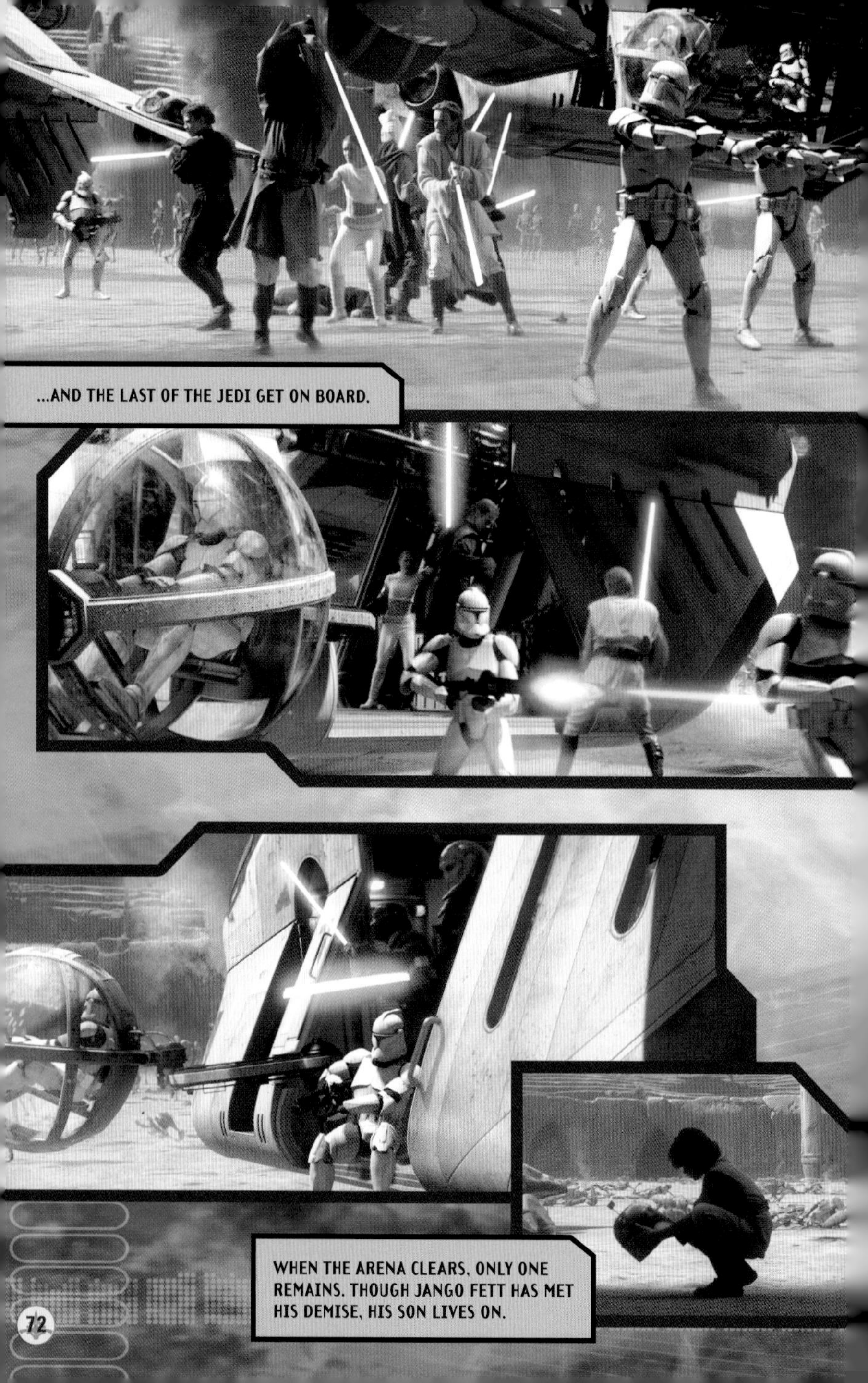
...AND THE LAST OF THE JEDI GET ON BOARD.
WHEN THE ARENA CLEARS, ONLY ONE REMAINS. THOUGH JANGO FETT HAS MET HIS DEMISE, HIS SON LIVES ON.

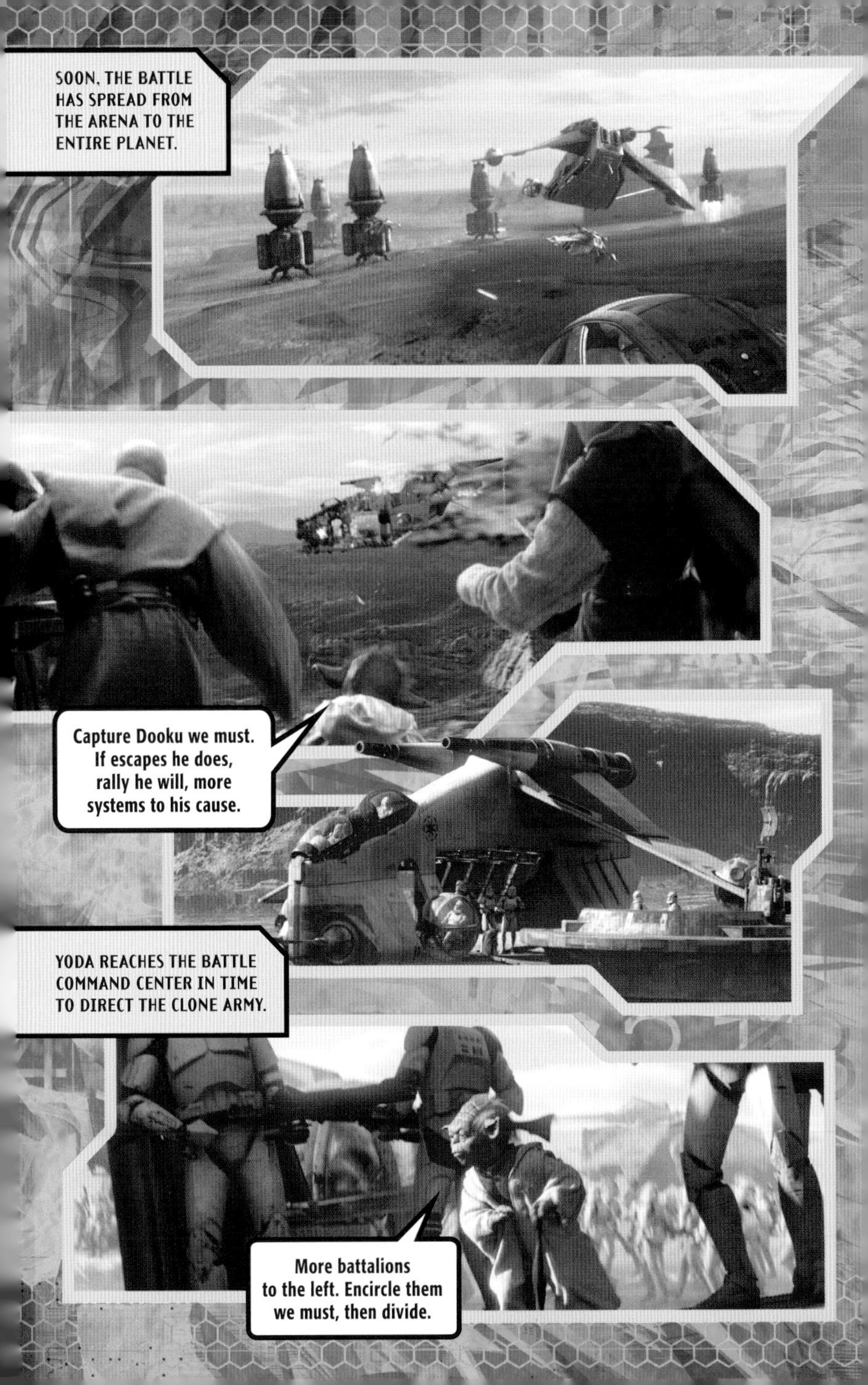
SOON, THE BATTLE HAS SPREAD FROM THE ARENA TO THE ENTIRE PLANET.
Capture Dooku we must. If escapes he does, rally he will, more systems to his cause.
YODA REACHES THE BATTLE COMMAND CENTER IN TIME TO DIRECT THE CLONE ARMY.
More battalions to the left. Encircle them we must, then divide.

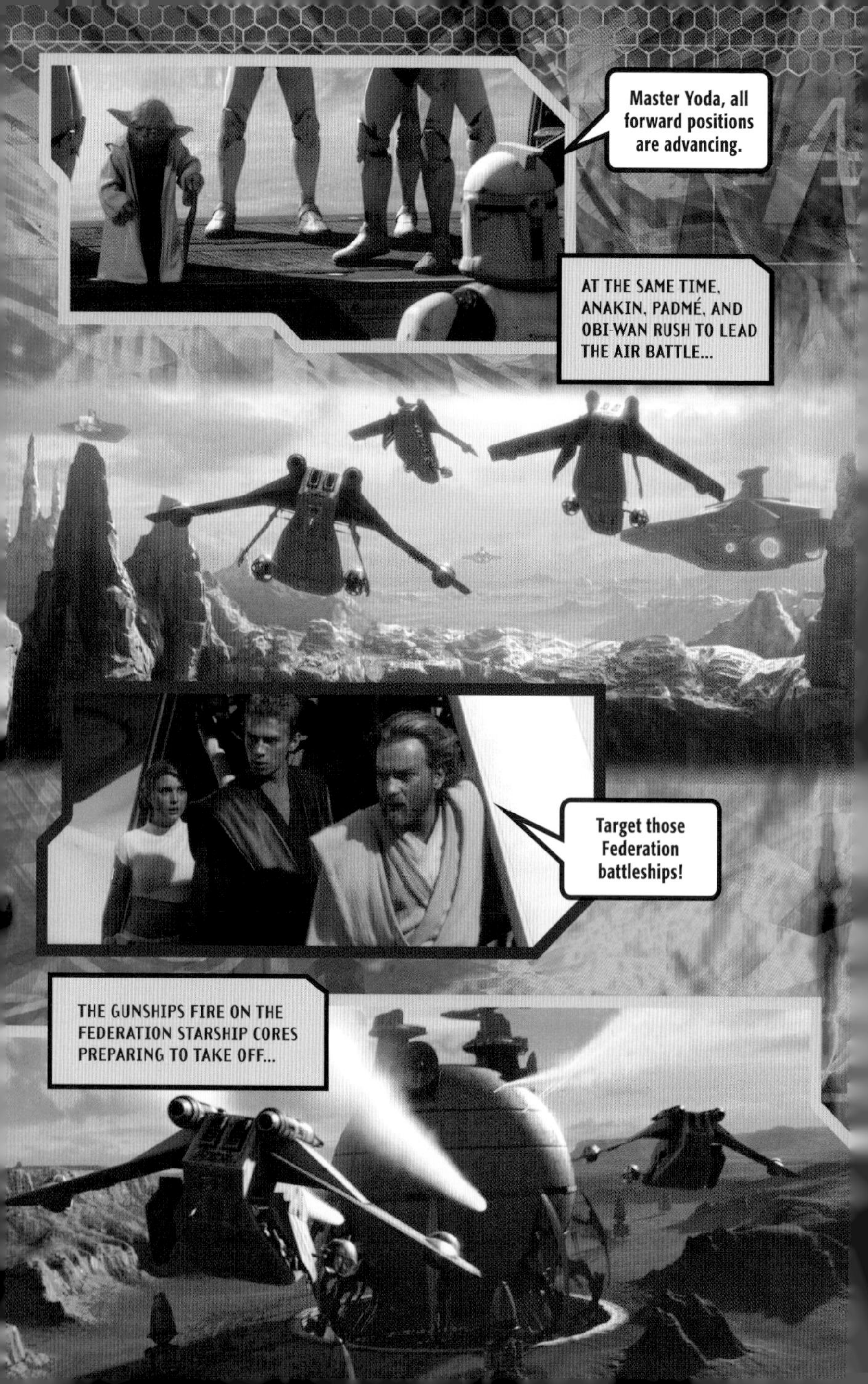
Master Yoda, all forward positions are advancing.
AT THE SAME TIME, ANAKIN, PADMÉ, AND OBI-WAN RUSH TO LEAD THE AIR BATTLE...
Target those Federation battleships!
THE GUNSHIPS FIRE ON THE FEDERATION STARSHIP CORES PREPARING TO TAKE OFF...

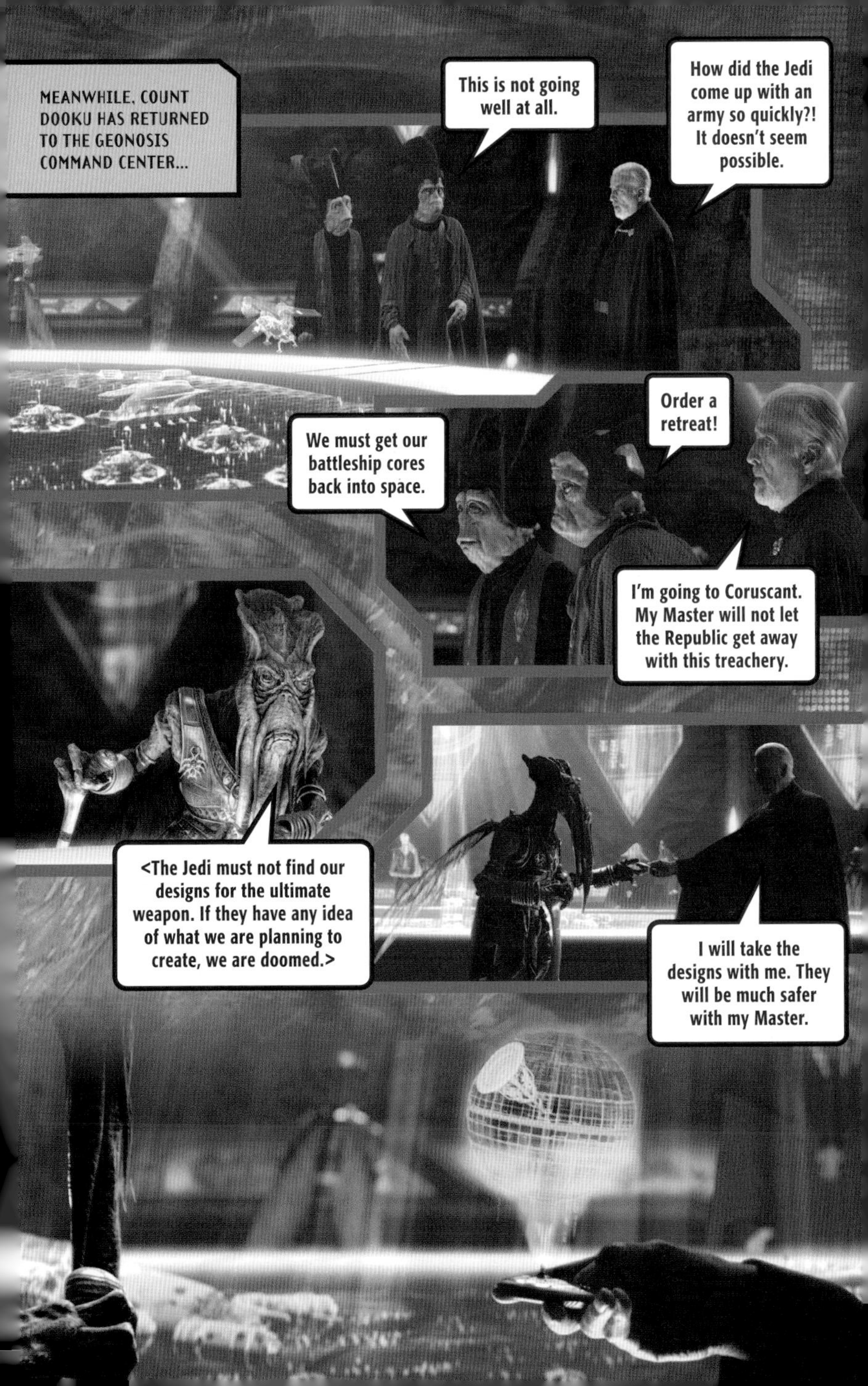
MEANWHILE, COUNT DOOKU HAS RETURNED TO THE GEONOSIS COMMAND CENTER...
This is not going well at all.
How did the Jedi come up with an army so quickly?! It doesn't seem possible.
We must get our battleship cores back into space.
Order a retreat!
I'm going to Coruscant. My Master will not let the Republic get away with this treachery.
<The Jedi must not find our designs for the ultimate weapon. If they have any idea of what we are planning to create, we are doomed.>
I will take the designs with me. They will be much safer with my Master.

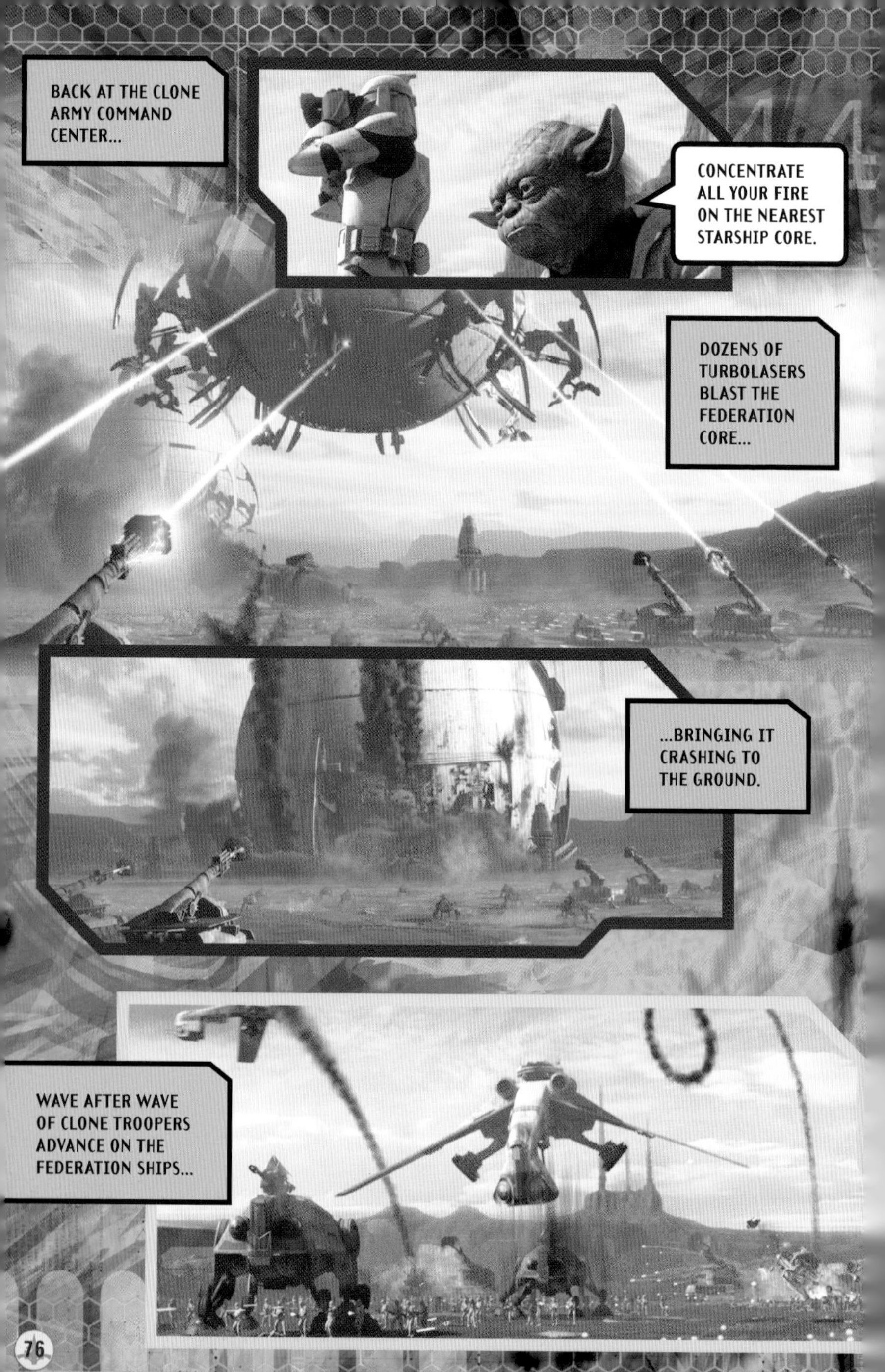
BACK AT THE CLONE ARMY COMMAND CENTER...
CONCENTRATE ALL YOUR FIRE ON THE NEAREST STARSHIP CORE.
DOZENS OF TURBOLASERS BLAST THE FEDERATION CORE...
...BRINGING IT CRASHING TO THE GROUND.
WAVE AFTER WAVE OF CLONE TROOPERS ADVANCE ON THE FEDERATION SHIPS...

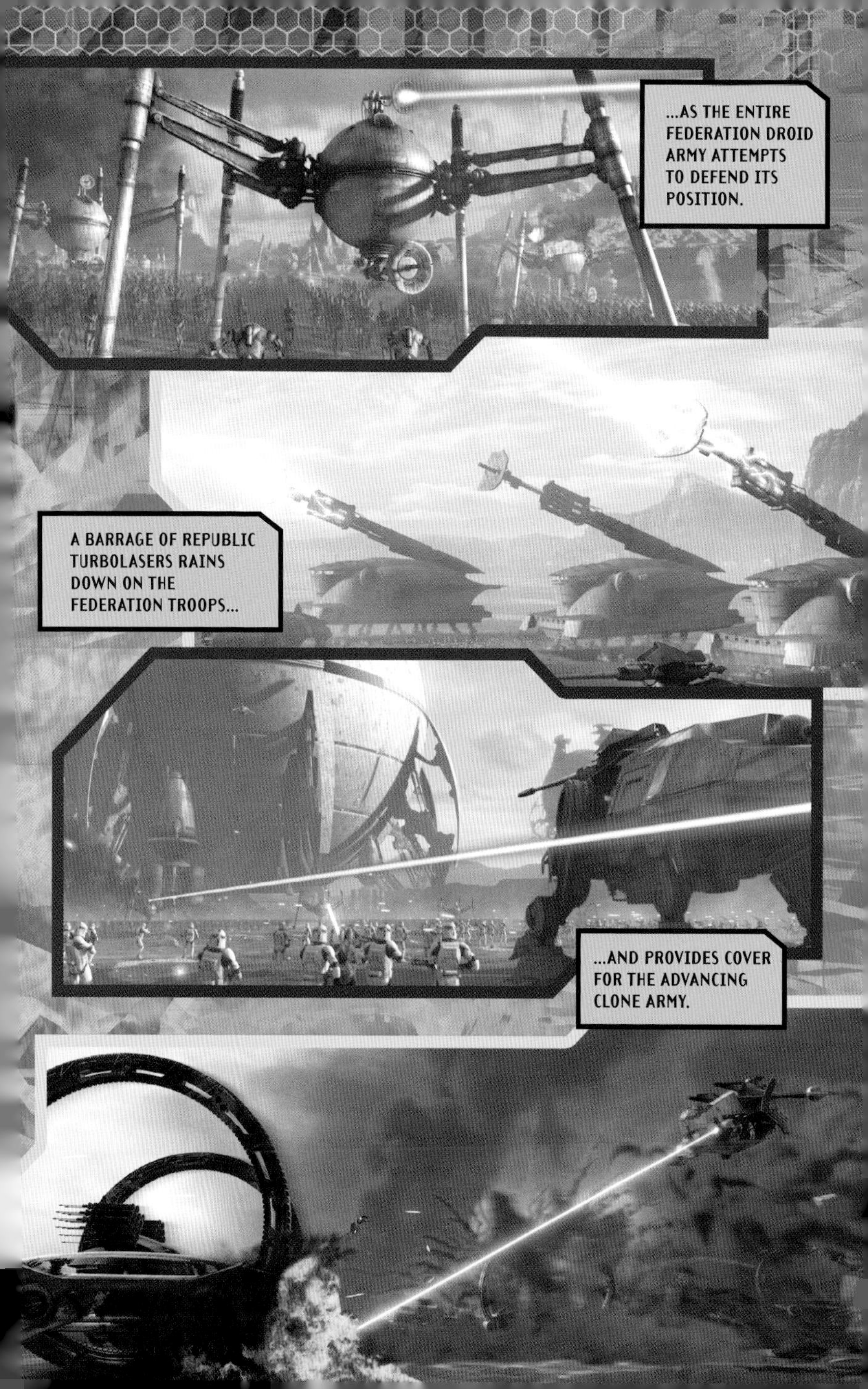
...AS THE ENTIRE FEDERATION DROID ARMY ATTEMPTS TO DEFEND ITS POSITION.
A BARRAGE OF REPUBLIC TURBOLASERS RAINS DOWN ON THE FEDERATION TROOPS...
...AND PROVIDES COVER FOR THE ADVANCING CLONE ARMY.

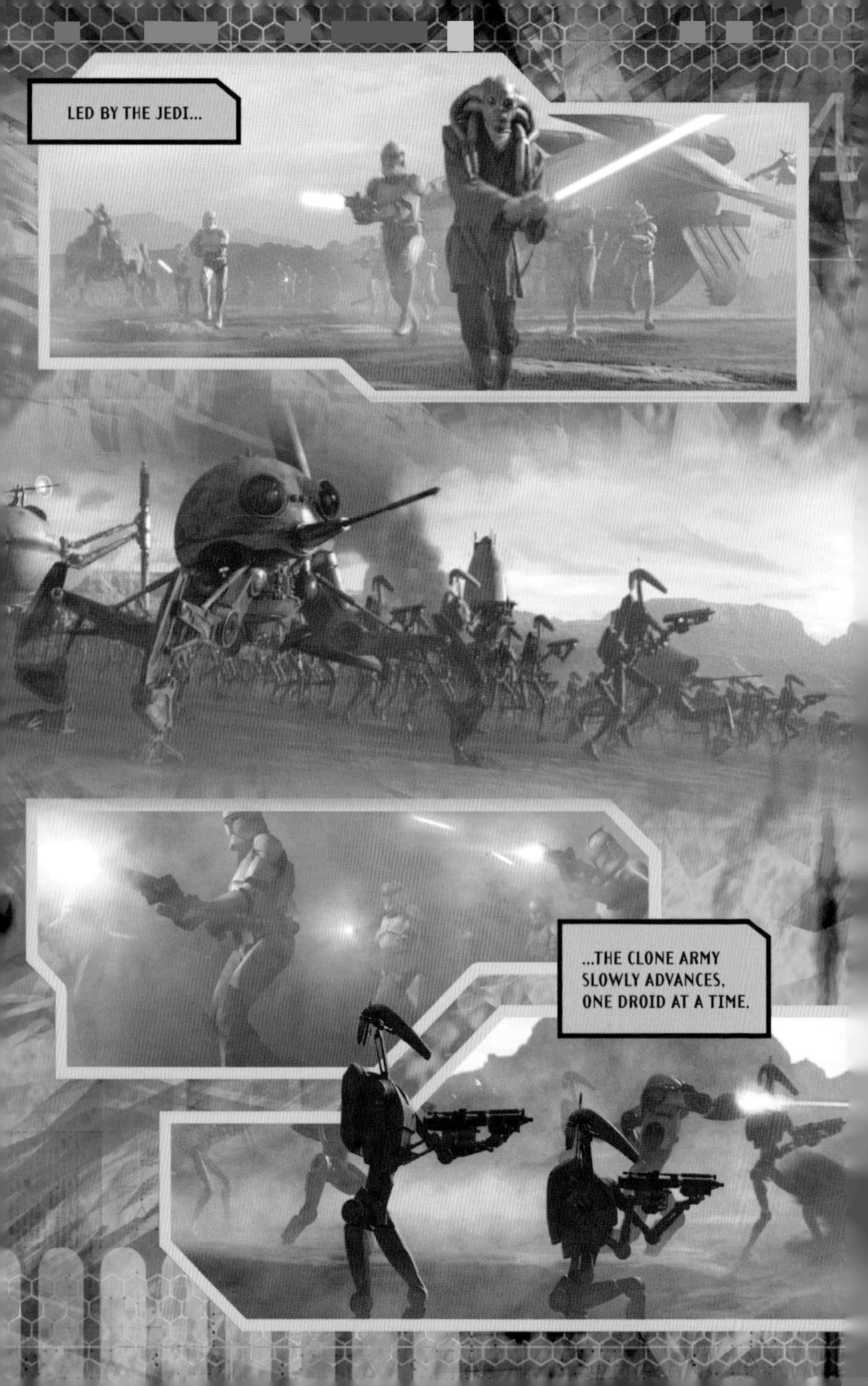
LED BY THE JEDI...
...THE CLONE ARMY SLOWLY ADVANCES, ONE DROID AT A TIME.

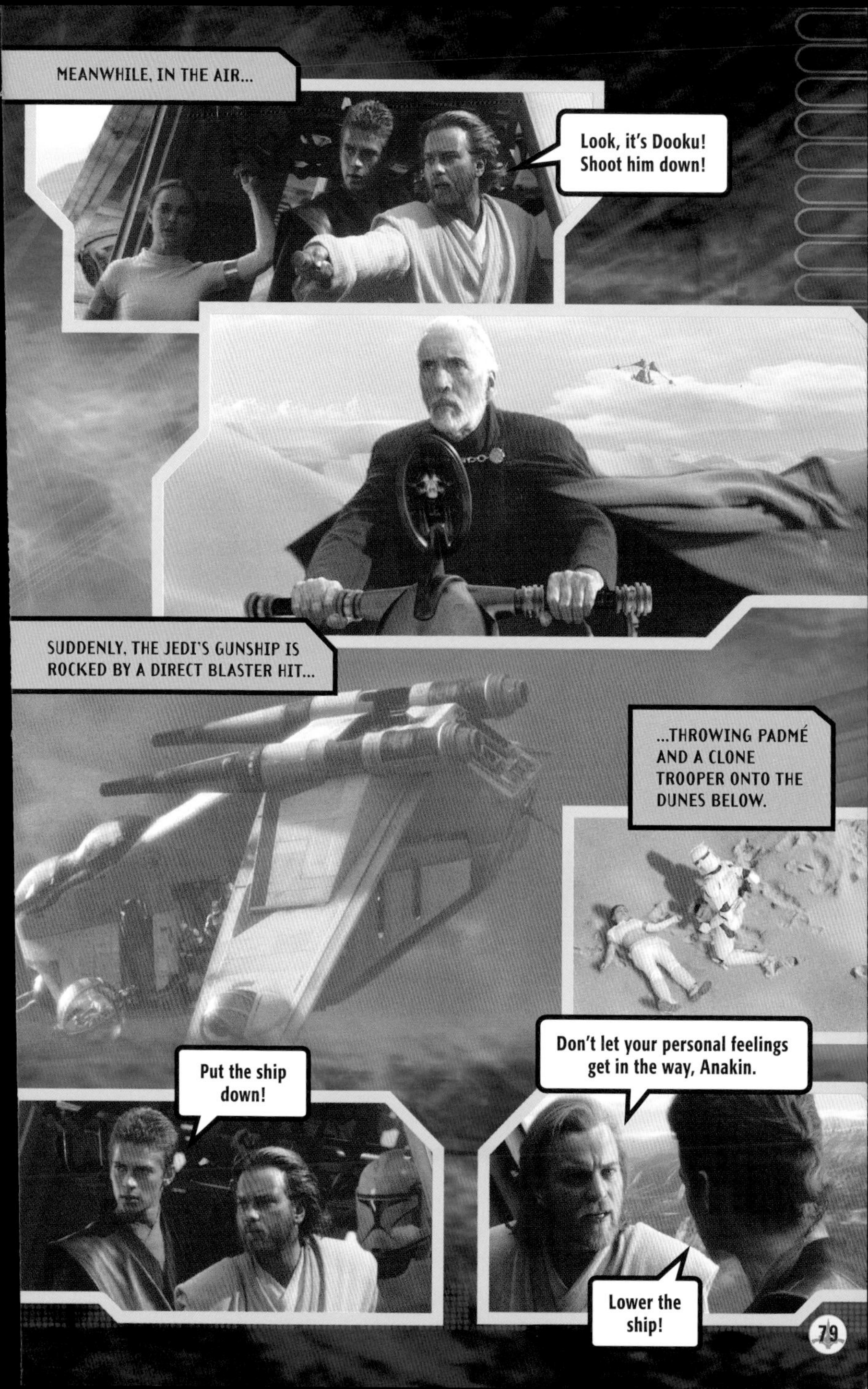
MEANWHILE, IN THE AIR...
Look, it's Dooku! Shoot him down!
SUDDENLY, THE JEDI'S GUNSHIP IS ROCKED BY A DIRECT BLASTER HIT...
...THROWING PADMÉ AND A CLONE TROOPER ONTO THE DUNES BELOW.
Put the ship down!
Don't let your personal feelings get in the way, Anakin.
Lower the ship!

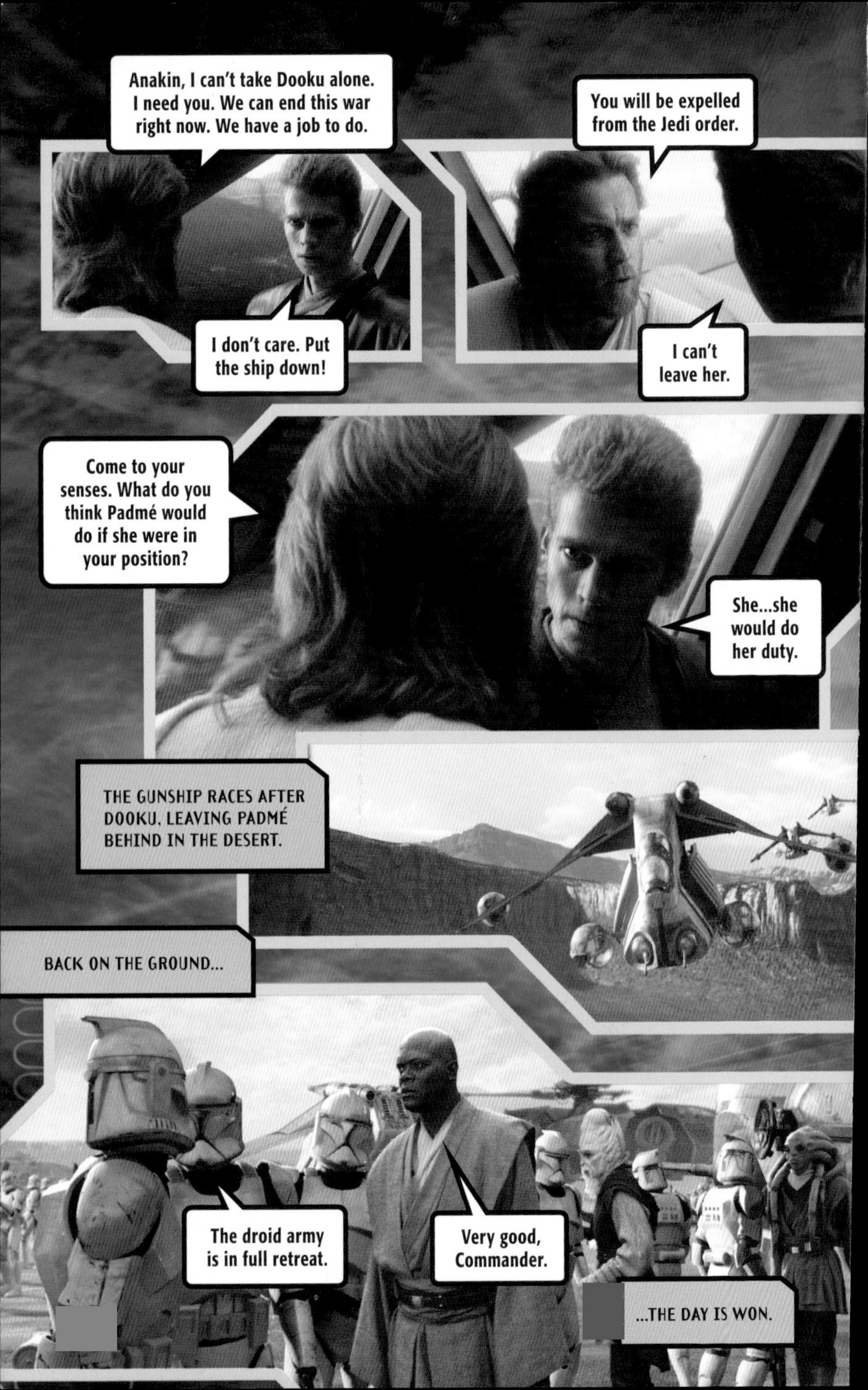
Anakin, I can't take Dooku alone. I need you. We can end this war right now. We have a job to do.
I don't care. Put the ship down!
You will be expelled from the Jedi order.
I can't leave her.
Come to your senses. What do you think Padmé would do if she were in your position?
She...she would do her duty.
THE GUNSHIP RACES AFTER DOOKU, LEAVING PADMÉ BEHIND IN THE DESERT.
BACK ON THE GROUND...
The droid army is in full retreat.
Very good, Commander.
...THE DAY IS WON.

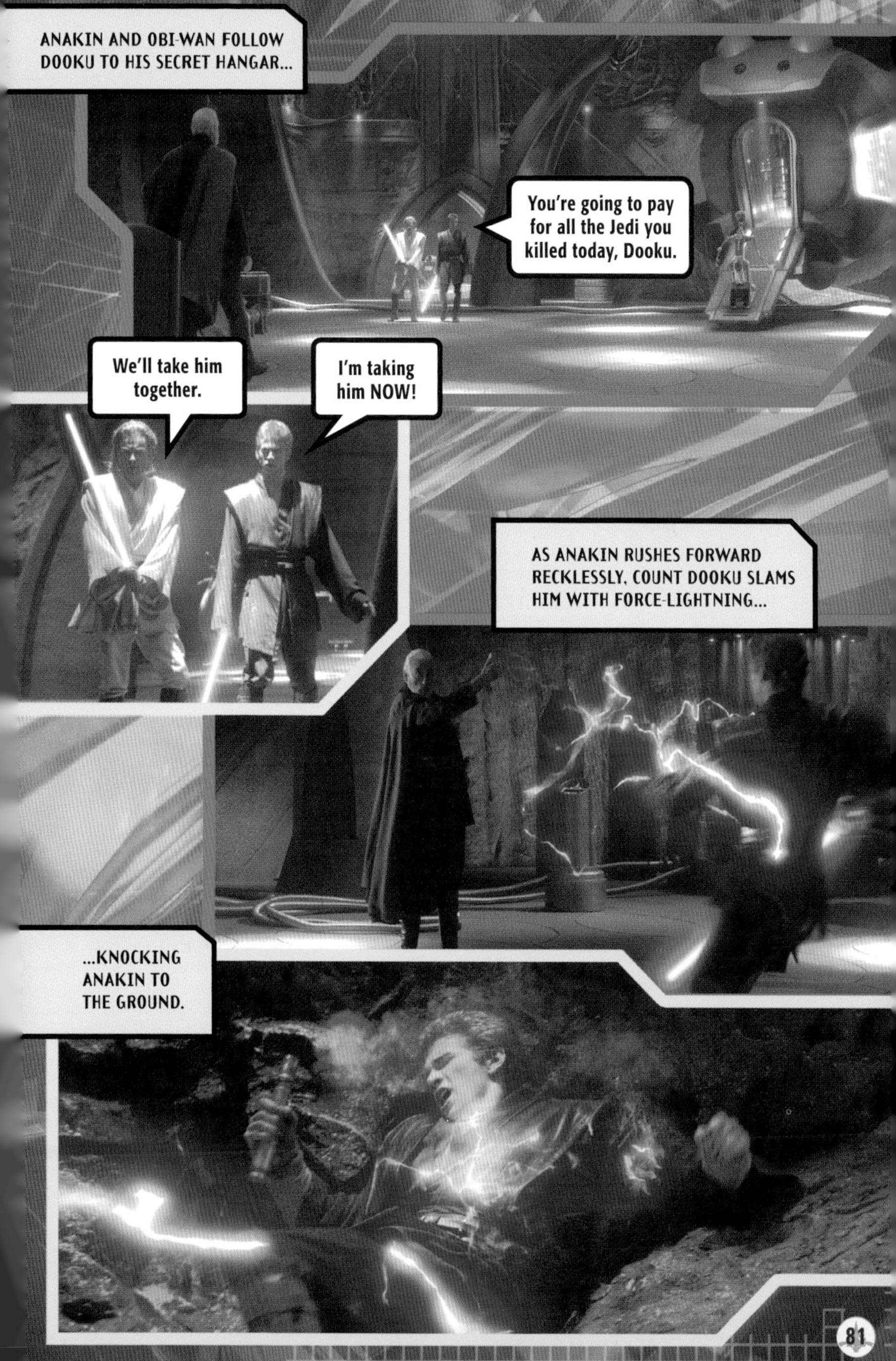
ANAKIN AND OBI-WAN FOLLOW DOOKU TO HIS SECRET HANGAR...
You're going to pay for all the Jedi you killed today, Dooku.
We'll take him together.
I'm taking him NOW!
AS ANAKIN RUSHES FORWARD RECKLESSLY, COUNT DOOKU SLAMS HIM WITH FORCE-LIGHTNING...
...KNOCKING ANAKIN TO THE GROUND.

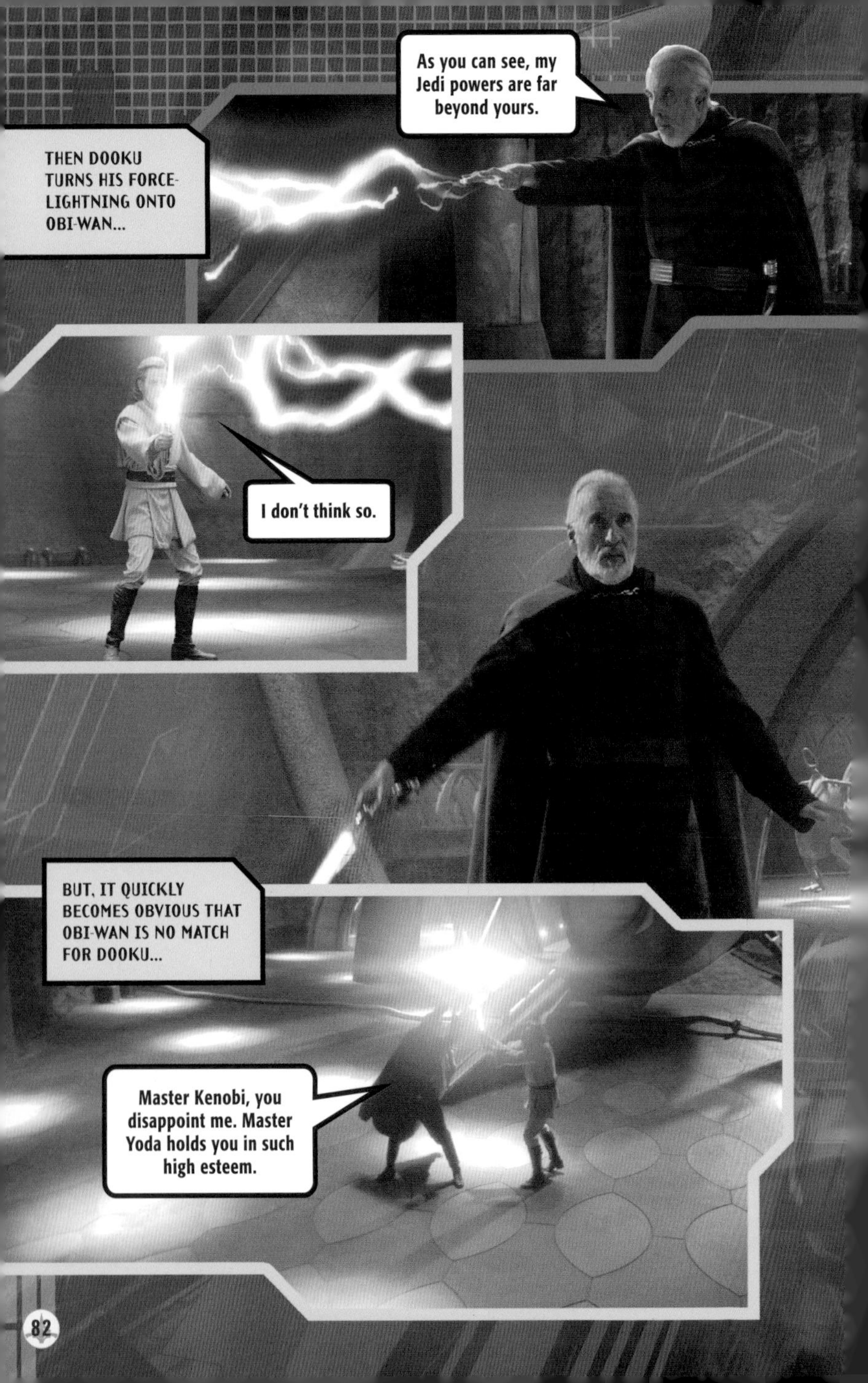
As you can see, my Jedi powers are far beyond yours.
THEN DOOKU TURNS HIS FORCE-LIGHTNING ONTO OBI-WAN...
I don't think so.
BUT, IT QUICKLY BECOMES OBVIOUS THAT OBI-WAN IS NO MATCH FOR DOOKU...
Master Kenobi, you disappoint me. Master Yoda holds you in such high esteem.

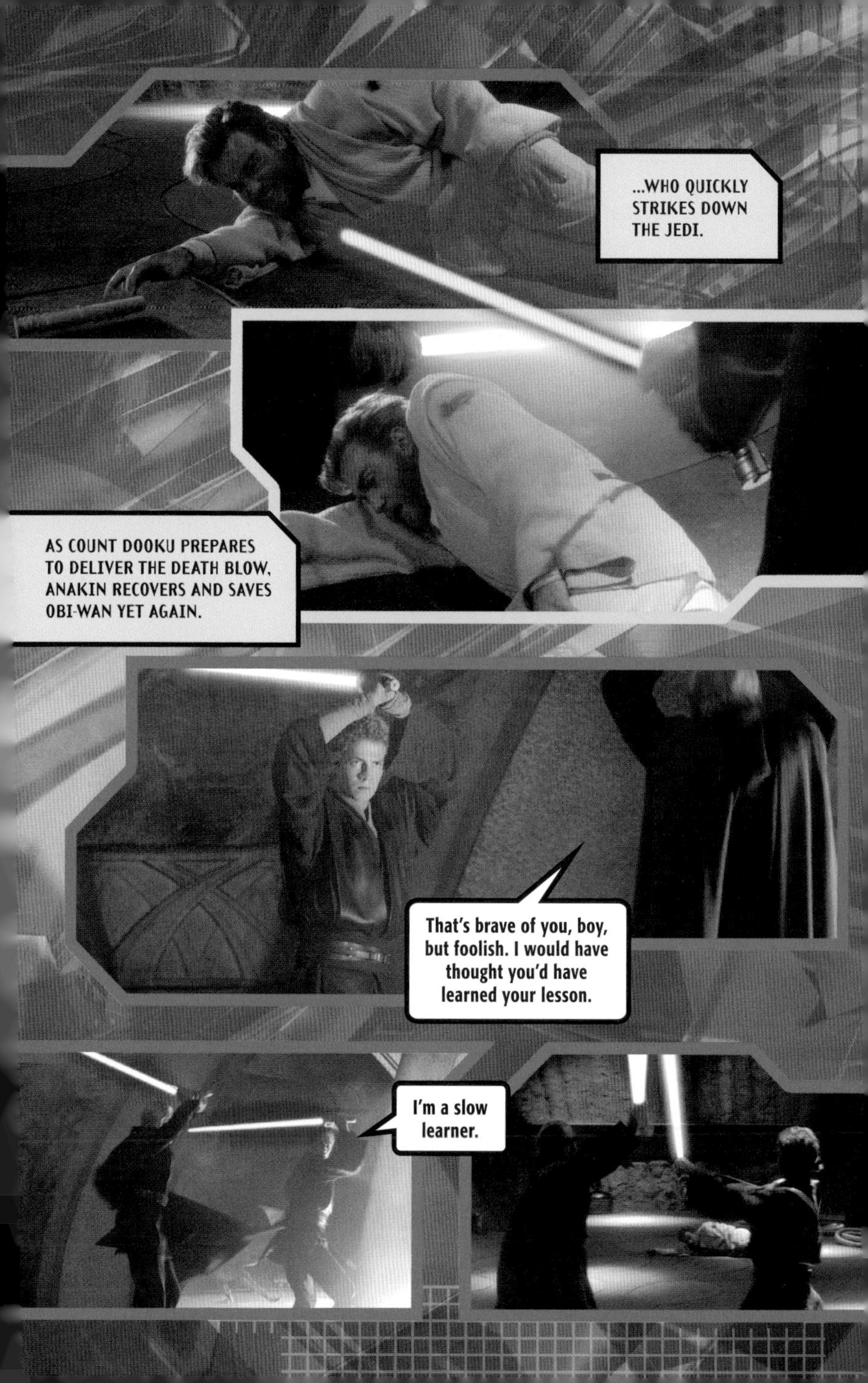
...WHO QUICKLY STRIKES DOWN THE JEDI.
AS COUNT DOOKU PREPARES TO DELIVER THE DEATH BLOW, ANAKIN RECOVERS AND SAVES OBI-WAN YET AGAIN.
That's brave of you, boy, but foolish. I would have thought you'd have learned your lesson.
I'm a slow learner.

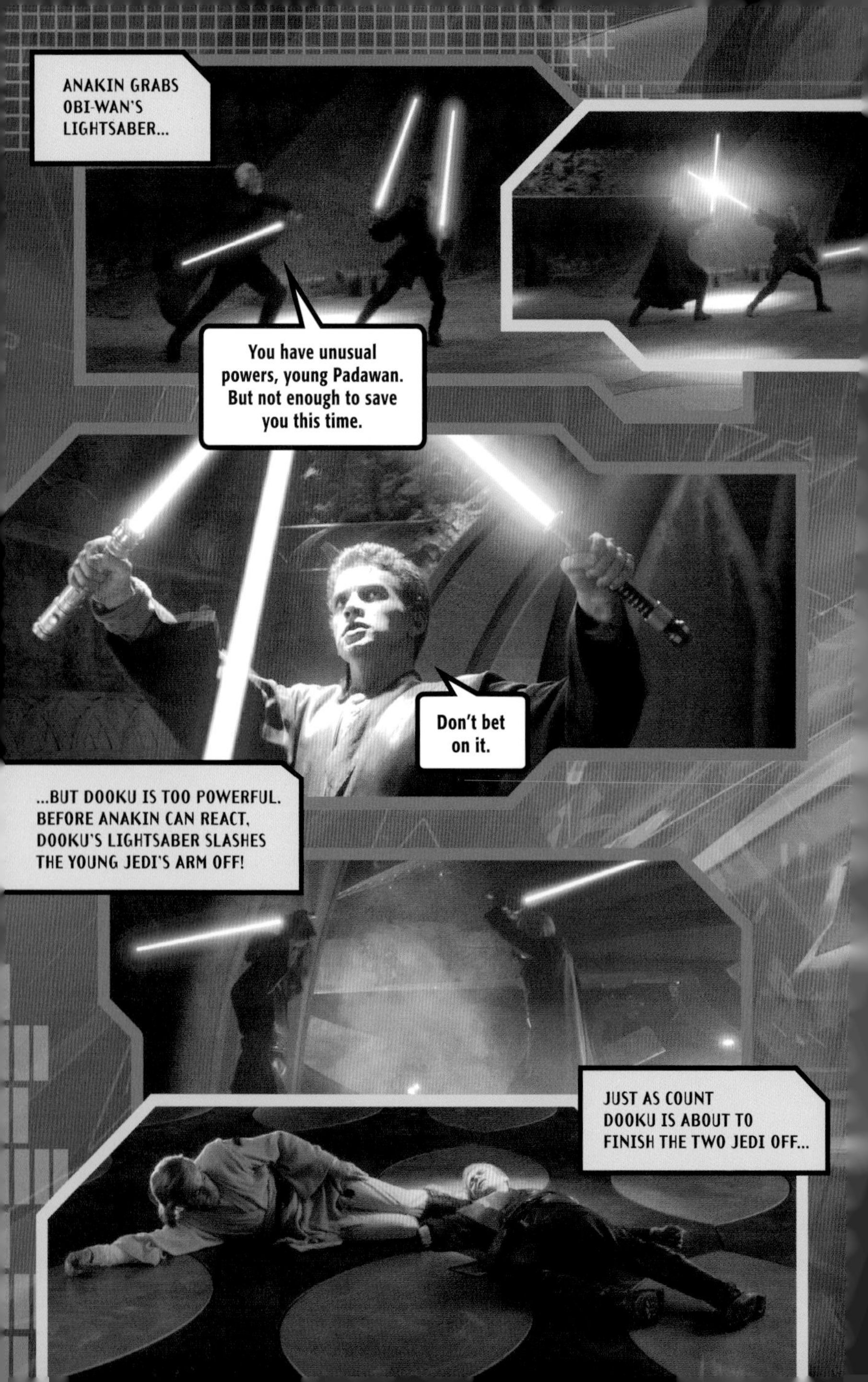
ANAKIN GRABS OBI-WAN'S LIGHTSABER...
You have unusual powers, young Padawan. But not enough to save you this time.
Don't bet on it.
...BUT DOOKU IS TOO POWERFUL. BEFORE ANAKIN CAN REACT, DOOKU'S LIGHTSABER SLASHES THE YOUNG JEDI'S ARM OFF!
JUST AS COUNT DOOKU IS ABOUT TO FINISH THE TWO JEDI OFF...

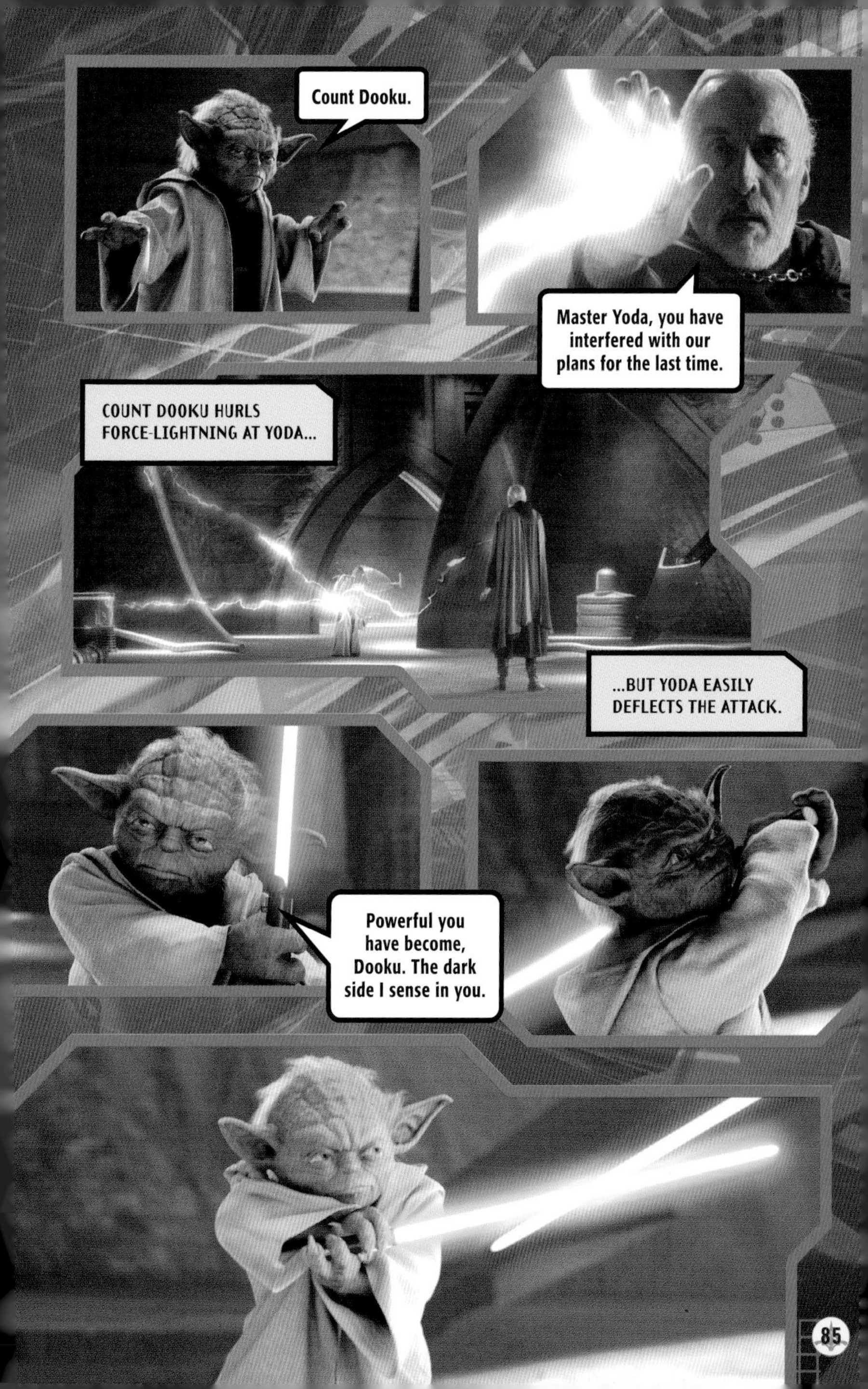
Count Dooku.
Master Yoda, you have interfered with our plans for the last time.
COUNT DOOKU HURLS FORCE-LIGHTNING AT YODA...
...BUT YODA EASILY DEFLECTS THE ATTACK.
Powerful you have become, Dooku. The dark side I sense in you.

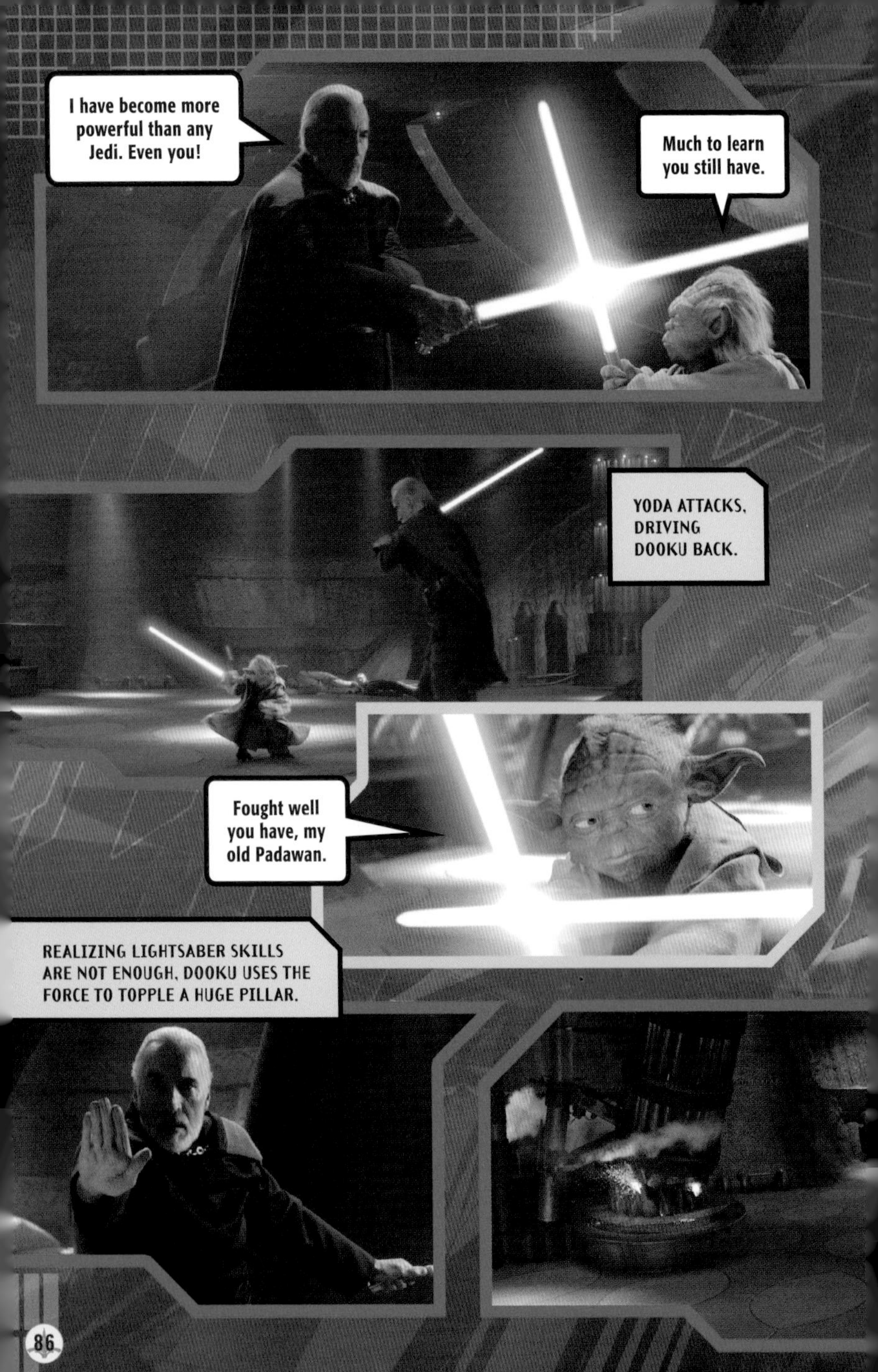
I have become more powerful than any Jedi. Even you!
Much to learn you still have.
YODA ATTACKS, DRIVING DOOKU BACK.
Fought well you have, my old Padawan.
REALIZING LIGHTSABER SKILLS ARE NOT ENOUGH, DOOKU USES THE FORCE TO TOPPLE A HUGE PILLAR.

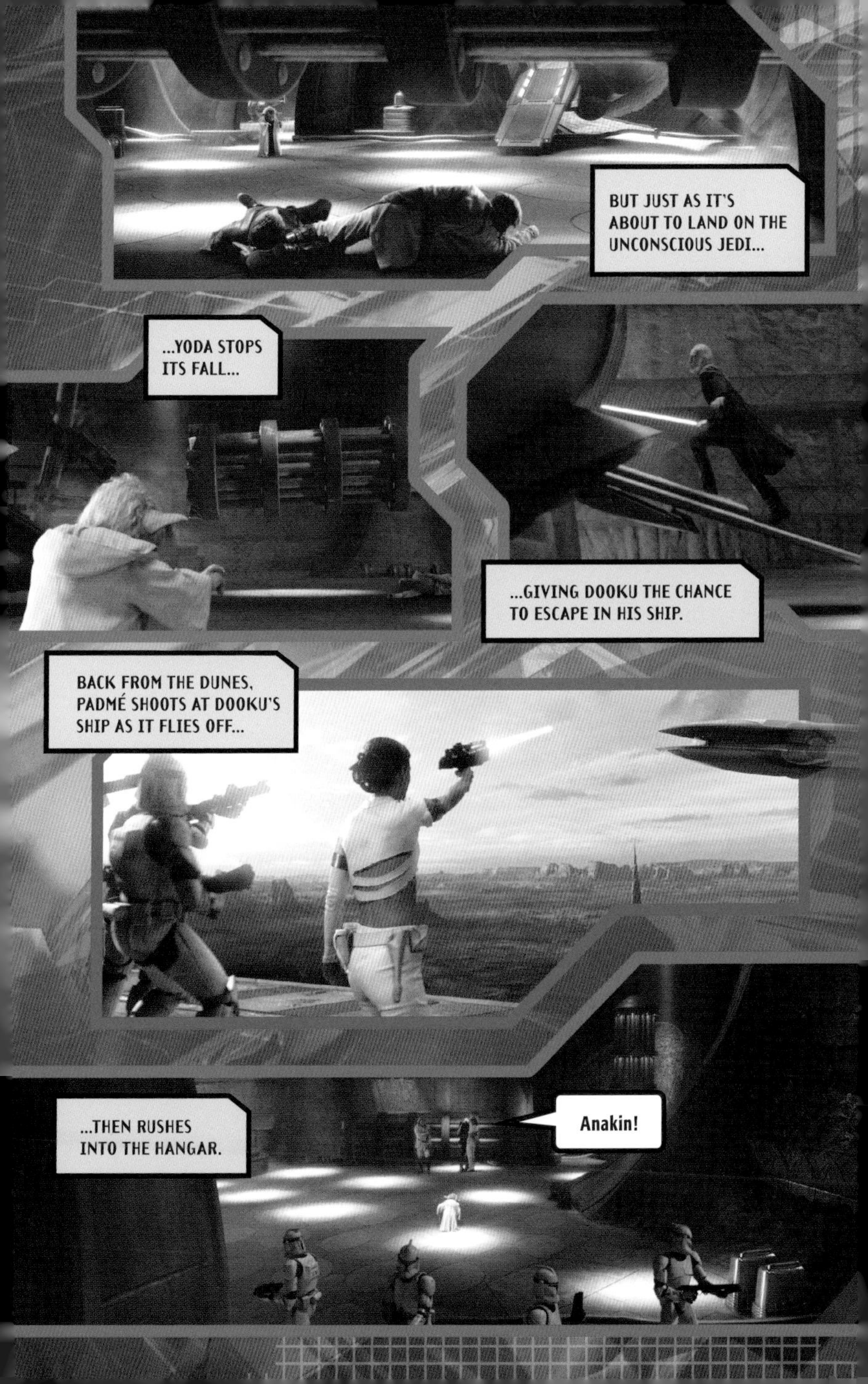
BUT JUST AS IT'S ABOUT TO LAND ON THE UNCONSCIOUS JEDI...
...YODA STOPS ITS FALL...
...GIVING DOOKU THE CHANCE TO ESCAPE IN HIS SHIP.
BACK FROM THE DUNES, PADMÉ SHOOTS AT DOOKU'S SHIP AS IT FLIES OFF...
...THEN RUSHES INTO THE HANGAR.
Anakin!

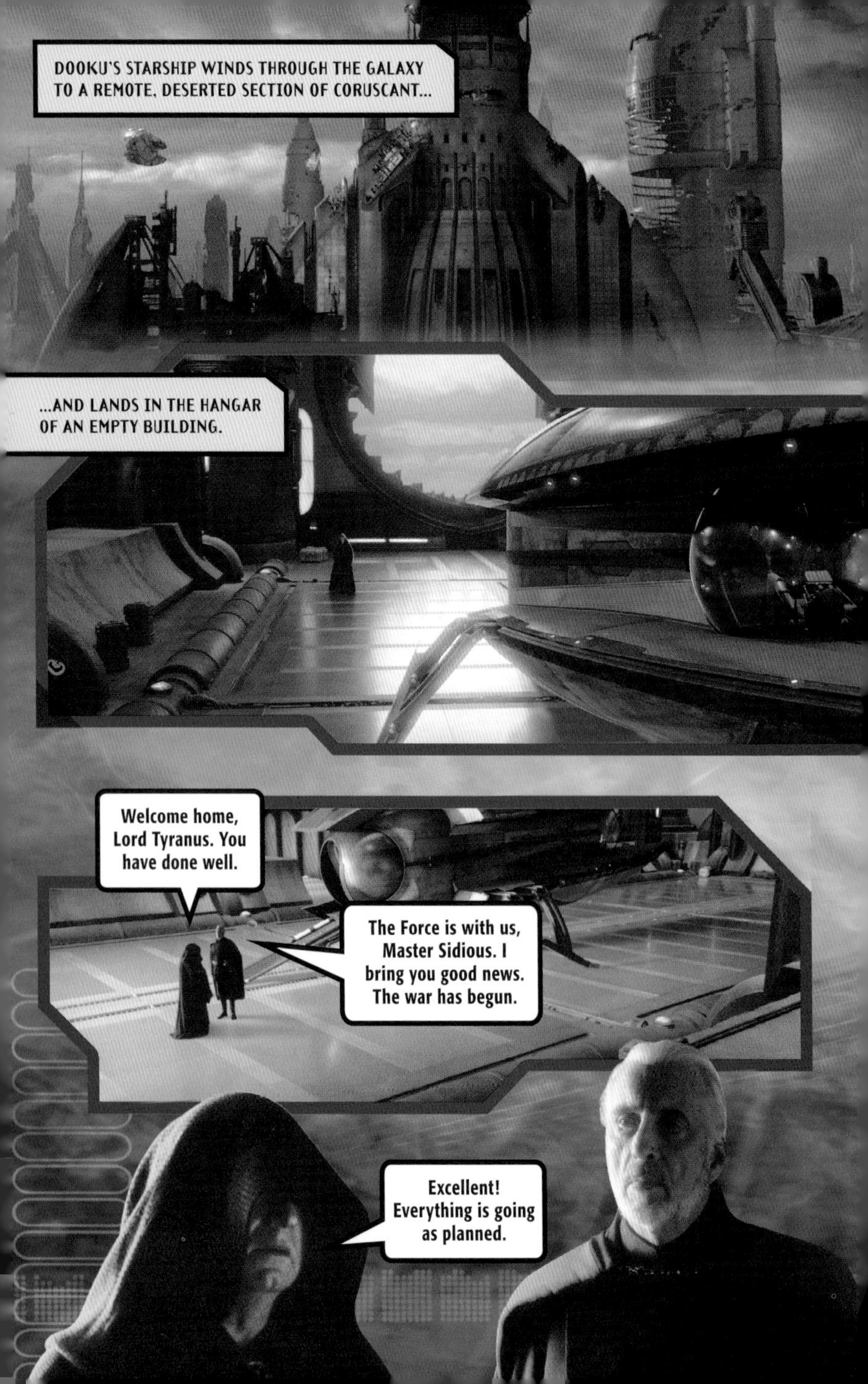

DOOKU'S STARSHIP WINDS THROUGH THE GALAXY TO A REMOTE, DESERTED SECTION OF CORUSCANT...
...AND LANDS IN THE HANGAR OF AN EMPTY BUILDING.
Welcome home, Lord Tyranus. You have done well.
The Force is with us, Master Sidious. I bring you good news. The war has begun.
Excellent! Everything is going as planned.

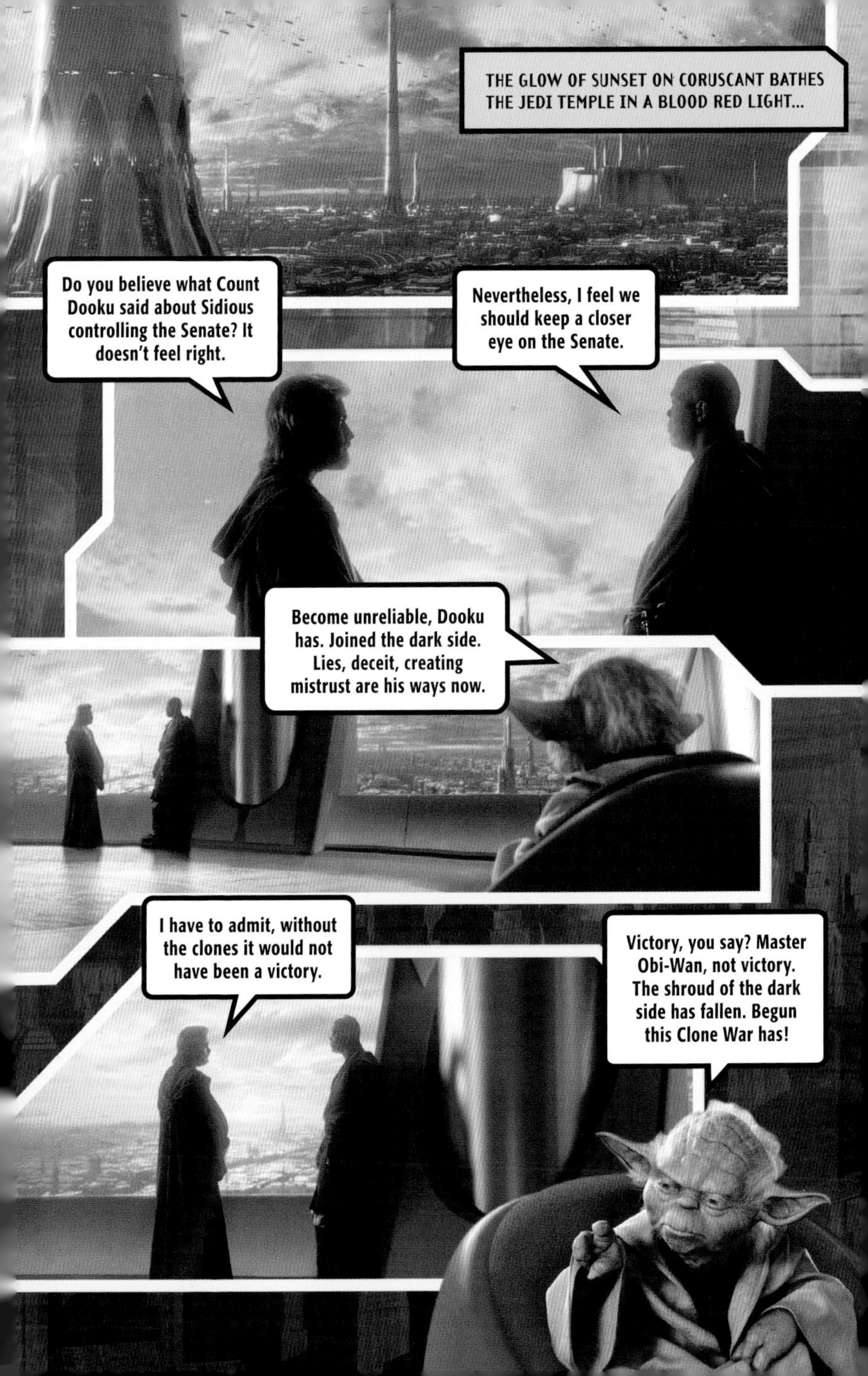
THE GLOW OF SUNSET ON CORUSCANT BATHES THE JEDI TEMPLE IN A BLOOD RED LIGHT...
Do you believe what Count Dooku said about Sidious controlling the Senate? It doesn't feel right.
Nevertheless, I feel we should keep a closer eye on the Senate.
Become unreliable, Dooku has. Joined the dark side. Lies, deceit, creating mistrust are his ways now.
I have to admit, without the clones it would not have been a victory.
Victory, you say? Master Obi-Wan, not victory. The shroud of the dark side has fallen. Begun this Clone War has!

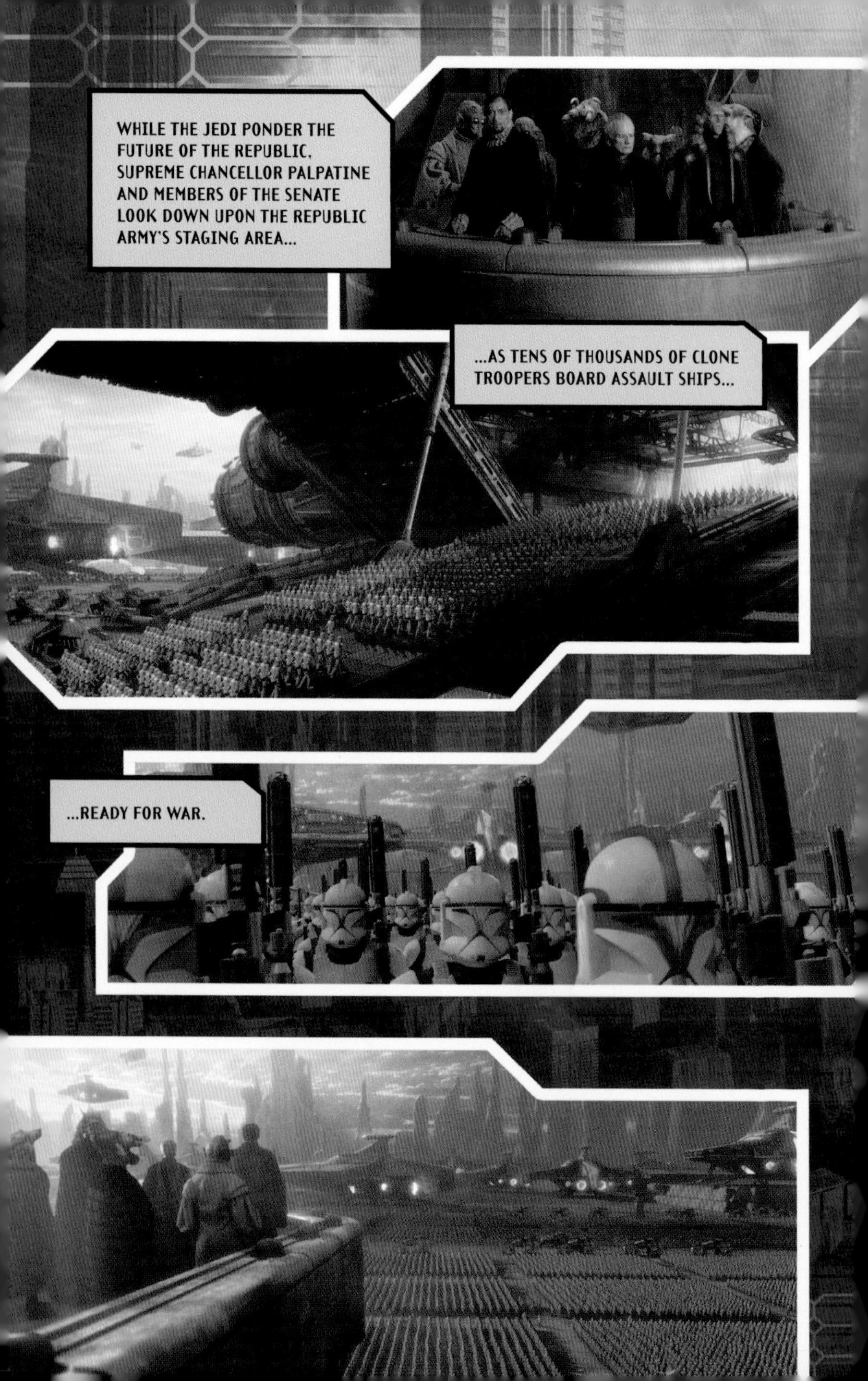
WHILE THE JEDI PONDER THE FUTURE OF THE REPUBLIC, SUPREME CHANCELLOR PALPATINE AND MEMBERS OF THE SENATE LOOK DOWN UPON THE REPUBLIC ARMY'S STAGING AREA...
...AS TENS OF THOUSANDS OF CLONE TROOPERS BOARD ASSAULT SHIPS...
...READY FOR WAR.

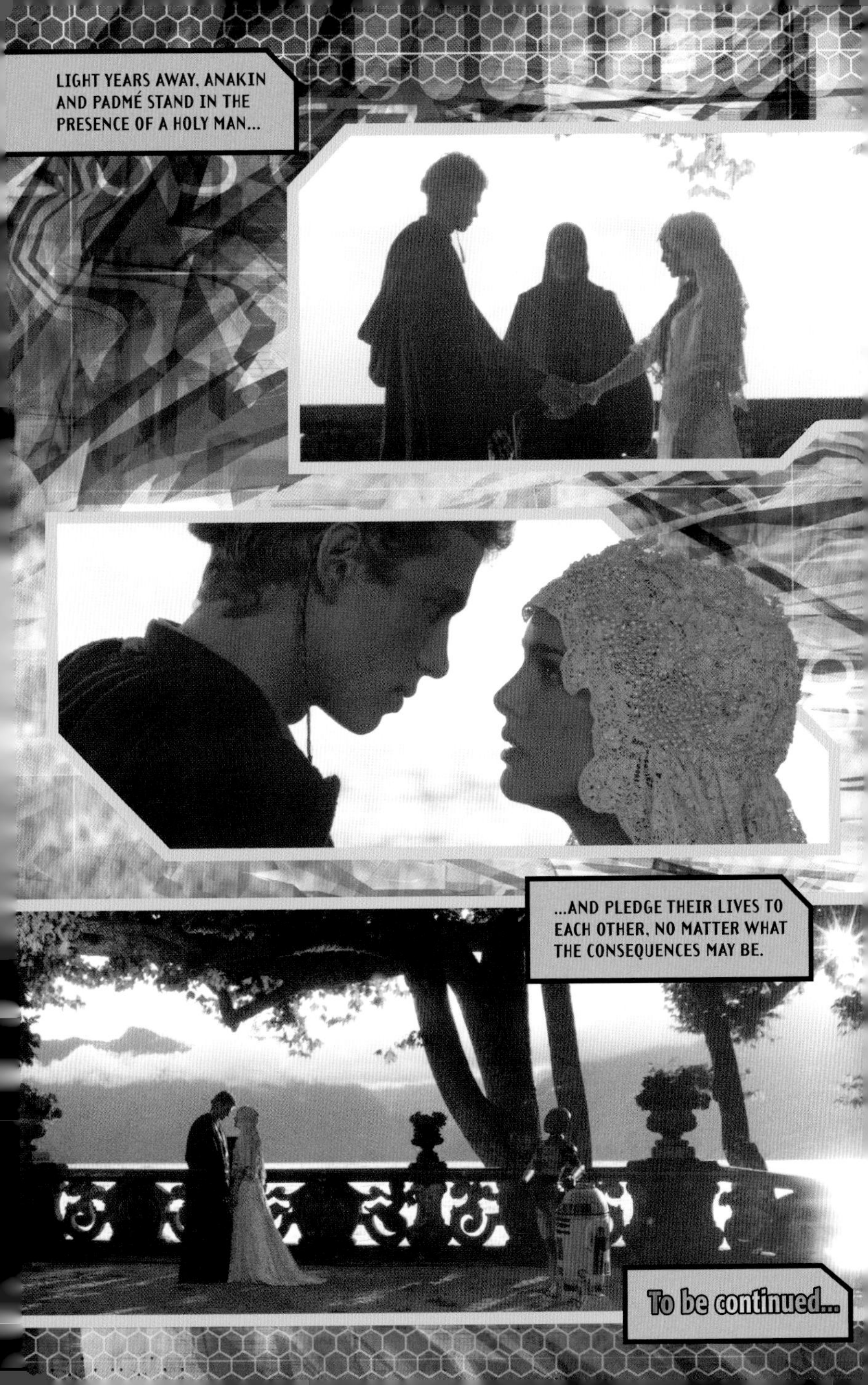
LIGHT YEARS AWAY, ANAKIN AND PADMÉ STAND IN THE PRESENCE OF A HOLY MAN...
...AND PLEDGE THEIR LIVES TO EACH OTHER, NO MATTER WHAT THE CONSEQUENCES MAY BE.
To be continued...

BONUS SECTION!

Vehicles of The Republic

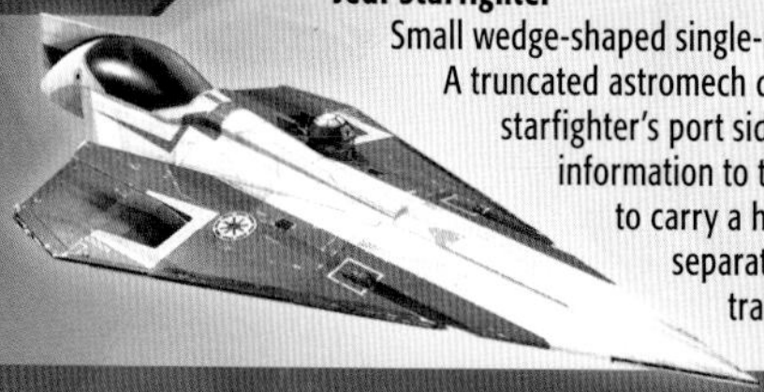

Jedi Starfighter

Small wedge-shaped single-pilot ship used by the Jedi order. A truncated astromech droid is hard-wired into the starfighter's port side, providing repair and navigation information to the Jedi pilot. The vessel is too small to carry a hyperdrive and instead relies on a separate hyperspace transport ring for transit through hyperspace.

Naboo Royal Cruiser

Senator Padmé Amidala's official starship. A majestic craft with smooth lines, an unblemished chromed surface, and a bold flying wing silhouette, the Naboo Royal Cruiser is unmistakable in its origins.

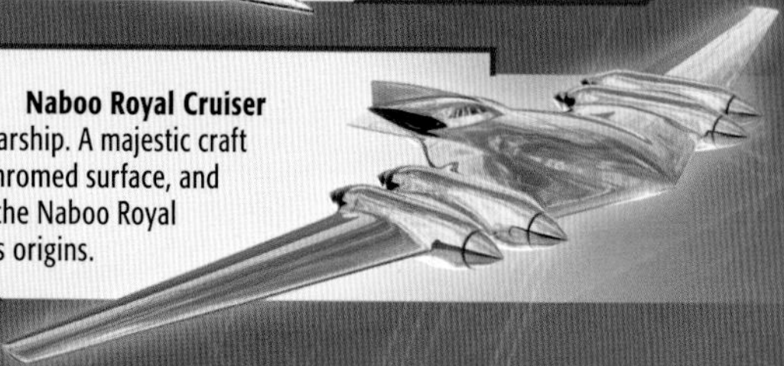

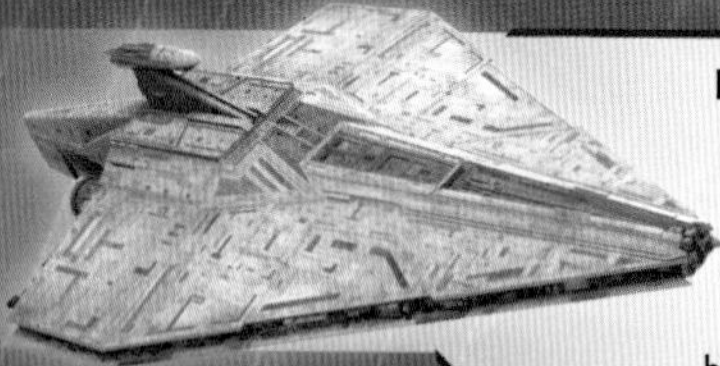

Republic Assault Ship

While the Kaminoans labored to perfect an indomitable clone army, the neighboring shipyards of Rothana were subcontracted to develop the hardware, armor and transports for the new infantry. The Republic uses these titan transport vessels to bring clone troopers to the battlefields of Geonosis.

SPHA-T Self-Propelled Heavy Artillery–Turbolaser

An armored juggernaut with incredible firepower, the SPHA-T is a self-propelled laser artillery tank. Rather than relying on a rotating turret, the entire vehicle can reposition itself by means of twelve articulated legs. Considerably larger than the AT-TE walker, the SPHA-T provides long-range surface-to-surface and surface-to-air fire, coordinated by a crack team of clone troopers.

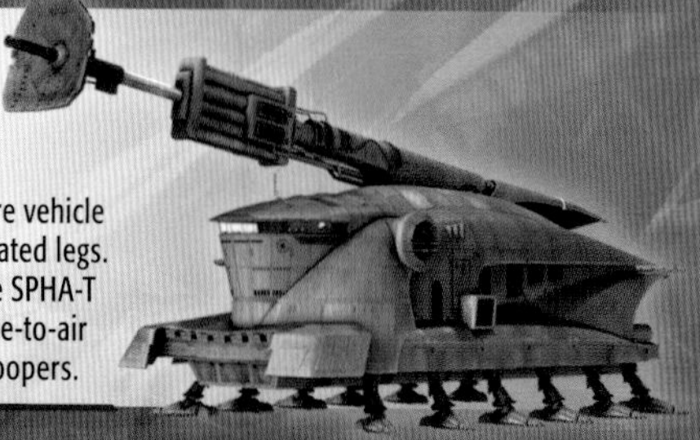

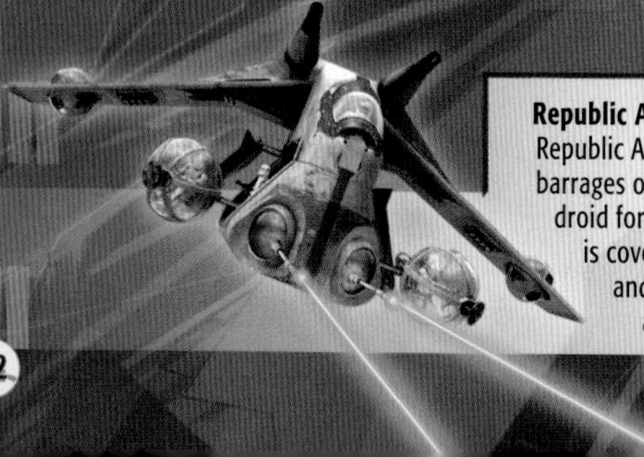

Republic Attack Gunship

Republic Attack Gunships rain down blistering barrages of laser and rocket retribution against the droid forces of the Separatists. Each winged gunship is covered in weapons, offering air-to-surface and air-to-air support as well as serving as an infantry transport.

Vehicles of The Federation

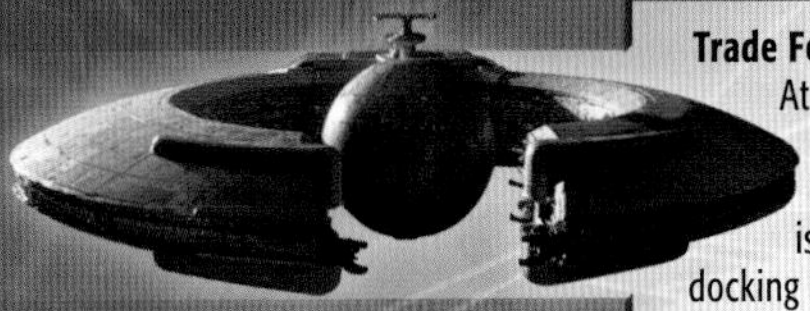

Trade Federation Battleship and Core

At over three kilometers in diameter, these enormous vessels resemble flattened disks with a central sphere containing the ship's bridge and landing core. The disk is broken at the front of the craft, revealing two mammoth docking bays lined with forward docking claws. The reclusive Neimoidian typically seal themselves in the ship's spacious bridge while their legions of droids handle the operation of the mighty craft.

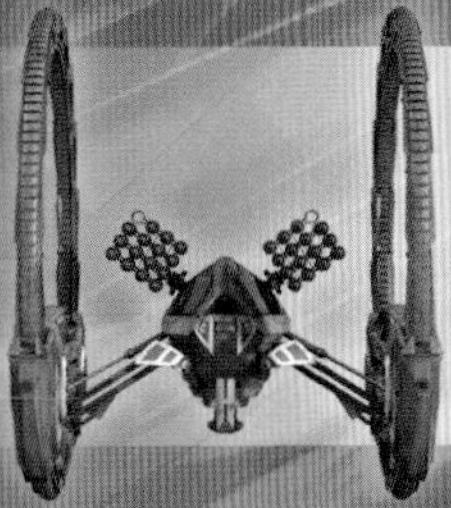

Hailfire Droid

A self-aware mobile missile platform used exclusively by the InterGalactic Banking Clan, hailfire droids deliver surface-to-surface and surface-to-air attacks with their stacked banks of thirty rocket warheads.

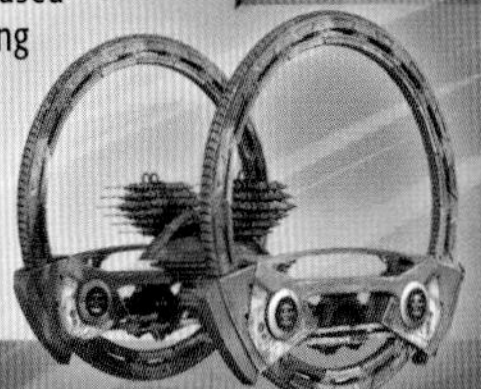

Slave I

The elliptical silhouette of the *Slave I* is the last thing any fugitive would want to see on their rear sensor display. The *Slave I's* sophisticated antidetection gear and stealth package ensure that very few fugitives ever see their captor coming. The vessel is armed with numerous laser cannons, as well as concealed projectile launchers and a seismic charge deployer.

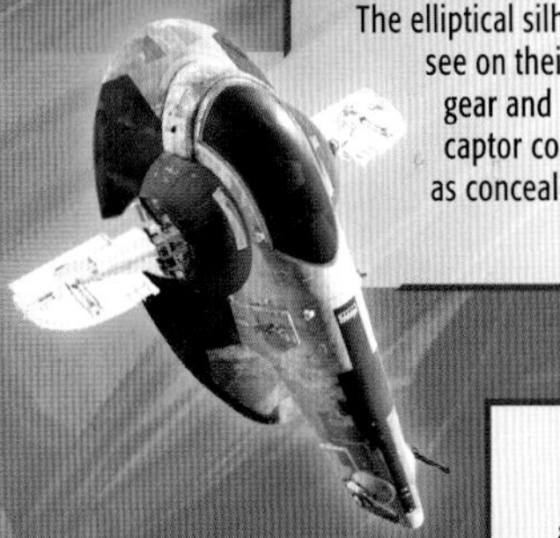

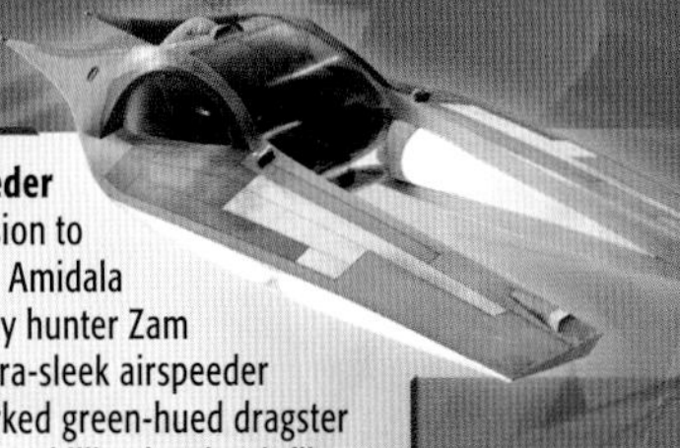

Zam Wesell's Airspeeder

During her mission to assassinate Senator Padmé Amidala on Coruscant, bounty hunter Zam Wesell employed an ultra-sleek airspeeder model. The wickedly forked green-hued dragster emits a chilling howl as it flies.

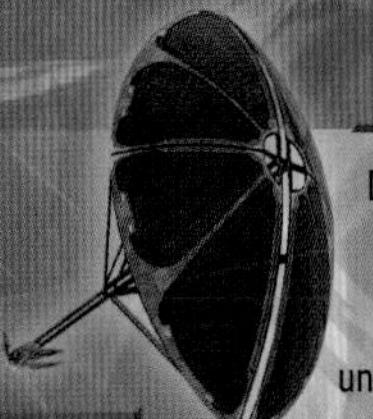

Geonosian Solar Sailer

An exotic, alien conveyance befitting Count Dooku's enigmatic character, the Geonosian solar sailer uses unique technology to propel the craft through both realspace and hyperspace. The vessel's carapace opens to expel its diaphanous sail, which unfurls into a parabolic chute that gathers energetic A-particles for propulsion.

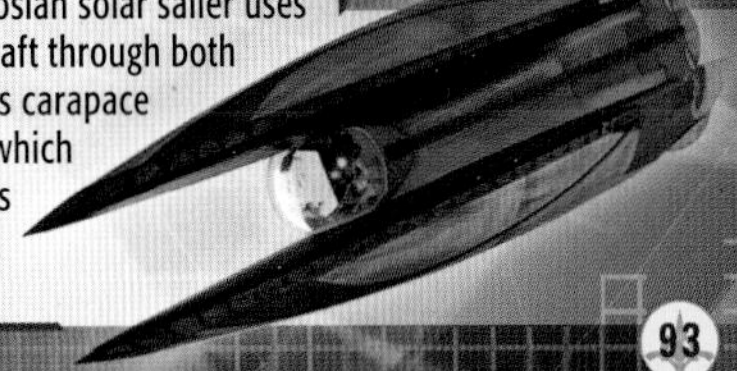

STAR WARS®

CLONE WARS ADVENTURES

Don't miss any of the action-packed adventures of your favorite **STAR WARS®** characters, available at comics shops and bookstores in a galaxy near you!

Volume 1
ISBN-10: 1-59307-243-0
ISBN-13: 978-1-59307-243-8

Volume 2
ISBN-10: 1-59307-271-6
ISBN-13: 978-1-59307-271-1

Volume 3
ISBN-10: 1-59307-307-0
ISBN-13: 978-1-59307-307-7

Volume 4
ISBN-10: 1-59307-402-6
ISBN-13: 978-1-59307-402-9

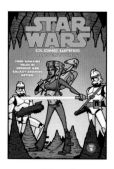

Volume 5
ISBN-10: 1-59307-483-2
ISBN-13: 978-1-59307-483-8

Volume 6
ISBN-10: 1-59307-567-7
ISBN-13: 978-1-59307-567-5

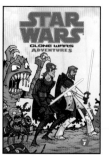

Volume 7
ISBN-10: 1-59307-678-9
ISBN-13: 978-1-59307-678-8

Volume 8
ISBN-10: 1-59307-680-0
ISBN-13: 978-1-59307-680-1
Coming in June!

$6.95 each!

READY TO TRY SOME OTHER GREAT STAR WARS® TITLES?

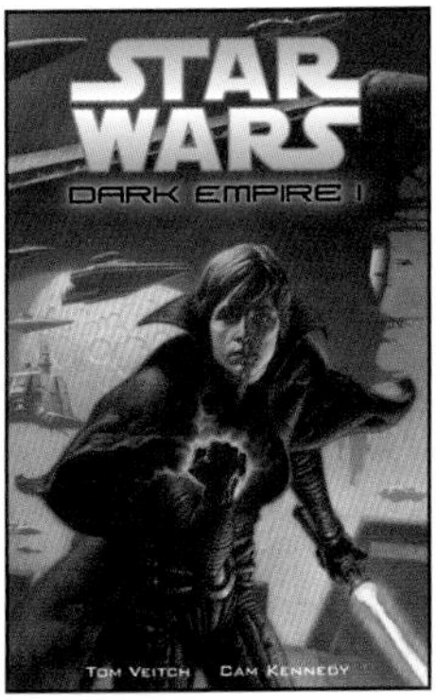
STAR WARS
DARK EMPIRE I
TOM VEITCH CAM KENNEDY

DARK EMPIRE

Join Luke, Leia, Han, and Chewie as they battle the Empire's latest super-weapons: the gigantic, planet-destroying World Devastators!

ISBN-10: 1-59307-039-X / ISBN-13: 978-1-59307-039-7

$16.95

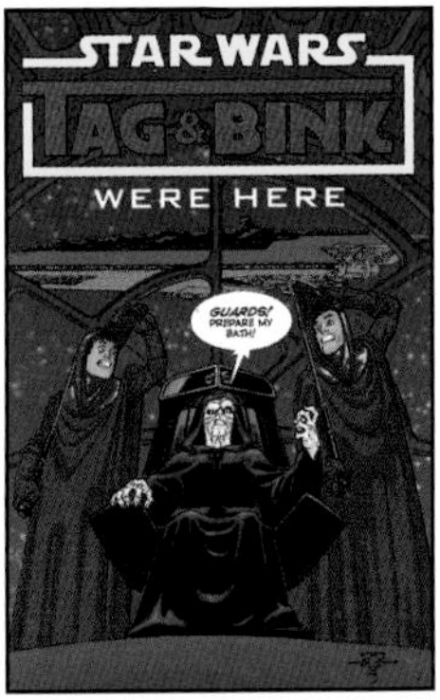
STAR WARS
TAG & BINK
WERE HERE
GUARDS! PREPARE MY BATH!

TAG AND BINK WERE HERE

Laugh yourself into orbit with the hilarious misadventures of a pair of hapless Rebel officers!

ISBN-10: 1-59307-641-X / ISBN-13: 978-1-59307-641-2

$14.95

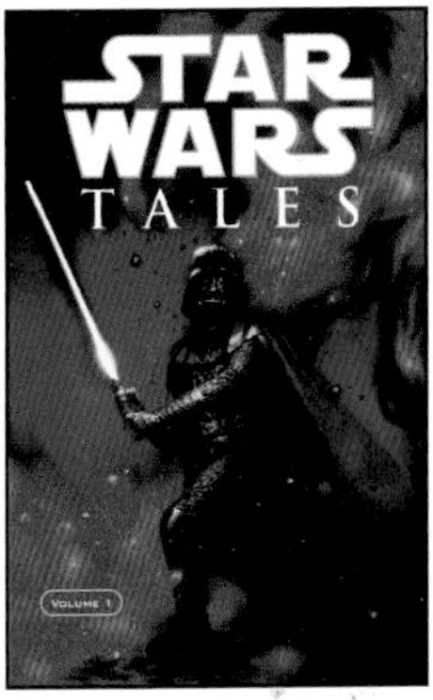
STAR WARS
TALES
VOLUME 1

TALES VOLUME 1

Read the first four issues of the quarterly anthology smash sensation that explores every corner of the *Star Wars* galaxy!

ISBN-10: 1-56971-619-6 / ISBN-13: 978-1-56971-619-9

$19.95

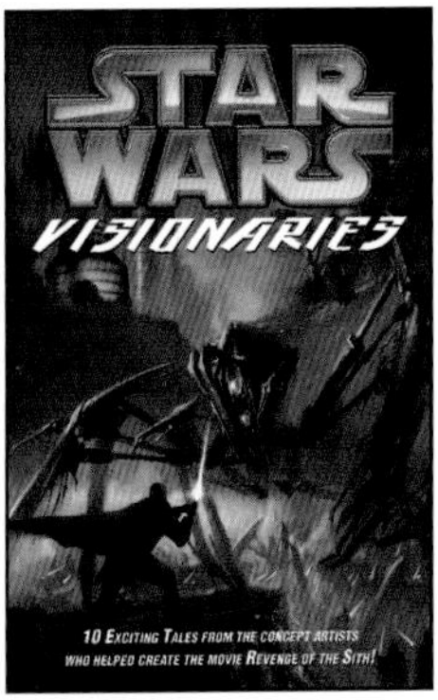
STAR WARS
VISIONARIES
10 EXCITING TALES FROM THE CONCEPT ARTISTS WHO HELPED CREATE THE MOVIE REVENGE OF THE SITH!

VISIONARIES

Ten exciting tales from the concept artists who helped create the movie *Revenge of the Sith*!

ISBN-10: 1-59307-311-9 / ISBN-13: 978-1-59307-311-4

$17.95

DARK HORSE BOOKS

AVAILABLE AT YOUR LOCAL COMICS SHOP OR BOOKSTORE!

To find a comics shop in your area, call 1-888-266-4226

For more information or to order direct visit darkhorse.com or call 1-800-862-0052 Mon.-Fri. 9 A.M. to 5 P.M. Pacific Time.

Prices and availability subject to change without notice.

STAR WARS GRAPHIC NOVEL TIMELINE (IN YEARS

Tales of the Jedi—5,000–3,986 BSW4
Knights of the Old Republic—3,964 BSW4
Jedi vs. Sith—1,000 BSW4
Jedi Council: Acts of War—33 BSW4
Prelude to Rebellion—33 BSW4
Darth Maul—33 BSW4
Episode I: The Phantom Menace—32 BSW4
Outlander—32 BSW4
Emissaries to Malastare—32 BSW4
Jango Fett: Open Seasons—32 BSW4
Twilight—31 BSW4
Bounty Hunters—31 BSW4
The Hunt for Aurra Sing—30 BSW4
Darkness—30 BSW4
The Stark Hyperspace War—30 BSW4
Rite of Passage—28 BSW4
Jango Fett—27 BSW4
Zam Wesell—27 BSW4
Honor and Duty—24 BSW4
Episode II: Attack of the Clones—22 BSW4
Clone Wars—22–19 BSW4
Clone Wars Adventures—22–19 BSW4
General Grievous—20 BSW4
Episode III: Revenge of the Sith—19 BSW4
Dark Times—19 BSW4
Droids—3 BSW4
Boba Fett: Enemy of the Empire—2 BSW4
Underworld—1 BSW4
Episode IV: A New Hope—SW4
Classic Star Wars—0–3 ASW4
A Long Time Ago . . . —0–4 ASW4
Empire—0 ASW4
Rebellion—0 ASW4
Vader's Quest—0 ASW4
Boba Fett: Man with a Mission—0 ASW4
Jabba the Hutt: The Art of the Deal—1 ASW4
Splinter of the Mind's Eye—1 ASW4
Episode V: The Empire Strikes Back—3 ASW4
Shadows of the Empire—3–5 ASW4
Episode VI: Return of the Jedi—4 ASW4
X-Wing Rogue Squadron—4–5 ASW4
Mara Jade: By the Emperor's Hand—4 ASW4
Heir to the Empire—9 ASW4
Dark Force Rising—9 ASW4
The Last Command—9 ASW4
Dark Empire—10 ASW4
Boba Fett: Death, Lies, and Treachery—11 ASW4
Crimson Empire—11 ASW4
Jedi Academy: Leviathan—13 ASW4
Union—20 ASW4
Chewbacca—25 ASW4
Legacy—130 ASW4

Old Republic Era
25,000 – 1000 years before
Star Wars: A New Hope

Rise of the Empire Era
1000 – 0 years before
Star Wars: A New Hope

Rebellion Era
0 – 5 years after
Star Wars: A New Hope

New Republic Era
5 – 25 years after
Star Wars: A New Hope

New Jedi Order Era
25+ years after
Star Wars: A New Hope

Legacy Era
130+ years after
Star Wars: A New Hope

Infinities
Does not apply to timeline

Sergio Aragonés Stomps Star Wars
Star Wars Tales
Star Wars Infinities
Tag and Bink
Star Wars Visionaries

BSW4 = before *Episode IV: A New Hope*. ASW4 = after *Episode IV: A New Hope*.